Animal Health

Health, Disease and Welfare of Farm Livestock

David Sainsbury M.A., Ph.D., B.Sc., M.R.C.V.S.

Lecturer in Animal Health, Department of Clinical Veterinary
Medicine, University of Cambridge

COLLINS
8 Grafton Street, London W1

Collins Professional and Technical Books
William Collins Sons & Co. Ltd
8 Grafton Street, London W1X 3LA

First published in Great Britain by Granada Publishing 1983
(ISBN 0-246-11625-0)
Reprinted by Collins Professional and Technical Books 1986

British Library Cataloguing in Publication Data
Sainsbury, David
Animal Health.
1. Livestock   2. Veterinary medicine
I. Title
636.089   SF91

ISBN 0-00-383356-9

Printed and bound in Great Britain by
Mackays of Chatham, Kent

Contents

Preface

The aim of this book is to give a concise account of the factors affecting the health of livestock under modern conditions of husbandry and describe the most important diseases. Many of the classic livestock diseases have either been completely eliminated or kept under control with vaccines or drugs. What is happening now under the conditions of modern husbandry is that animals are affected by less obvious but nevertheless serious and often chronic infections which can have immensely damaging effects on productivity. In addition, farm animals are increasingly afflicted with metabolic disorders. These are the conditions which cause severely adverse effects on production and health due to partial or total collapse of the animals' metabolic processes when 'pushed' beyond their normal capabilities. And in the field of contagious diseases the new problem of 'viral strike' is emerging; many apparently new virus diseases, borne by wind or vectors, travel through areas, causing some quite devastating effects for a time, especially in the larger livestock units. In no few cases these diseases so cripple the enterprise that it never recovers.

In particular I hope I can convey to the reader the need for an understanding of the way the various diseases exert their effect and the overriding necessity for their absolute prevention to give to the farmer the incalculable economic benefits of healthy livestock. Good health is the birthright of all animals and such an ideal lies completely within our grasp.

Acknowledgements

I am grateful to the following for the supply of illustrations:

Messrs Atcost Ltd, Tunbridge Wells, for Figs 1.1, 1.2, 1.3, 1.6, 1.12, 3.8, 4.7 and 7.5; Beacon of Penrith Ltd for Figs 3.8 and 5.1; Benham and Company, Surveyors, Chelmsford, for Figs 1.9, 1.10 and 5.2; Constrado for Fig. 4.8; Equine Veterinary Journal for 4.6; Glaxovet for Fig. 4.2; Gush and Dent Ltd for Fig. 3.6; Hallam of Nottingham Ltd for Figs 1.4, 1.5 and 7.1; Hoechst Ltd for Fig. 6.1; Imperial Chemical Industries Ltd for Figs 4.1 and 4.4; Maywick of Hanningfield Ltd for Fig. 1.13; Roche Products Ltd for Fig. 5.4; Turbair Ltd for Figs 7.6 and 7.7.

In thanking Professor W. Holmes, editor of *Grass* and his publishers Blackwells for permission to use Fig. 1.17, I would like to recommend that the reader studies this excellent treatise for a thorough grounding in such a vital agricultural topic.

No words of mine can adequately express my thanks to Miss Margaret McKean for her many hours of dedicated help in the preparation of this book. And finally my most grateful thanks go to Mr Richard Miles, Editorial Director of Granada Technical Books, who never seemed to tire in his persistent endeavours to strive for perfection in the production of the book. I would wish to couple these thanks with those to everyone in Granada who has done so much to make the time spent on *Animal Health* a pleasurable experience.

David Sainsbury

1 Health and the Environment

The changing health picture

Recent fundamental changes in farming practices have had a marked effect on the environmental influences on livestock health. These influences are now often the major factors affecting the economic viability of a farm.

In the first place, considerable advances in the control of animal infections have led to the effective elimination of many of the *traditional* causes of acute disease. This has been achieved by a combination of appropriate vaccine usage, good drug therapy and the development of disease-free strains of livestock. These advances have made it possible to keep animals in much larger groups and more densely housed than hitherto but the results have by no means led to a gradual disappearance of infectious diseases altogether.

On the contrary, a number of complex diseases has emerged, difficult to diagnose and induced by a multiplicity of pathogenic agents. Whilst these may cause an apparent or 'clinical' disease it is more likely that the effect will be less obvious and may only reduce the overall productivity of the livestock by, for example, slowing growth and reducing the food conversion efficiency. Animals may not die or even show any symptoms at all so that the farmer may be unaware of what is happening unless he keeps very careful records and uses them with more than the usual degree of skill. It is also a very common phenomenon that intensive production on a livestock unit may start efficiently and effectively, but deteriorate in time so gradually that it is not noticed until the consequences have become very serious and control becomes extremely difficult. The nature of these infections is of especial interest and concern because the environmental and housing conditions have a profound effect on their severity.

A second major problem is that of the *metabolic diseases*. These are a group of diseases that are caused intrinsically by the animals being called to produce an end product faster than the body can process its intake of feed. Enormous efforts are made to provide the right nutrients in an easily assimilated form but as the metabolic disease is rather different from a deficiency disease, this does not necessarily work. In a way the metabolic diseases are the inevitable outcome of the success in conquering the acute virulent diseases together with the advances made in improved genetics, nutrition and housing. These improvements have led to considerably increased growth and productivity but the capability of the animals to keep pace with these has outstripped the normal functioning process (or metabolism) of the body.

A good example of this is provided by studying the growth of broiler chickens. When the industry started in earnest it took about 13 weeks to produce a bird weighing 2 kg, at a food conversion efficiency of approximately 3:1 (that is, 3 kg of feed to produce 1 kg of live weight). The hazards in growing these birds at that time were innumerable, but were largely related to contagious and infectious diseases — viral, bacterial, mycoplasmal and parasitic. Mortalities were high, often up to 30%, and of course the diseases played their part in slowing growth and damaging the food conversion efficiency. Now the position is quite different. It takes little more than half the time for the birds to reach 2 kg: that is, about 7 weeks. Mortalities can average 4%, and contagious and infectious diseases are controlled largely by vaccines, drugs and good hygiene. But now we have a plethora of the so-called metabolic or production diseases. For example, birds are affected with excess fatty deposition, causing degeneration of the liver and kidney and heart attacks. The skeletal growth cannot keep pace with the rate of muscle development so that many locomotor disorders occur, such as twisted, rubbery and broken bones, and slipped tendons.

The type of diseases

An important factor influencing the incidence of disease in livestock today is the increasing immaturity of livestock. Improved performance has resulted in animals reaching market weight much earlier, whilst for genetic reasons, breeding animals are also younger on average than previously. Thus, in a livestock unit nowadays, there is usually a much higher proportion of young animals that are in a state of susceptibility to infectious agents whilst they are still developing the ability to naturally resist disease (natural immunity to disease) which will normally take place over a prolonged period (see Chapter

3). This difficult state of affairs is further exacerbated by the considerable size of many livestock units in which the young animals may have originated from various parents of very different backgrounds. In many cases the young or growing stock have come in from widely separated areas. They may have no resistance to local infections and will therefore be susceptible to them, whilst at the same time contributing a new burden of pathogenic organisms to the unit they have entered. Altogether the modern livestock unit may present at any one time a confusing immunological state and the basic design and its management will influence the success or otherwise of disease control (see Table 1.1).

Table 1.1 The disease pattern on the farm

Bad husbandry + Primary disease agent + Secondary disease agents
                     (often a virus)   (often bacteria or parasites)
= Sub-clinical or overt disease

Examples of bad husbandry
Overcrowding too many animals on a site
Mixed ages within a house or site
Excessive movement of animals
Poor ventilation and environmental control
Bad drainage and muck disposal
Insufficient bedding
Lack of thermal insulation in construction
Unhygienic or insufficient food and watering equipment
Absence of routine disinfection procedures
Faulty nutrition

It is appropriate to record the major groups of infections that contribute to these problems. Possibly the most widespread are the respiratory diseases. Many respiratory diseases are sub-clinical, have a widespread debilitating effect, and are caused by a large number of different infective agents even in any one disease incident. They may not respond satisfactorily to vaccines, antisera, antibiotics or any other drugs, so that the only way to approach their control is by environmental and hygienic measures (see Fig. 1.1).

Another significant group of diseases influenced similarly are enteric infections. These, as in the case of respiratory diseases, have many different primary causative agents, ranging from parasites to

Fig. 1.1 Large number of young cattle reared together must be kept under ideal environmental conditions if respiratory disease is to be kept at a low figure. This building has a very large area of spaced boarding at the gables and sides to give good air flow.

viruses and bacteria. The reasons for their increasingly harmful effects in recent years are not only those already listed earlier but also the general trend, for certain livestock, to eliminate the use of bedding, such as straw, which can be expensive to handle and store. Though the harmful effects of this may often be corrected by the use of good pen design, especially by the use of slatted or slotted floors, it is nevertheless rather more difficult to separate animals from their urine and faeces when the flooring is without litter, as the latter has a diluting and absorbent effect on the excreta.

One may also consider the several important bacterial infections that have tended to increase in large intensive units. Examples of these are *Salmonella* and *Clostridia* bacterial spores, together with *Escherichia coli* and *Pasteurella*. Many forms of these organisms are normal inhabitants of the animal's intestines in small numbers but excessive 'challenges' causing disease may build up under unhygienic intensive conditions, encouraged by buildings with poorly constructed surfaces which cannot be cleaned.

Livestock unit size

In addition to the risks of the gradual build-up of disease-causing agents within a livestock unit, the dangers of livestock groups becoming too large must be borne in mind. In all parts of the world where the development of large units has taken place there has emerged a number of viral diseases which tend to 'sweep' like a forest fire through areas with a high livestock population, leaving a trail of devastation. Often there is likely to be considerable loss over a concentrated period, after which the animal population either develops a natural immunity or artificial immunities are promoted by the use of vaccines. It is now known that contagious particles can travel great distances from infected sites — certainly distances of 50 miles have been virtually proven — but they may well travel much further than this. If livestock enterprises continue to grow in size then the dangers in this respect can only become greater. At the present time it is impossible to present soundly based objective advice as to the optimal unit size and in any event the factors that would lead to making proposals are highly complex. However, there is clear evidence that animals thrive less efficiently in large numbers even in the absence of obvious clinical disease (see Fig. 1.2).

However, it should be made clear that it may be possible and economic to keep very much greater numbers of *adult* animals or birds together than young stock, since there is nothing like the same number of contagious disease problems after the difficult growing stage and its immunological uncertainties are passed.

As to the maximum number of livestock that might be kept on a site, it will be appreciated that this will depend on a number of factors, apart from health considerations. Figures have been proposed which attempt to allow for all factors and those suggested are as follows:

- Dairy cows 200 and beef cattle up to 1 000.
- Breeding pigs 500 and fattening pigs 3 000.
- Sheep 1 500.
- Breeding poultry 3 000.
- Commercial egg layers 60 000 and broiler chickens 150 000.

Such figures can be no more than suggestions made in the light of

Fig. 1.2 A large cattle unit self feeding silage. Such systems give many opportunities for cross-infection of disease and also bullying, so yield per cow is usually adversely affected.

experience on the farm. In due time more scientific evidence may be available to establish a better degree of accuracy. It is certainly likely that the figures will require constant adjustment in the light of new developments in husbandry, housing and disease control and especially with the anticipated trend towards the increasing provision of live-stock free of specific diseases.

Design essentials to minimise the disease challenge
In addition to the size of the livestock unit, there are a number of other basic items which need to be considered in order to provide the bases of good health.

DEPOPULATION
One of the most important concepts in disease control is ensuring the periodic depopulation of a building or a site. The benefits of elimin-

ating the animal hosts to disease-causing agents are well understood and the virtue of being able to clean, disinfect and fumigate a building is also accepted. Nevertheless in practice the whole concept of the 'all-in', 'all-out' policy is more complex than the preceding sentences would indicate. Periodic depopulation is extremely important for young animals but is far less so for groups of older animals which have probably achieved an immunity to many contagious diseases. Much also depends on whether the herd or flock is a 'closed' one with few or no incoming animals or an 'open' one with a constant renewal of the animal population. If the latter is the case, then constant depopulation is of greater importance as there is little or no opportunity for natural immunities to develop and the regular removal of the 'build-up' of infection is of great assistance in ensuring the good health of the livestock.

THE HEALTH STATUS

The policy will also depend on the health status of the stock. At one extreme there are the so-called 'minimal disease' or 'specific pathogen-free' herds which have been developed to be free of most of the common disease-causing agents of that species. Here, depopulation is not so critical as is the isolation of the animals from outside infections. Since this danger is very serious in most localities it is important to sub-divide the animals in a unit into smaller groups, lessening the likelihood of a breakdown and/or enabling isolation and elimination of a group which may become infected. At the other extreme there are those units which have a constant intake of new animals from outside and of unknown disease status. In this case there is a constantly running risk — and more usually a near certainty — that some will be either clinically infected with, or carriers of, disease. Design specifications for such units should be quite different from those of the closed herd or flock so that defined areas of the unit should at least have groups of animals put through them in batches after which the area can be cleared, cleaned and sterilized. It is obviously preferable if the whole unit can be so treated since it ensures an absolute 'break' in the possible disease 'build-up' cycle.

Between these two extremes is the more usual case in which a herd or flock is of reasonable health status, though certainly not free of all the common diseases, and in which new livestock are added only occasionally. In such cases the precautions in the housing against disease 'build-up' and spread of infection can be relaxed, but there should still be proper provision for the isolation of incoming and sick animals.

GROUP SIZE

An important means of putting the housing on the right lines is to keep the animals in groups of minimal size. This may seem to be an out-dated policy that may eliminate all those advantages from automation that large units can give us, but this certainly need not be the case. If groups are small, it is usually easier to match the animals in them for size, weight and age, and it is well-established that growth under these circumstances is likely to be most even and economical. Behavioural abnormalities, such as fighting and bullying, are also kept to a minimum – indeed they may be prevented altogether (see Fig. 1.3).

Fig. 1.3 Kennels within a large generously ventilated building, a satisfactory combination of two housing systems, with the pigs in small groups.

Fighting amongst animals seems to be a highly contagious condition and under the most intensive management an almost casual accident that may draw some blood can escalate into a blood-bath. Pens which keep the animals in small groups will tend to reduce the occurrence of such disasters, and indeed with good management the removal of an animal that has accidentally injured itself or is off-colour and therefore prone to being bullied will stop the trouble before it ever has a chance to get going.

There is yet another advantage in keeping animals in small groups. It is obviously good practice for a farmer to keep his livestock some-where near the level that has been shown to be the densest possible for optimal productivity. For example, it is known that a broiler chicken will grow to its maximum potential at a stocking rate of about 15 birds to 1 m². If birds are kept in a house to allow a density such as this, it means that they should spread across the house evenly, so they do in effect occupy and use this area. In practice, however, this is rarely the case, especially when large numbers are housed together without any sub-divisions at all. Hence, the birds, or such other livestock as may be at risk, crowd in certain parts of the building which can lead to grossly over-stocked floor areas. This is bad enough in itself but it has further unfortunate side-effects which may be seen as obviously in beef animals and dairy cows as in pigs and sheep. If livestock crowd excessively in certain parts of a house, this area is likely to become more polluted with dung and exhalations to an abnormal and harmful degree; the humidity becomes high, proper air movement is impeded and the animals soon may become ill. Sick animals feeling cold tend to huddle together more, so the vicious circle is perpetuated and there is seemingly no end to it unless some measures are taken to ensure a better distribution of the stock. When this problem arises under practical conditions it may often be impossible to sub-divide the animals at once. An immediate trend in the right direction — that is, encouraging the animals to spread themselves more uniformly over the house — can often be achieved by heating the building and introducing some artificial heat. There are excellent portable gas radiant heaters and oil-fired and electrical blower heaters available which can do all that is wanted in this way if no permanent system is available.

When animals are penned in large numbers, the effects of a fright caused by an unusual disturbance can be extremely serious. It is almost impossible to guard against all the extraneous sounds and sights that may affect the stock. The best safeguard, therefore, is to have the animals housed in small groups so that the effect of a panic movement will be more limited and will never build up into highly dangerous proportions. Guiding standards for stocking rates for housed livestock are given in Table 1.2.

Table 1.2 Guiding standards for stocking rates of livestock

	Area per head m²
Cattle:	
Cows — loose — housed	6
Calves to 3 months of age	2
Young cattle 3—6 months of age	3
Young cattle 6—12 months of age	4.5
Bull pen	30
Pigs:	
Sow — loose — housed	3.5
Sow — with litter	8
Boar	5
Weaner pig to 1 month old	0.18
Fattening pig 3—6 months of age	0.54
Sheep:	
Ewe	1.2
Ewe with lambs	1.5
Hoggs up to 30 kg	0.7
Lamb creeps to 5 weeks of age	0.3
Domestic fowl:	
Floor rearing — light breeds	0.12
Floor rearing — heavy breeds	0.18
Floor rearing — broiler breeders	0.24
Broilers to 7 weeks of age	0.06
Layers — deep litter	0.27
Layers — slatted floors	0.09
Layers — caged	0.06
Layers — strawyard	0.27

FLOORS

The profound effect of the floor surface on the well-being of intensively managed livestock is well established. In those times when bedding was almost invariably used and it was a cheap commodity to hand there were relatively few problems related to flooring. Now

Fig. 1.4 Slatted floors can be a valuable aid to the efficient separation of animals from their excreta.

that the farmer must turn to housing systems without bedding and often with slatted or other form of perforated flooring in an attempt to produce economically a comfortable and clean environment for the animals, he finds himself facing a new set of problems. Though we are still far from being able to advise the ideal floor, it is possible by choosing a good combination of surface, and bedding where used, to provide the animals with a comfortable, warm, hygienic and well-drained surface (see Fig. 1.4).

The best solid flooring is usually based on concrete because when properly made and laid it is hard wearing, hygienic and impervious to fluid. Where an animal lies directly on the floor, without bedding, there should be an area of insulated concrete, most often incorporated by using 100–200 mm of lightweight or aerated concrete under the top screed.

The surface of the concrete must not be so smooth that the animals slip or injure themselves yet, on the other hand, if it is too rough it can cause abrasions and injuries. A happy medium is not easy to find but is usually achieved by using a wood float finish and by tamping the floor lightly with a brush. Also, very rarely are the 'falls' on the floor correct; again, they must be a nice balance between being steep enough to drain away liquids yet not so sharp the animals slip. With some animals the floor is made more comfortable by placing rubber mats on top; these are used with success with cattle, calves and pigs.

Some of the worst problems of injury, especially with cattle and pigs, have occurred with slatted or other forms of perforated floors. These have been particularly troublesome when the edges have been left too sharp or have worn leaving injurious protrusions. Great care is needed in choosing the correct flooring and making sure it is maintained properly.

BUILDING DESIGN SOPHISTICATION

It is possible to be too naive and uncritical in our attitude to so-called improvement in the design of livestock buildings. The author recently investigated the productivity of broiler chickens within an organisation which grows a total of 15 million birds per annum. Their first buildings were erected in 1958 and the latest in 1978. The results were examined from four crops of broilers in the period January to October 1979 representing 480 000 birds in the oldest site, with an exactly similar number in houses with much 'improved' construction, thermal insulation and ventilation, incorporating the accumulated experience of 20 years both within the organisation and outside. The results were as follows:

	No. of birds placed	Finishing age (days)	Finishing weight (kg)	Food conversion efficiency	Mortality (per cent)
Site erected in 1958	480 000	49	1.89 (4.16 lb)	2.1	3.7
Site erected in 1978	480 000	49	1.88 (4.14 lb)	2.1	3.8

So far as is possible under commercial conditions, each site had similar chicks, management and food. The results were precisely the same in biological terms in the old and new site. The main advantages in the new buildings have been in economy of fuel and labour costs but not in productivity or health. These results do illustrate the necessity for careful investigation of new systems under both experimental and practical conditions before they are advocated and adopted. They also show that good husbandry — which was certainly the case within this broiler organisation — transcends the deficiencies in housing and environment.

A housing classification in relation to health criteria

In a consideration of the relationship between health, environment and housing it is helpful to provide a classification that differentiates between the principal methods since they each require different schemes for environmental control. There are three essentially contrasting types of housing: (i) *climatic*, giving only a cover and protection from the elements; (ii) *controlled-environment*, which

Fig. 1.5 A large 'climatic' building with open ridge and generous side ventilation.

Fig. 1.6 A large cattle unit with outside feeding and inside accommodation in cubicles. Provided the site is well protected the free ventilation and open air feeding may assist in providing good health.

regulates the micro-climate as completely as is required for the particular stock being housed; and (iii) the *kennel*, which is in a sense a half-way house between the other two and gives two environments in the one building, allowing some free choice for the animal in the areas where they may go.

The methods of use of each of these types and their suitability for different countries, climatic regions and forms of livestock vary enormously and must be carefully defined. Some of the greatest errors in livestock housing are made by their incorrect application and it is vital to specify these essential needs and differences.

Climatic housing

The climatic house is most suited to the adult which has developed a large measure of adaptability to climatic stress (see Figs 1.5 and 1.6). The house can be cheap, as it is basically a cover only, but because of the lack of control of the climate, the space given to the animals must be much more generous than in other forms of housing, especially since it is exceptional to have powered ventilation. In general, stocking densities tend to be half or less than half of those in the controlled-environment house. A major problem is created by agriculturalists when they attempt to apply the highest stocking rates, suitable for the controlled-environment house, to the climatic house, as the building is unable to cope with the demands of the stock, and poor productivity and serious disease problems can result. It is usually the correct choice for cattle over six months of age, for sheep of all ages, for adult pigs which are bedded and very occasionally for poultry. Climatic housing often requires deep bedding for its success in cooler climates. This may be especially important because it is usual in climatic housing always to have a surplus of air flow and to have little ventilation control. Even though this may be devised without causing draughts on the animals, it does involve widely fluctuating conditions so that the animals may need to have their own protection from the cold (see Table 1.3 and Fig. 1.7).

Table 1.3 Essentials of good thermal insulation in an animal house

1.	High standard of insulation material, e.g. 100 mm thickness of glass fibre or 50 mm of polystyrene or polyurethene boarding.
2.	Protection from damp penetration by good outer cladding and vapour-seal on inside of insulation, or damp-proof course in floor below insulation.
3.	Inner cladding must protect insulation and withstand disinfectants.
4.	Lightweight materials must not be compressed.
5.	Incorporation of air spaces on each side of insulation advantageous.

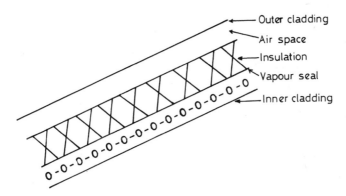

Fig. 1.7 Section through a well-insulated roof of an animal house.

The controlled environment house

This type of building (see Figs 1.8 and 1.9) is virtually the complete opposite in all respects of the climatic house. It may be used for all livestock but is especially appropriate for the young animal, the fattening pig, or chicken, the animal of almost any age housed without bedding, and livestock which require an environment with light control. It is also most economically viable with animals which are fed largely concentrate food rather than substantial quantities of

Fig. 1.8 A diagrammatic representation of the controlled environment house.

Fig. 1.9 Controlled environment livestock buildings with high standards of thermal insulation, light control and mechanical ventilation.

Fig. 1.10 The kennel or Monopitch house, with front ventilation only, controlled with ventilating flaps.

roughage, since the former is too expensive to be utilised as a form of energy. The housing is relatively expensive per unit area and sometimes extremely so in areas of climatic stress and where cooling devices are required. Because of the cost it is usually necessary to stock the buildings as densely as is practically possible to make them viable economically, and this can put the animals under a great health risk. The management to cope with their special requirements needs to be highly trained and efficient and unless these criteria can be satisfied the controlled-environment house is frequently an unwise choice. The rewards, at their best, can be great but the dangers are also enormous and both the planning of the building and management of the stock need to be of a higher standard than for the climatic house.

Kennel accommodation
This is an increasingly popular system (see Fig. 10) of housing which is a compromise between the climatic and controlled-environment systems, and attempts to combine the virtue of both at low cost. The essence of the system is that it keeps the animals in pens or groups which are sufficiently small to allow them to be closely confined, at least during their resting periods, without too great a danger from

Fig. 1.11 A group of calves in a Monopitch house. There are only about 12 calves in this house which with plenty of bedding forms an ideal environment.

respiratory or other disease. The close confinement makes it possible to keep the groups warm and draught-free generally by utilising their own body heat and by good insulation of the kennel and a limited cubic area (see Figs 1.11 and 1.12). This part of the accommodation approximates to the controlled-environment house and the rest is the climatic house and can be justified as this is the area where they will be freely moving about and will not normally be lying. It is likely to contain the dung and so must be freely ventilated, usually not by artificial means. In cold and exacting climates this area will be covered but in milder regions there may be no need for this and the 'yard' can be left uncovered, with benefit to health, probably to productivity, and without doubt to cost.

It is instructive to consider the arguments that can be advanced in favour of the kennel house. The capital cost can be as low as any system, especially if the yarding is uncovered. Good health is promoted by separation of the animals into small groups. The separation of the kennels one from another should be as complete as it possibly can be as this will limit the chance of a disease building up and spreading. It will also be of some assistance to the health of the animals if the muck is not in the warmer or closely confined resting area, a virtue which is easiest to fulfil with the naturally clean pig but which is certainly achievable at least in part by other livestock. It is often possible as well, by good design, to keep the dunging area separate so that the muck from different pens does not come together until after it has passed out of reach of the animals.

The cheapness of the housing is due largely to the fact that the environment is controlled only where it is absolutely necessary. It is certainly a distinct virtue if the dung can be in an area where the air is moving more freely and the temperature and the humidity may be much lower. Controlled-environment housing is becoming more and more expensive and there is no possible justification for this control to include the effluent from the animals which is not only a considerable cost but is also likely to intensify the disease risk.

Table 1.4 on page 20 summarises the foregoing paragraphs.

Artificial warmth as an aid to therapy

Under modern systems of management animals are often housed in very large groups. When an infection occurs, the illness usually

Fig. 1.12 Warmth in kennel housing is readily obtained by using bales of straw on the roof as a temporary measure. The straw can be used later for bedding.

Table 1.4 Ambient temperature ranges and housing systems suitable for housed livestock

Type of animal	Ambient temperature range	Housing system
Adult milking cattle	Milk production optimum 10°–15°C but little effect on yield from −7° to 21°C.	Climatic housing usual and generally satisfactory.
Beef cattle (from 3 months of age)	−7° to 15°C the optimum range.	Climatic housing appropriate but thermal insulation may be needed if bedding is absent.
Calves	10°–15°C at birth which may fall gradually thereafter. Higher temperatures, 15°–21°C are used in veal houses.	Kennel housing ideal, otherwise small units with some thermal insulation.
Lambs	4°–21°C	Controlled environment may be used if housing intensive otherwise kennels satisfactory.
Adult sheep	−7° to 30°C	Climatic, or kennels.
Adult pigs	4°–30°C	Climatic housing suitable where bedding is used, but not with individually housed adults without bedding when minimum temperature should be at least 15°C higher.
Fattening pigs	15°–27°C	Controlled environment or kennel housing required.
Young piglets	21°–27°C	Artificial heating needed to supplement controlled environment.
Brooding poultry	30°–35°C	Artificial heating, essential in controlled environment housing.
Broiler chickens	15°–30°C	Artificial heating essential in controlled environment housing.
Laying poultry	15°–24°C	Controlled environment housing required with high standard insulation or occasionally climatic housing with deep straw or other litter.

produces a sense of chill to the body and there is a tendency for the stock to huddle together in an endeavour to keep warm. This is the animal's natural instinct but though it may achieve a warmer environment it will also aggravate the challenge of infection. The air around the animals may become vitiated with greater numbers of disease-producing organisms and the floor itself with higher concentrations of excreta, which may also have its quota of infection. One remedial measure that may be taken to correct this is to apply artificial heat, so discouraging the need in the animals to huddle and indeed actively encouraging a dispersal. In addition, if extra warmth is applied it will enable more ventilation to be used which will also tend to produce a healthier climate, and will be of especial benefit to livestock affected with respiratory ailments (see Figs 1.13 and 1.14).

It is not always possible, however, for the farmer to have an artificial heating source available. Other ways may be taken towards the same end. Improved, possibly temporary, insulation will conserve the animal heat and lift up the temperature. Temporary measures may be no more than making use of a few bales of straw. Another way of increasing temperature is to regulate the ventilation more efficiently — and this does not mean necessarily the restriction of ventilation which may do more harm than good — but implies more

Fig. 1.13 Radiant gas heater ideal for the artificial heating of young or sick livestock.

Fig. 1.14 Maintenance of a satisfactory environment may be enhanced by heat conservation as in this two-storey prefabricated poultry house.

attention to the elimination of draughts and stale air pockets so that air flow is uniform throughout the building.

The importance of bedding

Within recent times there has been a tendency for animals to be kept housed without bedding on slatted or perforated floors. These have one principal advantage in that they allow for the automatic disposal of dung and, if the design is good, they will keep the livestock clear of their own excreta. However, there may be serious disadvantages in eliminating the use of bedding. Good bedding is an insulator and warmer of animals, and is probably the cheapest that there is. The air temperature of buildings can be lowered if bedding is used. When the bedding is straw it may be an acceptable, if not an essential adjunct, to the diet of the animal. The fibre may help digestion and create a sense of well-being. It keeps the animals occupied and assists in the prevention of vices. Bedding also provides just about the safest flooring for the animal, so reducing the danger of injuries to the body, particularly the limbs. It is also much more difficult to keep the floor dry when no bedding is used and if the animal's surface is kept wet there is a further chilling effect created by contact with a wet floor. It is also important to emphasise the health risk from undiluted muck which does not pass through slats but accumulates at some points, and the great risk to the respiratory system of man and animals from gases rising therefrom (see later in this chapter).

Not surprisingly, therefore, there has been a trend towards the advocacy of bedding for most animals (see Fig. 1.15). This is applauded though it will be of little benefit if the amount of bedding used is inadequate or its quality questionable.

Isolation facilities

There is an urgent need for better consideration to be given by the farmer to the isolation of sick animals. There is a large number of reasons why this should be done. First and foremost it removes some of the dangers of contagion to the normal animals. It also makes it much more likely that the sick animal will recover without the unwelcome attentions of the other animals who will always tend to act as bullies. In nature the sick animal usually separates itself from the rest of the herd or flock but it is often impossible for the housed

Fig. 1.15 The suckling pig. These pigs at about 10 days of age are in the cleanest of surroundings and have the comfort of copious bedding.

animal to do this. Also, under intensive management, more animals suffer from the aggression of their pen-mates and it is essential that such animals are removed to prevent them from suffering or being killed.

It is also easier, with an isolated animal, to give it such therapy as it requires and to give it any special environmental conditions, such as extra warmth. Thus with these various items attended to there is a far greater chance of the patient recovering. It is an interesting but important observation, known to most farmers, that if you take 'poor doers', perhaps animals suffering from sub-clinical disease, out of a group, and pen them with more space and extra comfort, they may thrive without any further attention. Nevertheless, with the addition of suitable therapy, the cure may be completed.

Many modern livestock units completely ignore the provision of facilities to isolate animals and much greater attention should be given to this need.

Health and the disposal of manure

The method used for manure disposal has potentially important effects on health − both human and animal. Whilst the smell of composted solid manure tends to be strong, it rarely travels far or creates a nuisance problem and there is little if any risk to the human or animal population from this form of manure under temperate climatic conditions.

Slurry, however, is quite a different matter. If placed straight on the land from the animal house or after holding in a tank anaerobically it has an extremely offensive smell. While masking agents are possible, they are too expensive at present to be considered economic. The worst smell comes from the pipeline and gun spreader, because the droplet size is small and light and particles may carry for considerable distances. Less smell arises from a tanker spreader because the slurry is much thicker and not spread by aerially-dispersed small droplets. The most satisfactory way to prevent the slurry from causing offence is to treat it aerobically in some way before spreading. Human and animal health problems may arise from the spreading of slurry and in particular dangers have been recognised from two groups of bacteria, the *Salmonella* and *Escherichia coli*. In surveys it has been found that potentially pathogenic bacteria were able to survive up to nearly three months in slurry kept under anaerobic conditions. Whilst the particular bacteria studied were *Salmonella* species and *E. coli*, there is little doubt that more resistant organisms, such as *Bacillus anthracis, Mycobacterium tuberculosis, clostridia* species and *leptospira* species could survive as long or probably very much longer. Thus there are three possible hazards from the distribution of anaerobically stored slurry: (i) smells objectionable to the human population; (ii) hazards to human health, and (iii) hazards to animal health. If the slurry should enter a river or stream, the pollution may have far-reaching and infinitely more serious effects. It is thus essential for all enterprises with slurry as the disposal system that either the slurry is placed on land where it cannot be a nuisance or health risk or it is so treated beforehand that the risks are removed. Safe methods for disposing of solid dung and slurry are shown in Fig. 1.16.

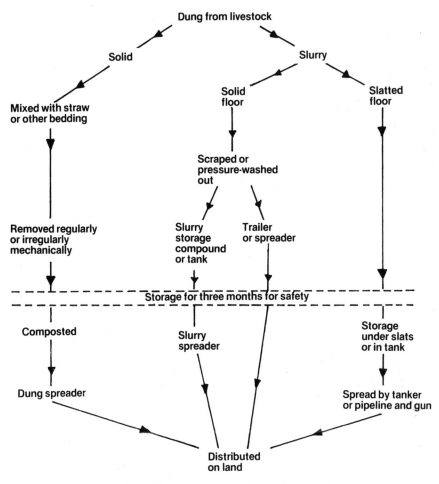

Fig. 1.16 Methods of disposing of dung safely.

The dangers from gases in farm buildings

Hazards associated with gases in and around livestock farms have been highlighted recently, particularly in association with gas effusions from slurry channels under perforated floors. Numerous fatalities have been recorded of livestock, and even of man, due to gas intoxication. There is, in addition, mounting evidence that there may be concentrations of gases in many livestock buildings that may affect production adversely by reducing feed consumption, lowering growth rates and the animals' susceptibility to invasion by pathogenic micro-organisms.

The most serious incidence of gas intoxication arises from areas of manure storage in slurry pits or channels under the stock, usually, but not always, associated with forms of perforated floors. The greatest risk arises when the manure is agitated for any reason, usually when it is removed. There is also an ever-present danger if a mechanical system of ventilation fails and this is the only method of moving air in the house. Several cases of poisoning have been reported when sluice gates are opened at the end of slurry channels and the movement of the liquid manure has forced gas up at one end into the building.

High concentrations of gases, chiefly ammonia, may also arise from built-up litter in animal housing. This is most likely in poultry housing, since the deep litter system is the most commonly used arrangement with broiler chicken and poultry breeders. The danger has undoubtedly been exacerbated within the past few years, owing to the necessity of maintaining relatively high ambient temperatures in order to reduce food costs, while at the same time there has been good evidence that higher temperatures than hitherto should be maintained for optimal productivity. Poultry farmers have often attempted to achieve such temperatures by restricting ventilation in the absence of good thermal insulation of the house surfaces, and the result can be generally harmful if not dangerous.

The most popular form of heating is by gas radiant heaters which are suspended from the ceiling. Well over half of all poultry housing is heated in this way, and because the cost of gas as a fuel appears in some respects to be improving in relation to that of other fuels, the system is being used more for pig housing and especially for piglets in the early weaning system. There is a risk that with inexpert use such heaters may be improperly serviced and the house insufficiently ventilated to give complete combustion and that toxic quantities of carbon monoxide may be produced.

The gases produced

The most important gases generated from stored manure are carbon dioxide, ammonia, hydrogen sulphide and methane; in addition there are a large number of trace organic compounds. Table 1.5 shows the limits of concentrations that are believed to be acceptable and these are expressed as threshold limit values (TLV) and given in parts per million (ppm).

Table 1.5 Acceptable limits (threshold limit value) for gases in the air of livestock buildings

Gas	Threshold limit value (TLV) (parts per million)
Carbon dioxide	5 000
Ammonia	50
Hydrogen sulphide	10
Carbon monoxide	50

Carbon dioxide: The TLV is about 5 000 ppm. Concentrations of 2 000 ppm can commonly be measured in normally ventilated controlled-environment houses. Fresh air contains about 300 ppm and more is released by respiration of animals and by manure decomposition. Most of the gas in bubbles coming from stored liquid manure is carbon dioxide. The gas in itself is not toxic but large quantities can contribute to oxygen deficiency and asphyxiation.

Ammonia: This is an important gas in animal housing. Ammonia is released from fresh manure and during anaerobic decomposition of organic matter. The problem is less with slatted flooring than with solid flooring because of the high solubility of ammonia in water. A TLV for man of 50 ppm has been set to protect against irritation to the eyes and mucous membranes of the respiratory tract. Air containing 50–100 ppm can be inhaled for some hours without any apparent effect. At 100–200 ppm it induces sneezing, salivation and loss of appetite. It is known that in the chicken such levels slow growth rate, induce kerato-conjunctivitis and reduce appetite, but even in the worst ventilated of poultry houses it is unlikely that levels higher than 50 ppm would be found, though modern practice in reducing ventilation to conserve heat makes the possibility distinctly greater.

Hydrogen sulphide: Hydrogen sulphide, with its highly characteristic smell of 'rotten eggs', is produced from the decomposition of organic wastes under anaerobic conditions. It is an extremely toxic gas and the TLV is 10 ppm. Dangerous concentrations can be released into a house if there is any form of agitation of stored slurry — concentrations of over 800 ppm have been found in livestock houses after slurry removal — and at this level unconsciousness and death in humans can result through respiratory paralysis.

Carbon monoxide: It is unlikely that carbon monoxide will appear in a livestock building other than due to the effect of incomplete combustion of gas burners. TLV is set at 50 ppm. There are a number of circumstances where this can occur. At certain times, as in brooding chickens or turkeys, the demands for heat are high but the need for ventilation is minimal. If management is careless, ventilators will be so closed that there is insufficient oxygen for the burners and substantial quantities of carbon monoxide rather than carbon dioxide are produced. Also, the maintenance of the burners may be neglected so that deposits of debris build up around the air inlets to the burners and starve the oxygen supply.

As a general conclusion it can be stated that there is adequate evidence that gases cause intoxication in and around animal buildings but there is little information as yet on the precise magnitude of the problem. Reports in recent years have tended to highlight the more extreme and spectacular dangers when, for example, ventilation fails, slurry is agitated or the combustion of burners is incomplete. Very much less is known about the effects of sub-lethal concentrations of gases on livestock given a prolonged or even a lifetime's exposure to them. It has been the author's experience that in buildings with poorly designed perforated floor systems, which allow the introduction of gases into the living area, there may be serious morbidity from respiratory disease and direct or indirect mortalities resulting on occasions. In contrast to the known harmful effects of gases there is little evidence that dust has any deleterious consequences on health at the normal concentrations found in piggeries.

Grazing management for health and productivity

The skilled management of grazing provides an adequate allowance of feed over the growing season, ensures efficient utilisation and maintains the productive capacity of the sward. There are several systems of grazing management which can give a range of optimal practices and in view of their health implications they are briefly considered in this chapter.

Grazing has a potential yield of dry matter ranging from 2 000 to 25 000 kilograms per hectare and the quality in terms of metabolisable energy ranges from 6 to 13 megajoules per kg dry matter (MJ per kg DM). Thus there is an enormous variation in the nutritional value of different quality swards.

The implications for health of the type and management of the pasture are numerous. In other chapters the relationship is shown between hypomagnesaemia, bloat, parasitic gastro-enteritis, husk and liver fluke and the management of grassland. Emphasis needs to be placed on the dangers of over-enthusiastic applications of nitrogenous and potash fertilisers and the increased risk of hypomagnesaemia created thereby. Great care must also be taken when animals are moved on to pasture in the spring or off it in the autumn. Changes must be gradual since abrupt alterations can cause severe scour, metabolic problems and excessive effects from parasitic infestation. Over-stocking of pasture and the running of young stock on pasture contaminated by the droppings of older animals also commonly create serious disease hazards.

The effect of the animal on pasture

The frequency and severity of grazing will influence the botanical composition of the pasture. Frequent close grazing encourages prostrate species and in British conditions results in a dense sward of perennial ryegrass and white clover. In contrast, infrequent grazing or cutting results in a less dense sward and encourages tall and stemmy plants such as cocksfoot.

With rotational grazing management, the frequency of grazing is largely dictated by the length of the rotation cycle. On continuous stocking, frequency increases as herbage allowance declines.

TREADING AND POACHING

Grazing animals exert pressure on the sward and compaction is more severe when the soil is wet. The effect of treading depends on the stocking rate, soil type and rainfall. Pasture species vary in resistance to treading, perennial ryegrass being one of the most resistant. In wet conditions, treading may break the surface sward, cause poaching, impairment of the drainage and seriously reduce the production of the sward.

DUNG AND URINE

The daily production of faeces from stock varies, ranging from 2.5 to 3.5 kg DM for dairy cows; 1.2 to 2.0 kg DM for young cattle and 0.3 to 0.6 kg DM for sheep. Adult cattle faeces may cover 0.5 to 1.5 m² per day with proportionately smaller areas for smaller animals. A cow will void from 6 to 25 litres of urine daily.

Dung contributes considerably to the fertility of the soil but because of the uneven distribution and the low availability of the nitrogen (about 25% in the first year), the dung is of little immediate fertiliser value. Grass surrounding dung pats is often rejected. Urine immediately contributes to plant growth and does not cause rejection.

Slurries from housed cattle, pigs or poultry are often applied. It is better if they are applied to arable land or grass to be cut for conservation. When applied to pasture they should be allowed at least 5 weeks before grazing. Great care should be taken in applying the correct quanitities of slurry. Disease hazards have been referred to earlier in this chapter.

STOCKING RATE

Full production from pasture is achieved only when the needs of the animals and the productive capacity of the pasture are in balance. Stocking rate, which affects intake and animal performance, has therefore a major influence on pasture utilisation.

The stocking rate is normally expressed as numbers of animals per hectare for a given time period. A more precise measure is the weight, or for comparing animals of different sizes, the metabolic weight ($W^{0.75}$) per hectare.

The influence of herbage allowance in the short term and of stocking rate in the long term has been examined in many investigations. When herbage allowance is high animal production is maximal and as the allowance declines, production per animal declines. Over the normal range production per animal declines linearly with increasing stocking rate.

EFFICIENCY OF GRAZING

The herbage harvested by cutting either for one growth or for the whole season may be compared with that harvested by grazing.

Direct comparison with rotational methods of grazing are feasible since the quantities of herbage present before and after grazing can be estimated but comparison with continuous methods of stocking is more difficult. Efficiency of grazing varies from 50% to 90%.

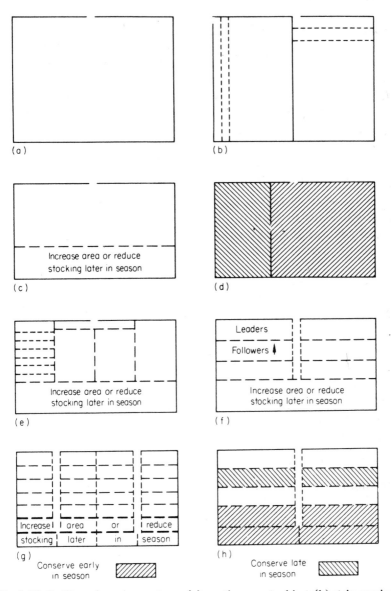

Fig. 1.17 Outline of grazing systems. (a) continuous stocking; (b) strip grazing (alternative methods); (c) intensive continuous stocking; (d) integrated grazing and conservation; (e) rigid rotational grazing; (f) leader and follower rotational grazing; (g) daily rotational paddocks; (h) flexible rotational paddocks. Permanent fence ———, temporary fence ————, movable electric fence -----. (From *Grass* edited by W. Holmes (Blackwell). Reproduced by permission.)

Grazing systems

Grazing practices (see Fig. 1.17) vary widely in the degree of control
which they provide, their requirements for capital and labour and
their influence on animal production and health and on pasture
utilisation.

Recently there has been a return by many farmers to simple
grazing systems. The major distinction is between continuous and
rotational methods. These methods have different effects on the
swards. Continuous stocking tends to encourage the development of
a dense sward with little bare ground and may encourage the maintenance of clover in the sward. In contrast, rotational methods,
especially with long grazing cycles, tend to develop a more open
sward which may be equally or more productive, but may be more
sensitive to damage from poaching and less suitable for the maintenance of white clover.

Continuous stocking

This is when a group of stock has access to one area of pasture for
the whole grazing season. It exists in its pure form only in extensive
conditions where the stocking rate in relation to pasture production
is low. There are, therefore, periods when grass growth exceeds the
needs of the animals and the herbage becomes mature, dies and
dilutes the available feed. Conventional hill grazing systems may
approach continuous stocking. If the overall herbage allowance is
high, grassland is under-utilised, coarse grasses dominate, shrubs or
trees may establish and the nutritive value of the pasture deteriorates.
If the overall herbage allowance is low, pasture is severely grazed,
poaching or erosion may occur and the stock are under-nourished
and may be parasitised.

Intensive continuous stocking

The simplicity of continuous stocking which makes few demands on
fencing, water supplies or labour, and allows the stock some choice
in the selection of feed and shelter, coupled with the realisation that
the stocking rate is the dominant factor affecting grazing output, has
led to the widespread adoption of intensive continuous stocking,
both with sheep and cattle. The stock are allowed access to an area
of pasture for the early part of the season with numbers so adjusted
that grass production and utilisation are in balance. To allow for the
lower rate of production of grass towards the end of the year, stock
requirements are reduced by the sale of fat stock and the removal to

other pastures of dry cows or ewes, or of weaned calves or lambs. Alternatively, the area available may be expanded by including regrowth from areas previously cut for hay or silage, or by the inclusion of pasture sown in the spring which becomes productive in mid-season. These methods are widely used for all cattle and sheep. Risks of parasitic infestation are considerable if the pasture is ever over-stocked.

Integrated grazing and conservation
Also referred to as the '1:2:3' or 'full-graze' system. It combines some advantages of continuous stocking with some of rotational grazing. An area of pasture is allotted to a group of stock and sub-divided in two in a ratio of between 33:67 and 40:60 by the grouping of existing fields or by dividing one large field. At the beginning of the grazing season the larger area may be grazed for one or two weeks. During the period of maximal herbage growth (mid-April to mid-June) the smaller area is grazed and the larger area allowed to grow for five to seven weeks and then cut for silage. During the middle of the growing season (mid-June to mid-August) the larger area is grazed while the smaller area, including any residues left when grazing ceased, is fertilised, allowed to grow for five to seven weeks and then cut for silage. After mid-August the stock has access to the whole area. The area available increased in the ratio 1:2:3, hence the name. It is simple to operate and economical on fences and water. It allows the stock freedom of choice and if surplus grass accumulates it can be cut and conserved. It also allows vigorous growth and build-up of root reserves and the fact that each area is free from stock for a period of five to seven weeks helps to reduce the incidence of parasitic worms. The method is specially suitable for young growing cattle and can also be adopted for milking cows and suckler cows.

Rotational grazing
A greater degree of management control is provided by rotational methods of grazing which may also facilitate greater grass production, although the benefits are only in the order of 5–10%. The risk of parasitic infestation can be reduced to a minimum with rotational systems.

The *rotational* or *grazing cycle* is the total number of days elapsing from the beginning of one grazing period to the beginning of the next in a particular area.

The number of. days within a cycle that each paddock is unoccupied by animals is called the 'rest period'. Experience has shown that the grazing cycle in British conditions should be within 20 to 30 days.

Rotational grazing systems are classified as follows:

(i) RIGID ROTATIONAL GRAZING

Here stock spend a similar time in each paddock of similar size and move according to a predetermined time-table, irrespective of the defoliation of the sward.

A typical system is the Wye College system which includes four paddocks each grazed for one week and rested for three. For dairy cows it is preferable that each paddock is divided by a temporary electric fence to give a fresh allocation on each day of the week. The system is simple to operate and at appropriate stocking rates can achieve high performance with minimum effect. It is a system that promotes good health by reducing the challenge from parasites.

(ii) FLEXIBLE ROTATIONAL GRAZING

Adjustments to the variation in pasture growth rate are possible by varying the number of days within a paddock, depending on the quantity of grass present and/or conserving some of the paddocks.

It is, however, not usually so efficient as the rigid rotational systems or 1:2:3 systems. For it is vital that in the first half of the season the cycle remains within 2 to 28 days. Attempts to achieve apparently efficient utilisation of the first paddocks to be grazed may result in the later paddocks reaching too advanced a stage of growth. It is also vital that conservation of surplus paddocks is so arranged that a continuous supply of fresh grass for grazing is maintained.

(iii) PADDOCK GRAZING

This describes either rigid or flexible rotational grazing with a large number of paddocks (20–30) where normally stock occupy each paddock for only one day.

(iv) STRIP GRAZING

This is the fresh allocation of pasture daily by moving an electric fence. It is best organised within a cycle of rotational paddocks but may be employed in one field, for the early bite, autumn saved pastures and in times of pasture scarcity. In these circumstances a back fence should be provided so that the crop is not re-grazed too soon. This helps pasture growth and reduces the risk of parasitism.

(v) LEADER AND FOLLOWER ROTATIONAL GRAZING

Within the rotational pattern successive groups of stock of differing nutrient requirements may rotate. More than two groups complicate the operation and may restrict the recovery period. For ewes with lambs, two age groups of young beef cattle, or of growing heifers, the practice is useful. The animals which need the highest quality of diet should be the leaders. With sheep and lambs, forward creep grazing is the descriptive term. An eight paddock, 24-day cycle is preferred, lambs are encouraged to creep ahead, through specially constructed gaps in the fences where they choose a high quality diet and are possibly less exposed to worm larvae. Leader-follower systems always tend to reduce the incidence of worms.

2 The Animal Body

The skeleton

The skeleton is the part of the body which gives it its fundamental shape. It is rigid and permanent and consists largely of bone, but it also includes cartilage and teeth. With few exceptions bones start as cartilage.

The skeleton also forms the structure to which the muscles are attached. The bones are composed largely of minerals, the carbonates and phosphates of calcium and magnesium. The bone consists of a hard, outer part and a softer core – the marrow cavity – part of which is a honeycomb of spongy bone, particularly near the ends of the bones.

The backbone is the basal foundation of the skeleton and consists of small bones called vertebrae, and articulation between these bones enables the animal to bend its back. The rest of the skeleton essentially articulates on the backbone and consists of the skull – made up of the cranium and the jaw bone – the long and short bones, separated by joints which form the framework of the fore and hind limbs, and paired ribs forming a hooped cage. Each of the ribs articulate with a vertebra at one end and fuse with the breast bone at the other end.

The typical long bones of the body consist of a shaft which is partly hollow and which is swollen out at the ends. The marrow cavity in the shaft is filled by blood vessels and soft fatty tissue. The dense bone consists of a matrix of white organic fibres impregnated and strengthened with mineral salts, chiefly salts of calcium and phosphorus. In this matrix are cells which are sustained by a capillary blood supply. Red blood corpuscles are formed in the marrow.

The skeleton has the following functions. It protects the organs of the body. The central nervous system is protected by the skull and vertebral column, the heart and lungs by the rib cage and the urino-genital system by the pelvis. In movement, it is the particular way in which muscles are attached to bones which enables the animal to move. Muscles always work in pairs because each muscle is capable of a pulling action. Thus one muscle pulls the bones in one direction and the opposite number in the pair pulls it back again (one is known as a 'flexor' and the other as the 'extensor'). The skeleton also serves as a storage for minerals, particularly calcium and phosphorus, which can be called upon when required as in pregnancy, milk production and egg laying.

Joints (Articulations)

Where bones adjoin and there is movement between them, to reduce friction and wear the ends of the bones are coated with very smooth cartilage; the joint is lubricated by fluid secreted by the synovial membrane within the walls of the joint (see Fig. 2.1).

The bones are also held together by tough bands of fibrous tissue, the ligaments. The whole area of the joint is a peculiarly vulnerable part of the animal body and is often attacked by pathogenic organisms, or may be easily injured, especially in the very young or old animal. In the fast-growing animal the joints are also sometimes incapable of developing quickly enough to sustain proper movement of the limbs.

Correct growth and function of the joints are assisted by good nutrition, especially the provision of the correct quantities and balance of minerals and vitamins.

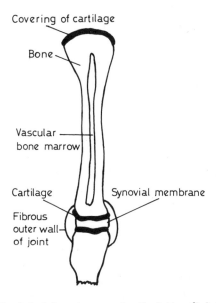

Covering of cartilage

Bone

Vascular bone marrow

Cartilage

Synovial membrane

Fibrous outer wall of joint

Fig. 2.1 A long bone and articulation (joint).

Teeth

There are three types of teeth, incisors, canines and molars. The incisors are the front teeth, then comes the canine or tusk; the back teech are the molars. All mammals have a set of temporary teeth which are succeeded later by the permanent teeth. Not all the molar positions are filled in the temporary set, the latter being known as pre-molars. As the numbers vary between different species a dental formula is used which indicates the various teeth to be found on each side of the mouth for any species. In the ruminants a hard pad, the dental pad, exists instead of the incisors on the upper jaw. The lower incisors tear herbage by gripping it between the lower incisors and the dental pad.

Ageing of animals by teeth is usually carried out by reference to the incisor teeth only. It is done on the basis of the time of eruption and subsequently the characteristics of the wear that takes place.

The muscular system

The function of the muscles is to move parts of the body. Some muscles are under the control of the will and are called voluntary muscles. Others operate outside the animal's control and are described as involuntary muscles.

The typical voluntary muscle has a tendon at each end with the body of the muscle between. Tendons are composed of tough fibrous material because they have to take the strain when the muscle contracts by swelling laterally. The tendons of the muscles of the limbs are inserted into bone so, if one of the bones is considered to be stationary, the other must move when the muscle contracts. Many muscles are not attached to bone — for example, those which move the skin, and those which are involuntary in nature and move the stomach, intestinal walls, and also the heart.

The digestive system

There are clear distinctions between the digestive systems of the single-stomached animals like the pig; the ruminant, such as the cow and sheep; and poultry, e.g. the domestic fowl.

In all cases, however, the basic arrangement is similar. The digestive system consists of a long tube, known as the alimentary canal, with a number of accessory organs associated with digestion, such as the liver and the pancreas. The canal starts at the mouth, continues as the pharynx or throat and then passes through to the oesophagus (gullet) which takes the food, which has in most cases been chewed or masticated, to the stomach or stomachs. The food then goes on to the small or large intestines for the major processes of digestion, and finally undigested material is voided at the anus (or cloaca in the bird). In the process of dealing with food there are the processes of mastication — breaking up the feed — which is done by the teeth in mammals, but in the gizzard in the case of chickens. The food is then digested by chemicals which break down the proteins, carbohydrates and fat in the food into products that are simple enough to be absorbed through the intestinal wall. Digestion is brought about by enzymes which are secreted by glands such as the pancreas and pass into the alimentary canal.

All the organs of the body are delicate and need protection, either as they move against each other or as material passes along the alimentary canal. Both protection and lubrication is supplied by membranes which line the organs.

The lining of passages which communicate with the exterior, such as those in the alimentary canal or respiratory system, are called mucous membranes. Those which cover surfaces closed from the exterior are called serous membranes. Membranes vary considerably in their strength and thickness: for example, the mucous membrane lining the mouth is tough as the food may be quite coarse and damaging, whereas that lining the intestine is much thinner as the food is now soft and wet. All mucous membranes secrete mucus, a slimy lubricant, but in illness the absence of secretion may be an early feature. The serous membranes lining the body cavities are the peritoneum round the abdomen and its organs, the pleura round the lungs and the pericardium around the heart.

An outline of the digestive process

THE SINGLE STOMACH ANIMAL

Food passes into the mouth, is masticated with teeth, moved with the tongue and has secretions from the salivary glands containing the enzymes which commence the process of digestion. At the rear of the mouth is the pharynx, which has several openings including that from the nose; and at the base is the entrance to the trachea (windpipe) and thence the lungs, and also the entrance to the gullet or oesophagus (see Fig. 2.2). The food passes down the oesophagus to the stomach. Here food is further digested and stored and is released into the intestines in controlled amounts.

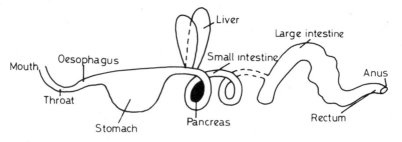

Fig. 2.2 Alimentary system of a pig.

The intestines are up to 30 metres long in the pig and are divided into the small intestines (duodenum, jejunum and ileum) and large intestines (caecum, colon and rectum). Most food is actually absorbed in the small intestine. Enzymes pass from the pancreas into the duodenum and from the liver via the bile gland and duct. In the large intestines much of the water is absorbed leaving relatively dry faeces to pass out via the anus.

THE RUMINANT

The ruminant (see Fig. 2.3) has four stomachs. The first is the large *rumen* which can occupy up to half the abdomen and will hold as much as 250 litres in cattle. From here the food passes to the *reticulum*, then the *omasum* and finally the *abomasum* which is the organ having the same function as the stomach of the single stomach animals.

The complexity of this system is to enable the ruminant to deal with coarse and fibrous feed. Food is swallowed firstly without any real mastication and regurgitated later in mouthfuls and ground between the molar teeth.

There is great activity all the time in the ruminant's stomach, producing much heat and gas with constant eructations of the latter.

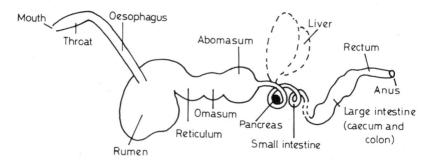

Fig. 2.3 Alimentary system of a ruminant.

THE FOWL

The fowl is different in the nature of its digestive system (see Fig. 2.4). The beak gathers the food material and at its edges are tactile cells by which the bird decides whether it will accept the food or reject it. The food is swallowed whole, with a little saliva added, passes down the oesophagus to the crop which is basically a container only for bulky food. Here the fibre is well softened and the food acidified. From the crop the food passes to the proventriculus which secretes hydrochloric acid and pepsin, and then to the gizzard – a strong muscular organ which contracts powerfully, reducing the contents to a thick paste-like mass with the aid of the insoluble grit present within it. The food then passes to the small and large intestines and finally the faeces go to the cloaca which is also concerned with the excretion of urine, the acceptance or delivery of semen, and the passage of the egg.

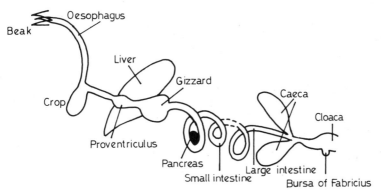

Fig. 2.4 Alimentary system of a fowl.

The respiratory system

The respiratory system's function is essentially to enable oxygen to be brought into the blood and remove the carbon dioxide and water from it (see Fig. 2.5).

The fresh air that is so vital for life passes through the nostrils. Mammalian nostrils are lined with turbinate bones which are thin plates arranged in cylindrical fashion. These bones are lined with highly vascular mucous membranes and also equipped with small hairs (cilia). The vascularity helps to warm air before it enters the lungs and the cilia help to trap dust and germs. However, their vulnerability makes the turbinate bones very susceptible to damage epitomised in the pig where it inflames and destroys the tissue (e.g. atrophic rhinitis in pigs).

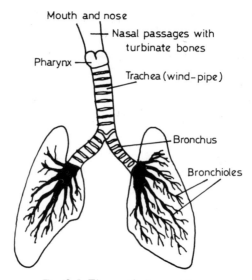

Mouth and nose

Nasal passages with
turbinate bones

Pharynx

Trachea (wind-pipe)

Bronchus

Bronchioles

Fig. 2.5 The respiratory system.

At the back of the throat is the larynx which is the gateway to
the trachea. The trachea is constructed largely of rings of cartilage
which safely maintain its rigidity. When the trachea reaches the
lungs it divides into two bronchi which then divide and sub-divide
into numerous branches known as bronchioles which then go into
terminal air spaces called alveoli. This is where the exchange of
oxygen and carbon dioxide and water vapour takes place. The lungs
are favoured areas for the lodgement and multiplication of many
pathogenic organisms.

The circulatory system

The blood is the transport mechanism that gathers the oxygen from
the lungs and the food products absorbed from the intestines and
also releases carbon dixoide through the lungs and other waste
products chiefly through the kidneys. Blood also regulates the heat
of the body.

The blood circulates via the heart, arteries, veins and capillaries.
Arteries convey the blood from the heart, veins bring blood back
towards the heart.

The main artery leaving the heart, the *aorta*, distributes via various
branches the blood to all parts of the body (see Fig. 2.6). Arteries go
on constantly dividing until they become the smallest, the arterioles,
and from there to the very small capillaries which are the links in the

tissues between the arterioles and the venules which are the corresponding part of the venous system whereby the blood is returned to the heart. It is by means of the capillaries that the exchange of gases, nutrients and waste products takes place. From the venules, the blood passes to the veins which eventually take all the blood back to the heart.

Arteries are strong, elastic, muscular tubes as they must withstand the powerful force of the heart beat which drives the blood through them, while veins have a passive role of conveying the blood back to the heart. The arteries supplement the force of the heart, and expand and contract to help the blood on its way.

Where the arteries leave the heart one-way valves prevent the blood flowing backwards as the heart expands for its next quota of blood. These are the only arterial valves but valves are frequent in veins to prevent the blood flowing back from the heart. Arterial blood which is oxygenated is bright red, and venous blood darker.

The heart and lungs

The powerful heart situated nearly in the centre of the thorax (chest) consists of four cavities — two on each side. There is no direct contact between left and right except in the foetus when the functionless lungs are short-circuited. The upper cavities are known as the auricles and below, separated by valves, as the ventricles.

Blood from the whole body enters the right auricle and passes through the one-way valve to the right ventricle as the auricle contracts and then, as the ventricle contracts, blood is forced into

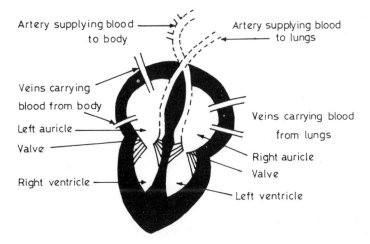

Fig. 2.6 The heart.

the pulmonary artery leading to the lungs. After passing through the lung capillaries, where carbon dioxide is released and oxygen collected, the blood travels via the pulmonary vein to the left auricle. Contraction of the two sides of the heart is simultaneous and from the left ventricle blood is pumped via the aorta to all parts of the body.

Blood

Mammalian blood is composed of fluid and cells. The fluid, blood plasma, is a solution of nutrients and salts and includes carbon dioxide, mostly in the form of bicarbonates.

The red colour is due to the red blood cells, present at the rate of about 6–10 million per cubic millilitre. They have no nucleus except in the youngest stages and their total life in the blood-stream is about 6 weeks. The red colour is a protein called haemoglobin and this contains iron. Haemoglobin readily takes up oxygen (from the lungs) and gives it up to the tissues as required.

White blood cells are present in the blood at the rate of about 8 000 to 17 000 cells per ml^3 (ruminants contain much less than pigs). There are many different types and their main function is to protect the animal against invasion by pathogenic microbes. The two main types of white blood cells are the lymphocytes and the polymorphonuclear leucocytes: the latter can alter their shape and they will pass through the walls of capillaries in areas of inflammation and engulf invading organisms in order to digest them.

There are also blood platelets – about 200 000 per ml^3 – small cells which are concerned with the clotting mechanism. If bleeding occurs the platelets fracture, release an enzyme, resulting in the formation of fibrin, a stringy material which adheres to the walls of wounds and enmeshes escaping blood cells. The fibrin contracts and draws the cells together, thus tending to seal the wound and stop the haemorrhage.

The lymphatic system

Lymph is a cloudy fluid produced in the tissue spaces from the blood plasma which passes out of the capillaries to assist the function of the individual cells. The tubes of the system join up as the veins do but they are much smaller. Ultimately lymph finds its way into the anterior vena cava near the heart. Along the lymphatics are the nodes where lymphocytes are generated. Any foreign material not dealt with at the site of entry will find its way along the lymphatics and each lymph node acts as a barrier to further advance. Invading bacteria will usually have to overcome several of these barriers before

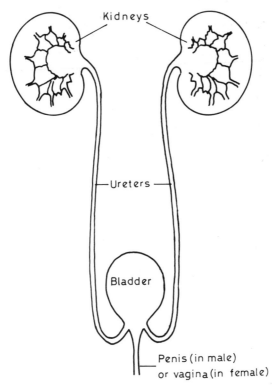

Fig. 2.7 The urinary system.

reaching the blood-stream for general circulation. The lymph nodes become enlarged, tender and inflamed when dealing with an invasion.

The urinary system

The urinary system (see Fig. 2.7) consists in the mammal of two kidneys, two ureters, the bladder and the urethra. The kidneys are situated under the lumbar vertebrae and are extremely well supplied with blood. Their function is to remove all the waste products of metabolism which are carried away in the urine. The exchange of products takes place by diffusion. This occurs in many glomeruli situated in the outer part of the kidney the cortex. A glomerulus (see Fig. 2.8) looks like the head of a flower in cross section. Capillaries ramify in the glomerulus and the space around the capillaries is the beginning of a urinary tubule which leads to the centre of kidney from whençe a tube known as a ureter leads to the bladder. Water passes from the blood capillaries of the glomeruli into the

Fig. 2.8 Schematic diagram of a section through a glomerulus.

urinary tubules and in it are the end products of metabolism and minerals.

Urine is continually produced in the kidneys and trickles down the ureter on each side to enter the bladder situated on the floor of the pelvis. The bladder is a storage organ composed of highly muscular tissue, and is pear-shaped with the narrow end pointing hindwards ending in a sphincter muscle which leads into the urethra. The sphincter muscle is normally closed but as the bladder becomes distended nerve impulses lead to the releasing of the sphincter and contraction of the muscle of the bladder to assist in the elimination of the urine.

The bladder leads to the urethra. The female urethra is short with a wide passage and opens into the vagina just above the bladder. The vagina is a common passage with the genital system which opens to the exterior through the vulva, an opening situated immediately below the anus.

The male urethra is a long, narrow tube directed backwards from the bladder along the floor of the pelvis and then curled down and forward under the pelvis to continue in the substance of the penis.

The genital organs

The male

Sperm for reproduction is produced in the pair of testicles which are situated in the scrotum (see Fig. 2.9). Nerves and blood vessels serving the testicles enter the scrotum in the spermatic cord which also includes the vas deferens, the tube along which sperm travel from the testicle. In farm animals such as the bull, ram and boar, the scrotum is suspended under the abdomen, though in the boar the scrotum is held close to the body.

The testicles orginate inside the abdomen of the foetus and travel down sometime near parturition through an opening between muscles on each side. In passing out of the abdomen into the scrotum, each testicle takes with it a fold of peritoneum. Thus there is a risk of hernia — i.e. the passing of abdominal contents, in this case intestines, into the scrotum. Hernia is most common in the pig. In some cases the testicle fails to enter the scrotum. It may come later or be permanently retained in the abdomen. A male animal with this defect is called a *rigg*. Most male farm animals are adversely affected in the production of fertile spermatozoa if the environment is too warm, and the testicles — themselves being outside the abdominal cavity proper — are more than normally vulnerable.

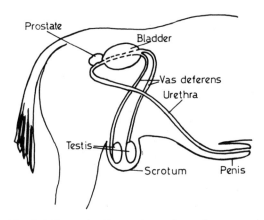

Fig. 2.9 Reproductive system of a male mammal.

The vas deferens, after leaving the testicles and passing up the spermatic cord, continues over the bladder to enter the urethra before it enters the penis which is normally held within the prepuce — a fold of protective skin. The penis has much elasticity and contains spaces within it which are part of the blood circulatory system. Under sexual stimulus these spaces become engorged with blood, resulting in a substantial lengthening and stiffening of the penis so that it protrudes from the prepuce — an essential process in copulation.

The female

Ova, the primary female cells in reproduction, are produced in the paired ovaries situated high in the abdominal cavity. They are small bodies varying in size and shape during the sexual cycle. In the substance of the young ovary are many follicles, each containing one large cell, the ovum. Most of the follicles are at any time quiescent but enlargement occurs before any follicle bursts to release an ovum into the fallopian tube or oviduct, a much convoluted narrow tube which leads to the uterus (or womb).

The uterus is an organ of greatly variable size, for it is here the young develop before birth. The uterus has a cervix (the neck), a body and two horns. Each fallopian tube enters a horn. The two horns form the main part of the uterus and one or both become greatly distended during pregnancy. The horns join to form the short body and the cervix is the area of the complex sphincter muscle which is normally closed, opening slightly during oestrus and subject to great distension at the time of parturition. The wall of the uterus is muscular. During pregnancy the muscle increases in size and power. The foetal membranes are attached in various ways to the uterus and by this means receive nutrients.

Passing back from the cervix is the short but very distendable vagina which opens to the exterior at the vulva (see Fig. 2.10).

Reproduction

At puberty animals become sexually active. The male seeks the opportunity for mating and the female commences the cyclic period of oestrus or heat when she is receptive to the male. As puberty approaches, the secondary sex characteristics develop. This is most noticeable in the features and shape and form of the head, but the whole male frame is bigger and somewhat coarser.

Oestrus is the state of heat when a female will accept a male. This happens in regular cycles. The cycle is about 21 days in the cow, 17 days in the ewe and 21 days in the sow. Oestrus itself lasts up to about 24 hours in the cow and up to 2 days in the ewe and sow. Oestrus is controlled from the ovaries, the animal coming into

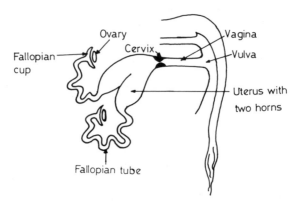

Fig. 2.10 Reproductive system of a female mammal.

Empty follicles

Albumin-secreting region

Isthmus,with incomplete egg, where shell membrane is deposited

Uterus or shell gland forming the shell

Vagina

Cloaca

Fig. 2.11 Ovary and oviduct of a chicken (after Romanoff).

oestrus as a follicle approaches maturity just prior to releasing an ovum into the fallopian tube. After rupture of the follicle slight bleeding occurs and a clot forms in the ovary which shortly becomes organised into the corpus luteum. This corpus luteum grows during the first part of the oestrus cycle and disappears before the next oestrus. If the animal becomes pregnant the corpus luteum continues to grow slowly and only recedes in the second half of the pregnancy. The presence of the corpus luteum inhibits oestrus and delays the development of any more ovarian follicles.

Cows and sows have oestrus cycles at all seasons but in sheep the oetrus cycles are limited to a definite season. There is considerable variation in the factors that induce a return to oestrus cycles after a parturition.

The reproductive system of the fowl is essentially the same as in the mammal but with certain notable differences. The testes of the male remain within the abdominal cavity near the kidneys. In the hen, only one ovary, the left, develops and becomes functional. In the functional female the ovary contains 5 to 6 large developing egg yolks (follicles) and a large number of small white follicles which represent immature undeveloped yolks. The large convoluted oviduct (see Fig. 2.11) is the site of egg white secretion, shell membrane and egg shell formation. As the yolk passes down the oviduct, therefore, the remainder of the egg is formed and then is 'laid', after which most of the development of the embryo takes place if the egg is 'incubated' for 21 days at about 37.5°C.

Sexual activity in birds is stimulated by increasing amounts of light, as in spring time, whereas decreasing amounts, as in the autumn, tend to put birds off lay and lead to a moult. Most hens will produce about 150 fertile eggs in a season.

Signs of oestrus vary. In the ewe they are slight unless a ram is present and he is probably attracted by smell. The sow when in season become quiet and it is possible to sit on her back, whereas at other times she is not likely to accept this. An important essential with pigs is to place boars within sight, sound and smell of the sows.

In cows the signs of heat are as follows. One cow may ride another, but either may be on heat. The cow on heat is restive, may try to break out, and is noisy. The vulva is usually swollen and there is a stringy mucous discharge.

Pregnancy

At mating the tadpole-like sperms move vigorously up the female tract into the fallopian tube where, if fertilisation is to take place, the sperm and ovum (the female egg) join together to form the embryo. During pregnancy certain changes take place. Oestrus cycles cease. Abdominal enlargement takes place. Various techniques exist to determine very early pregnancy, including palpation, hormone determination and sonic recorders.

The upper mammary glands also gradually enlarge in preparation for the supply of milk. Pregnant animals also tend to put on weight gradually and their temperament often improves and they become more docile.

The nervous system

The central nervous system is the name given to the brain and spinal cord. The rest of the nerves are described as being peripheral. The cells of the nervous system have processes which carry impulses or messages. There may be several short processes to receive messages but only one process takes impulses from the cells and this may be extremely long, extending right down a limb. These long processes are extremely fine individually, but large numbers of them are bound together to form the nerve which can be seen by the naked eye.

All conscious action and thought is centred in the right and left hemispheres of the brain. Subconscious control may be effected from the cerebellum at the back of the brain, below which the medulla oblongata leads into the spinal cord, which runs through the spinal column.

Nerves leave the brain to serve the head and the special organs of sight, hearing and smell. Branches leave the spinal cord behind the arch of each vertebra in pairs, one each side (see Fig. 2.12). The main nerve trunk of the limbs, such as the radial in the fore limb and the sciatic in the hind limb, are derived from several branches of the spinal cord. The nerves in their bundles are of two types, *afferent* nerves bringing messages into the brain, sensations of touch and temperature and *efferent* nerves taking messages from the brain which result in action. All parts of the body are served by both types of nerves.

The autonomic nervous system

In addition to the nerves serving centres in the brain, a whole system of nerves governs the involuntary activities of the body (see Fig. 2.12). These autonomic nerves are linked to each other and have connections with the spinal cord. They control the activities of glands, the involuntary muscles of the digestive and other systems, the heart muscle and the pupil of the eye.

The autonomous nerves are in two groups working antagonistically

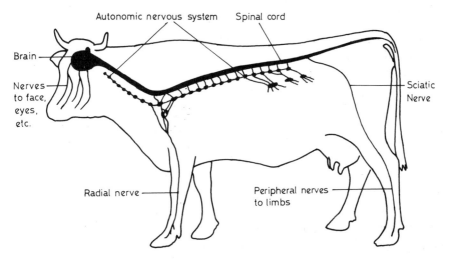

Fig. 2.12 Diagrammatic representation of the central nervous system and autonomic (sympathetic and parasympathetic) nervous system.

to meet the varying needs of the body. One group, the sympathetic nervous system, produces effects similar to those produced by the hormone adrenalin. It reduces the activity of the digestive system, stimulates the heart muscle and tends to concentrate the blood in the areas of action. The sympathetic nerves are therefore in the ascendancy in emergency. The other group, the parasympathetic nerves, stimulate muscular and glandular activities in the digestive system, urinary and sexual activity and have a depressing effect on the heart muscle. Afferent nerves from all over the body can bring impulses resulting from touch, pressure, temperature and pain, but certain organs are responsible for special senses which are of great importance to the animal – the eyes, the ears and the centres responsible for smell and taste.

The skin

The skin is the protective outer layer of the body. It is richly supplied with nerve endings responsible for sensations of touch, heat, cold and pain. The skin is continuous with the mucous membranes at all the natural orifices of the body. It varies greatly in thickness and toughness and sensitivity, depending on the needs of the situation. The outermost layer of the skin, the epidermis, is a thick mass of cells with neither blood supply nor nerve endings. These cells are continuously being shed. Underneath is the true skin, the dermis, with both blood and nerve supply. It contains hair follicles (see Fig. 2.13) together with sebaceous glands which produce an oily protective

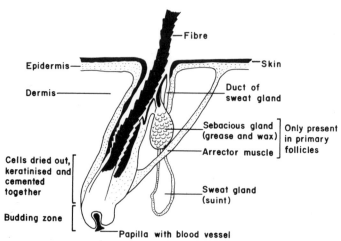

Fig. 2.13 Cross-section of a hair follicle, also showing structure of skin. (Courtesy of Dr D C Dalton.)

material. Sweat glands are also present in the skin which assist in the heat-control mechanism.

Hair and wool are modifications of skin — a hard protein substance which serves as a means of protection. Hair is continually being shed and thicker hair will grow to respond to cooler conditions. Hoof and horn are also modifications of skin composed of hard protein.

The endocrine organs

The endocrine organs — also called ductless glands — produce secretions but instead of being led by ducts to their point-of-use, they pass directly into the blood stream where they can travel to all areas as required. These secretions are called hormones. The glands and their main functions are as follows.

Thyroid gland

The thyroid gland is situated in the neck close to the larynx. Thyroxin, the hormone it produces, contains iodine which is an essential element in its production. Thyroxin is a general long-term metabolic stimulant — it is a master gland in its effect on metabolism. A deficiency results in a fat, sluggish individual that loses its hair. Excessive thyroxin increases growth rate, activity and appetite.

Hypothyroidism occurs in areas of low iodine — such as Derbyshire. Hence, correct levels of iodine are most important in the ration for the correct functioning of thyroxin.

Parathyroid glands

These are very small glands situated within the substance of the thyroid. They are concerned with calcium metabolism.

Adrenal glands

These are small paired glands beside each kidney. They consist of two quite distinct parts. The outer part is the cortex, which produces a large number of fatty substances known as corticosteroids. These have three main functions — they control the mineral and the carbohydrate metabolism and reduce sensitivity and immunity reactions. The latter is a usage which is widely practised in human and veterinary medicine to assist the body's recovery, prevent over-reaction and allergies to infections and foreign substances. The inner part — the medulla — produces adrenaline, the hormone of 'fright, flight and fight', i.e. it prepares the body for reaction to catastrophes and stresses.

The pancreas

Much of the tissue of the pancreas is concerned with digestion and in this respect the gland has a duct but within the gland are the Islets of Langerhans which act as an endocrine gland. They produce insulin which converts the glucose in the blood into glycogen — an insoluble carbohydrate which is stored as a reserve in the liver and muscles. Insulin and adrenalin act in an antagonistic way which produce a balance — insulin arranging the storage of potential energy and adrenalin making it available.

The pituitary gland

This is a small gland situated at the base of the brain. It produces a number of hormones, most of which activate other endocrine organs. Hormones largely control the development of reproductive organs, the reproductive cycle, successful pregnancy, the development of the udder and the let-down of milk. The pituitary is responsible for initiating this activity but also influences other endocrine organs, particularly the thyroid and adrenal cortex.

One hormone from the pituitary with little effect on the reproductive organs is the growth hormone — the rate of secretion during the growing period being largely responsible for the ultimate size of the individual.

THE REPRODUCTIVE HORMONES OF THE PITUITARY

1. *The follicle stimulating hormone (FSH).* Before puberty this helps growth of the reproductive organs in the male and female. After puberty FSH brings the ovarian follicle to maturity.

2. *Luteinising hormone (LH).* The LH causes the follicle to burst, releasing the ovum. It then supplies the stimulus for the production of the corpus luteum in the crater resulting from the burst follicle. The follicular fluid and the corpus luteum produce further hormones. In the male FSH is responsible for the development of sperm and LH stimulates the growth of the supporting tissue in the testicles where the sperm are produced.

3. *Oxytocin.* Oxytocin is a hormone from the pituitary which has a number of effects. It acts rapidly, on the udder tissue particularly, causing a let-down of milk into the cistern above the teat. The secretion is influenced by any action or noise associated with the process. For example, the noise of the piglets or butting of the

udder, or in cows any action associated with the normal milking routine.

The reproductive organ hormones

Oestrogen causes oestrus. The principal one occurs in the follicular fluid of the ovary. The hormone is, in fact, already being produced in small quantities early in life, even in foetal life and results in the female conformation. When a follicle becomes large the increased production of oestrogen has an effect on the uterus and above all results in the behaviour known as oestrus or heat. When a follicle bursts the oestrogen is lost but the corpus luteum which replaces it secretes progesterone which causes a quiescent state in the muscles of the uterine wall and at the same time stimulates production of nutriment from the uterine wall and other activities in preparation of the embryo. If conception takes place the corpus luteum persists and progesterone continues to act as a stimulus to enlargement of the uterus and also leads to an increase in milk-secreting tissue in the udder.

Progesterone has an antagonistic effect on the pituitary gland tending to suppress the production of FSH and LH so that during pregnancy ovarian follicles remain quiescent and oestrus does not occur, a rule with only the rarest exceptions. Pregnancy can usually be ended if the corpus luteum is squeezed off the ovary of the cow by manipulation through the wall of the rectum.

When conception does not take place the corpus luteum only develops for about half the oestrus cycle and then regresses. Progesterone is then secreted in ever-decreasing amounts, the pituitary becomes more active and one or more follicles enlarge as oestrus occurs. Fig. 2.14 illustrates diagrammatically the oestrous cycle of the sow.

Testosterone is produced in the male testicles and brings about the male characteristics and the development of the secondary male organs such as the prostate gland.

Prostaglandins are important hormones produced by the reproductive organs of both sexes. Their functions of practical interest are in female reproduction but many tissues have been found to produce prostaglandins. They are inducive to both oestrus and parturition. Prostaglandins are frequently used to induce parturition and also to stimulate oestrus.

The development of the foetus

The foetus begins as a fertilised ovum which then divides and goes on so doing. The embryo, as it is now called, comes to reside in a horn of the uterus where further nutriment is derived from the secretions of the glands in the uterine wall. The first differentiation is into three tissue layers which develop as follows.

The ectoderm gives rise to the skin and central nervous system, the endoderm gives rise to the alimentary canal and the mesoderm to the organs and tissues in between. At an early stage the layers fold over as if to form a cylinder and the ectoderm, as its name implies, becomes continuous on the outside except for the area of the umbilicus whence the foetal membranes are rapidly formed. The membranes are initially a fluid-containing sac which grows up over the top of the foetus from each end. When the two ends meet fusion occurs in such a way as to produce two separate membranes round the foetus, each containing liquid. Thereafter the foetus is suspended in this double fluid container, which protects it from buffeting. The two membranes are together known as the placenta. At parturition they become the 'afterbirth'. The different tissues and organs of the foetus develop with great rapidity.

As the female approaches the end of her pregnancy the udder enlarges and milk will begin to be secreted. The vulva becomes enlarged and up to 48 hours before parturition the sacro-sciatic ligament will slacken. The animal, if free, will tend to draw away alone from her fellows and will often cease to feed. Sows will make nests if given the opportunity. Labour pains mark the beginning of parturition — these being due to the contraction of the uterine muscles.

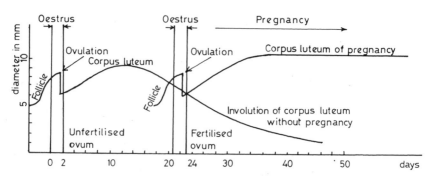

Fig. 2.14 The oestrous cycle of the sow (after Corner). Note the enlargement of the follicle and the regression of the corpus luteum if fertilisation does not occur. If the follicle is fertilised, the corpus luteum enlarges and persists during pregnancy.

Fig. 2.15 Normal position of calf in the uterus before delivery.

Labour pains come in spasms, the interval between them becoming less and less as parturition progresses. Sows grunt, sheep bleat and cows bellow.

The cervix must open and the vagina dilate. Under the pressure of the uterine muscles, the fluid-filled placenta firstly enters the cervical canal. This placental sac is known as the water-bag, it tends to go through the vagina and then extends outside the vulva. The bag usually bursts to be followed by the birth of the young. After the young are born the afterbirth is expelled.

Fig. 2.15 shows the normal position of a calf before delivery, but there are many abnormalities in parturition. For example, the presentation being backwards; limbs being retracted; the head being retained in a sideways position. In general, difficult mal-presentations should be dealt with by the veterinary surgeon.

3 Disease, Immunity and Welfare

Organisms causing infections

A substantial number of micro-organisms cause disease in livestock and it may be helpful to give a classification of these.

The smallest of them are the viruses, below 300 mμ in size, but many are well below this. For example, the foot-and-mouth disease viruses are 10 to 27 mμ (1 μ = 0.001 mm and 1 mμ = 0.000001 mm). Viruses cannot usually be seen under the ordinary microscope but can be photographed by the electron microscope. They are simple organisms that can only multiply within living cells, and this property distinguishes them from bacteria. Viruses are classified into a substantial number of different groups, e.g. reoviruses, adenoviruses, herpesviruses.

Bacteria are relatively large organisms, compared with viruses, and can multiply and grow outside living tissues. In size, for example, cocci (round) bacteria measure 0.8 to 1.2 μ, rods (bacilli) are 0.2 to 2 μ, and the spiral-shaped spirella up to 50 μ. They are visible under the ordinary microscope. Many types, once outside the animal body, may sporulate to form a protective coat so that they can live many years in buildings, soil or elsewhere and can still be capable of infecting animal life. For example, the spores of anthrax and clostridium can live for 20 years or more under favourable circumstances.

Mycoplasma are smaller organisms than bacteria, being about 0.25 to 0.5 μ (or 250 to 500 mμ). They are rather like oversize viruses but, unlike viruses, they can be cultured on artificial media.

Rickettsia are of somewhat smaller size to mycoplasma, being 0.25 to 0.4 μ, but they cannot be grown in ordinary culture media and will only multiply intracellularly, like viruses.

All these organisms are from the vegetable kingdom and can be joined by the yeasts (moulds and fungi) which are larger than bacteria and a few varieties of which cause diseases in animals and man.

There are also many simple organisms from the animal kingdom, known as parasites, that cause disease in farm livestock. These range from the single-cell protozoa, such as the coccidial parasite, to parasites of ever increasing size and complexity, culminating in such relatively complicated organisms as the roundworms (helminths), lice, flies and ticks.

Table 3.1 A summary of the living organisms causing disease

Organism	Size range	Main characteristics
Viruses	From 10 mμ (0.00001 mm) to 300 mμ	The smallest group of pathogenic organisms. Can only multiply in living cells. Often very contagious. Quite vulnerable to destruction outside body.
Bacteria	From 0.1 μ (0.001 mm)	Relatively large. Great variety of size and shape. Can multiply and grow outside animal cells. Can form spores to resist destruction for many years. Contagious but less so than viruses.
Mycoplasma	0.25 to 0.5 μ	Resemble large viruses but they can multiply outside animal cells like bacteria. Moderately contagious in nature.
Rickettsia	0.25 to 0.4 μ	Similar in size to mycoplasma but only multiply in cells like viruses.
Fungus	0.1 μ to 5 mm	Rapid multiplication under warm damp conditions. Easy survival. Quite resistant to disinfection.
Parasites	From 1 μ to 300 mm	From animal kingdom. Live whole or part of their lives on or within animals. Life cycles often complex with secondary hosts. Range from single cell protozoa, such as coccidia to parasites of ever increasing size and complexity, e.g. helminths, lice, flies and ticks.

Organisms from these groups are the main cause of infectious disease in farm livestock. The only other agents causing disease and which are not infectious are the metabolic diseases, poisons, deficiencies, excesses and injuries, examples of which are found throughout the book.

Immunity

In our understanding of the mechanism of disease control it is essential to know the principles of the animal's immunological disease control system and the way in which we make use of such products as vaccines and sera to boost it as necessary. This is best understood by studying the cycle of events in any animal's life.

When an animal is born it is relatively free of disease organisms but it has what is known as *passive immunity*, which it receives from the mother whilst still *in utero*. If the mother has been vaccinated against a disease or has had an experience of the actual disease, then her immunological system will produce the antibodies that are capable of resisting the disease. These antibodies circulate in the blood and will also be transferred to the foetus. The antibodies themselves are effective only for about 2–3 weeks before they disappear.

The young animal can produce only its own antibodies and thus develop what is known as *active immunity* if it has experienced the disease in question, or has been vaccinated against it. It should be stressed that an animal will have some passive immunity only to those particular infections experienced by the mother. These may be quite limited and 'local'. This is a good argument for rearing an animal in the environment in which it is conceived and a good reason for not transporting young animals too early in life before they have some better ability to resist a 'foreign' disease challenge. Passive immunity in mammals is fortified immediately after birth by the young drawing the first milk (or colostrum) from the dam. Colostrum is especially rich in antibodies and also nutrients.

As the passive immunity the young animal receives from its mother wanes it may be replaced by an active immunity if the young animal is vaccinated or has some challenge from the organisms that can cause disease. Under practical conditions the aim is to make sure that any natural challenge of potentially pathogenic organisms is mild or gradual, not massive and overwhelming.

Sometimes it is perfectly satisfactory to allow the animals to receive a 'natural' challenge from the environment, but this is at the best inexact and at its worst ineffective. Thus, various methods of

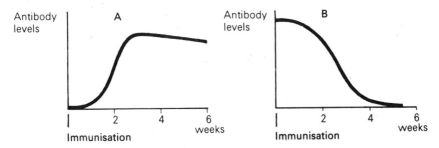

Fig. 3.1 Immunity. The curves in the diagrams represent antibody levels produced by active and passive immunisation. (A) shows the gradual development of antibodies after active immunisation, as with a vaccine. (B) shows the immediate but short-lived protection from passive immunity, as with hyperimmune serum.

induced immunity are given, either *passive* or *active* (see Fig. 3.1). The passive immunity is induced by injecting into the animal hyperimmune antiserum prepared from the serum of animals which have experienced the actual infection and have recovered. This serum may be used for treatment of the disease and for passive immunity but has only a transitory effect lasting about three weeks, similar to the natural immunity received by the young animal from its mother.

For an active immunity, vaccines are used. A vaccine is a way of activating the body's defence mechanism by challenging it with the pathogenic organisms so modified that they are just active enough to produce an immunity but not the disease itself. The modification is done in very many ways — by adding chemicals, by growth of the organism in special media or livestock of a different species or by irradiation. Sometimes no modification is required as an organism can be used which is sufficiently closely related to induce immunity but not disease.

The production of vaccines is a very sophisticated process but can induce an enormously efficient protection for the animal. Vaccines must be used by skilled hands at the right time in the correct dose and repeated as necessary since the immunities developed vary according to the infection. It should be borne in mind that when a vaccine is given the immunity takes time to develop — somewhere in the order of three weeks — so it may be necessary to protect an animal during that time by antisera, antibiotics or simply by isolation. Some vaccines are of live organisms, others are dead. In general the live vaccine may give a stronger immunity more quickly but it is not necessarily any longer lasting and it may induce more reaction. Dead vaccines in an oil or other special base are very effective for long-term immunities and are increasingly widely used. It should be emphasised that when a vaccine is administered to an animal it causes a degree of illness and during the period of immunological development the animal is experiencing stress and is *more* susceptible to infection than at other times. Thus it is necessary to practise even better management at the time of vaccination. Very often this factor is not appreciated and a failure that is unjustifiably ascribed to the vaccine is essentially due to mismanagement of the animals.

Drugs

Vaccines and sera are used to protect or treat animals for specific diseases. They should be used wherever they can be in the prevention of infections but in many cases no serum or vaccine exists and we must deal with illness using one or many of a wide choice of drugs. Also, many of the disease conditions we are dealing with are caused by a number of different organisms. Often these are primary viral agents and secondary bacterial ones and, indeed, their identity may not be known definitely. Frequently the urgent need for treatment demands that a drug is used before laboratory examinations have elucidated the cause, and we must rely on the clinical skill of the veterinarian to judge the correct drug to use. When the results of the tests are known, an appropriate change in treatment may be indicated.

Drugs can be given to have an almost immediate action. One administration may have an effect for only a few hours or in some cases for a few days but usually, in order to keep the levels up within the blood stream of the animal, there must be a constant boosting of levels. It cannot be emphasised too strongly that the full course of treatment prescribed should be completed and levels maintained correctly or the benefits may be lost and drug resistant organisms produced: this possibility is one of the worst outcomes of the use of drugs. Care must also be taken in the agricultural use of drugs to observe certain conditions of use. For example, with many drugs a compulsory withdrawal period is required before animals can be sent for slaughter, varying from about 5–10 days, and milk from cows being treated for mastitis must also not be mixed with normal milk for specified periods. Ignorance of the correct procedure can be disastrous.

The majority of drugs used for the prevention and treatment of disease are *chemotherapeutics* — the term implying the use of chemicals that have either been synthesised, such as the sulphonamides, or produced by the action of living organisms, these being the antibiotics. Modern research is continually producing new drugs and great credit is due to the active research in this field which makes available the vast armoury of safe materials for use in livestock husbandry.

The routes by which drugs are given vary from injection by the intravenous, intramuscular or subcutaneous routes to oral dosing and incorporation in feed or drinking water. With so many drugs available and the routes and methods of administration being so variable it is perhaps inevitable that careless and abusive use occurs. One cannot do more than emphasise that the prescribing of drugs requires a high degree of skill and their administration an abundance of diligence and competence.

Growth promoters

For many years the livestock industry has made use of antibiotics and other substances which, when incorporated in very small amounts in the ration, tend to increase the growth rate of livestock and improve food conversion efficiency. In the early days of use of these materials, the same antibiotics were used for growth promotion as for the treatment of disease. Since drugs as growth promoters are used at a much lower level than for therapeutic use, the incorporation of antibiotics in a low level in the feed is a disaster since drug resistant organisms will soon emerge and not only will the antibiotics no longer be of use as growth promoters but they will also have lost their value for therapeutic purposes. Because of this there is now a clear separation, legally enforced, between the use of antibiotics for these two purposes. Those antibiotics that are used as growth promoters (e.g. zinc bacitracin, Flavomycin and Virginiamycin) have no other use and are not used for any therapeutic purposes. Furthermore, the therapeutic antibiotics are used only for prevention and treatment of disease and are available only on veterinary prescription to be used under the control of the veterinary surgeon.

This problem of resistance is not the only one in connection with the use of the feeding of growth-promoting antibiotics. These substances have their greatest effect when the hygiene or husbandry system is less than ideal. Under really good management practices they may do little good at all. Thus they tend to 'mask' bad husbandry and this is a dangerous characteristic since such an effect will not last for ever; the bad practices, however, will not only last for ever but will tend to have a cumulative effect on results. It may sometimes be argued that the use of growth promoters is altogether to be deprecated but this I would not subscribe to because it must always be borne in mind that it is impossible, under commercial conditions, for everything to be always ideal. Better, therefore, to use them as an aid but not to rely on them absolutely.

There is still no absolute certainty as to the means by which growth-promoting antibiotics exert their effects but it seems most likely they are due to their favourable action on the balance of bacteria in the intestines, reducing the harmful ones and promoting the beneficial ones and thereby increasing the efficiency of food utilisation and production.

The importance of disinfection

All livestock are now housed much more intensively than hitherto. This involves not only the stocking of animals more densely but equally an increased size of units and the more efficient use of building space. It is rare for a livestock pen to be without stock; if there is a break between batches then it is usually a short-lived one. In the days before the use of antibiotic therapy, intensive methods tended to collapse under the burden of disease. Now they are again under threat because an increasing number of disease-producing organisms are resistant to drugs and also the cost of almost continuous antibiotic therapy is becoming an economically damaging burden to the stock keeper.

It is now appreciated that there is one viable alternative to this, and it is to institute a very efficient programme of cleaning and disinfection of the buildings. Let us be quite clear, however: disinfection needs to be done in a carefully organised way and must not be, as so often is the case, an application of some disinfectant chosen at random in the hope that it will kill the pathogens. Firstly, it is imperative — at least with young livestock — to plan the enterprise in such a way that a building or even a site is totally depopulated of stock before the cleaning and disinfection takes place. This is necessary because the live animal — and it might be literally only one — is potentially a much greater reservoir of infection than the building itself. So, the complete emptying of a house can be more important than the disinfection process itself. The disinfection process in sequence is shown in Table 3.2.

Then there must be a careful consideration of the different requirements in respect of the young and the old housed animal. Young animals are born only with a limited immunity to infection and this

Table 3.2 The disinfection process in sequence

---

1. Empty the pen and preferably the house of all livestock.

2. Clean out all 'organic matter' — dung, bedding, old feed, any other material that could contain pathogenic microorganisms. Remove totally from the area of the buildings.

3. Remove all portable equipment for cleaning and disinfecting outside the building.

4. Wash down with heavy duty detergent-steriliser. Use a power washer wherever possible.

5. Apply a disinfectant appropriate to the type of infections being dealt with. Usually required is a mixture active against viruses, bacteria, parasites and insects which may carry infection from one batch of livestock to another.

6. Wherever possible fumigate with a formaldehyde-active material after the equipment and litter have been reassembled.

7. Dry out and rest for a day or two before restocking.

---

can very quickly wane. It is usually essential that the young animal receives a very limited challenge of disease in the first few weeks of life particularly and this is best achieved if it is born in very clean quarters. Thus it is something of an essential in limiting the challenge to have buildings of small size, thereby reducing the number of animals, and also animals of only one age group, if possible. These are more likely to have the same levels of immunity and they can build up this immunity together without competition.

With much older animals and in particular the adult, the position may be totally different. The animals may have a considerable degree of immunity to local pathogens so that there is no merit in giving them totally clean buildings. What may be wanted here may be a rather different standard of underlying good hygiene to prevent gross infection and contamination.

Practical hygiene

How does one go about setting up the hygienic programme in practice? There will probably be some difference first of all in the construction of the building. With the animal which is very young, or in poultry the hatchery and incubator, almost total sterilisation is the aim. This can be achieved only by raising the standard of construction of the surfaces which must be both smooth and impervious so that they can be thoroughly cleaned (see Fig. 3.2).

Fig. 3.2 The application of a smooth rendering on an under-surface insulation layer ensures cleanliness, warmth and less likelihood of condensation.

With knowledge of the diseases that are causing risk to the animals, a suitable range of disinfectants can be chosen; such a programme of disinfectants may well include the application of disinfectants *and* fumigants. Disinfection is likely to involve the elimination of viruses, bacteria, fungi and parasites. With the housing of adults, however, the position is rather different. Because the disease risk is less, the construction of the buildings may not be to such a high standard. For example, timber construction may be widespread and floors may be of earth or chalk rather than impervious concrete. Furthermore, the range of infections under consideration may be less comprehensive, bacterial agents possibly being the worst that have to be dealt with, but the animal may already have a fairly high degree of immunity, for example, to viruses. Thus it can be said that whilst measures may not be so complicated, it is still very important to choose the right agent and apply it in the correct way (see Figs 3.3, 3.4 and 3.5).

Signs of health and disease

Early recognition of illness is particularly vital in the intensive unit because the risk of spread of anything that is contagious is very great. Early recognition increases the opportunity for successful treatment, enables the affected stock to be isolated and speeds any laboratory diagnostic work. It also helps in the good welfare of the animals since sick animals are often maltreated by their neighbours. All in all, it will also generally reduce losses to a minimum, thus being of sound economic sense.

The following are the signs to look for, in general:

1. FEEDING

One of the earliest and surest signs of illness is a lack of interest in feed (anorexia) or a capricious appetite, though occasionally it is the feed itself which is at fault and requires investigation.

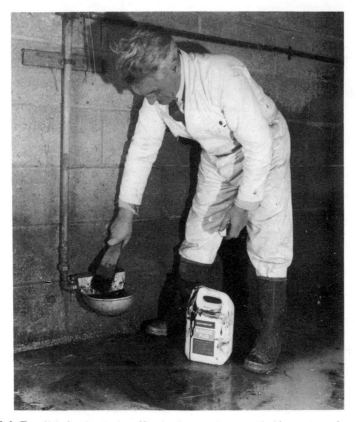

Fig. 3.3 For disinfection to be effective it must be preceded by proper cleansing.

Fig. 3.4 Modern disinfectant solution applied to clean surfaces, even if porous, can be effective if allowed sufficient time to act.

Fig. 3.5 The disinfected foot dip is a valuable aid to sanitation on the livestock farm.

2. SEPARATION FROM THE GROUP
Such animals will usually separate from the others and hide in a corner or bury themselves in bedding, if available.

3. EXCRETA
This may be 'abnormal'. Sick animals often have scour (diarrhoea) or, more usually in the earliest stages of disease, they will be constipated, especially if there is a fever. In other circumstances the faeces may contain blood (dysentery) or may be of abnormal colour (which sometimes happens in cases of poisoning, for example).

4. URINE
This may show abnormalities such as the presence of blood, or may be cloudy or yellow (jaundiced). Normal urine is pale and straw-coloured.

5. POSTURE
Sick animals may find it impossible to rise, or may hold themselves uncomfortably, and may be lame. The nature of the abnormality of posture may indicate the organ affected.

6. APPEARANCE
Sick animals will often have a droopy head, with dull eyes and dry muzzle and possibly discharge from the nose and watery or catarrhal eyes. All mucous membranes may be discoloured.

7. SKIN AND COAT
A healthy coat is clean and glossy. Abnormal coats may be 'hide-bound' which is when dehydration makes it difficult to move the skin over the underlying tissues. Sick animals may have bald, scurfy, staring, 'lousy', mangy or scabby skin, and the animals may scratch or rub. The skin, coat and feathers are very good indicators of disease.

8. COUGHING
Most abnormalities of the respiratory system produce coughing in animals and the nature of the cough will often be diagnostic of certain conditions.

9. PAIN
The presence of pain shows in a number of ways: grunts, groans, grinding of the teeth, squealing or crying, arching of the back.

10. TEMPERATURE

An abnormally high temperature usually indicates an infection; an abnormally low one may be due to a metabolic defect, a poisoning or simply the later or terminal stages of an infection. Normal temperatures and respirations are set out in Table 3.3.

Table 3.3 Normal temperatures and respiration rates

	Temperatures		Respirations
	°F	°C	per minute
Cattle	101.5	38.7	12–20
Sheep	103.0	39.4	12–30
Pig	102.5	39.2	10–18
Fowl	106.5	41.5	12–28

Respirations tend to be accelerated by infectious diseases and slowed by others though the nature of the breathing will also be vastly affected and may change from the deep to the shallow on the occurrence of illness.

11. PULSE RATES

This is normally only studied by the veterinarian, but the normal rates are set out in Table 3.4.

Table 3.4 Normal pulse rates

	Pulse rate per minute
Cattle	45 to 50
Sheep	70 to 90
Pig	70 to 80
Fowl	130 to 140

Animal welfare and animal health

A recent phenomenon has been widespread disquiet questioning the humanity of some of the more modern and intensive methods of rearing livestock. Under critical attack from so-called 'welfare groups' have been certain systems, especially chickens kept in battery cages, calves housed in crates for the production of veal and sows closely tethered in stalls during pregnancy. Having been personally involved in this controversy since it started and now in the position of looking back on 30 years' involvement in the management of intensive live-stock, I am convinced that the dispute has been beneficial since it has thrown a very sharp light on methods and forced everyone involved to think carefully about what they are doing. It is now leading rather belatedly to active research and investigation which may answer some of our doubts. Table 3.5 summarises the essentials of livestock welfare.

Table 3.5 The essentials for welfare

1. Enough space to be provided for the animals to move around freely — to stretch their limbs or wings, to turn round and groom or preen themselves.

2. All surfaces, especially flooring, must be comfortable and unlikely to cause injury.

3. A suitable 'micro-climate' to be provided, that is, appropriate ambient temperatures, humidities, air movement and ventilation.

4. All measures must be taken to ensure healthy stock.

5. A balanced ration should be available in sufficient quantity and of a suitable consistency for the animals' digestive system. Clean water should always be accessible.

6. Groups of animals should be evenly matched. If animals are kept individually they should have sight of others.

7. All sick animals and 'bullies' must be removed and isolated from healthy stock.

8. There should be adequate provision to cope with emergencies such as fire and electrical or mechanical failures.

9. Wherever possible bedding should be provided such as clean straw or wood shavings.

10. Mutilations on animals, such as beak-trimming of birds or de-tailing of pigs, should not be undertaken except under exceptional circumstances when more suffering might result if it were *not* done. Alternative husbandry systems which do not require mutilations should be considered.

11. Lighting should be generous for the management of the animals and adequate at all other times.

Animal welfare is also very pertinent to the question of health since there is no dispute that one of the essential criteria for the provision of good welfare is the maintenance of health in the animals. It has also become apparent from recent activities in the research field that the eventual goal of establishing what constitutes good welfare in a scientific way is going to be very difficult indeed, if not impossible. Thus we shall have to continue to rely, at least in the foreseeable future, on the overall knowledge, expertise and even instinct of the persons concerned with the management and care of the animals, these being the farmers, stockmen, and husbandry and veterinary advisers. It is essential to keep in the forefront of one's mind the overriding importance of welfare and humanity to animals on all occasions. Anyone who has closely observed sick animals can understand what constitutes 'misery' in the animal kingdom and contrast this with the alert and buoyant appearance of an animal in good health.

A feature of this controversial field which has been particularly beneficial is the way in which it has forced us to enquire whether it is

Fig. 3.6 Perforated pig flooring — a form of mesh which is self-cleaning but with risks of disease and welfare emphasised in the text.

Fig. 3.7 This livestock transporter reduces the stress on the stock by its mechanical hoist and powered ventilation.

necessary to house animals using methods which involve an abnormal degree of restriction on their movement. There has been a search for alternatives which has been fruitful insofar as it appears to indicate that there may be less need for the extremes of intensification than has been alleged and indeed it may be economically preferable to have systems which are more in harmony with the overall agricultural scene.

Very large and intensive livestock enterprises have often been unsuccessful and even disastrous for three principal reasons. Firstly, the management of large numbers of *living beings* is not easily organised on the large scale. Stockmanship is partly science and partly art, and art must rely heavily on the individual. If only one small item goes wrong or is overlooked it can lead to a very serious chain of events on the large scale.

The second reason is that disease is much more likely to have a serious deleterious effect in the large unit — in sub-clinical or clinical forms. The failure of many units can be ascribed to their inability to control disease so that the economic viability of the unit has been totally destroyed (see Chapter 1).

Fig. 3.8 Tethered sows in a large building of approximately 200 sows. Note the partly slatted floors and passageway. The design allows good inspection facilities.

The third reason is the heavy cost of buying in or bringing in fodder and moving out the muck in such enterprises. It is common for the highly intensive unit to be totally dependent on food from outside the farm or the locality and faced with great difficulty in disposing of all the waste products. In smaller units the crops can be used to feed the livestock and the 'muck' they generate is of great value to the land; energy is conserved and this is agriculture of a totally balanced sort.

It may also be stated that the welfare standards that are gradually emerging across the world are based on evidence which, as far as is possible, is not in conflict with economics. For example, if animals are housed at concentrations and intensities above those advised, it is likely that their productivity will fall. Particularly is this so when it comes to stocking density and its relationship to growth, production and the efficiency of food utilisation. Good welfare standards can be used, therefore, as a husbandry standard with some confidence.

The key to good welfare is a high standard of stockmanship and if this is to function then good facilities must be provided for the stockman. Many systems that have been developed in recent years completely ignore this. The essentials are as follows:

- Plenty of room for the stockman to *see* the stock whenever he needs to.
- Good lighting and no undue saving on passage space.
- Facilities for isolation of sick stock.
- Easy access by the stockman to the pen and, above all, a very high standard of handling facilities so that it is easy to medicate or treat the animals in any way necessary.

Disease legislation

In Great Britain, under the Diseases of Animals Act, there is a substantial number of Orders relating essentially to the State's interest in animal disease control. These regulations cover a wide spectrum of activity. For example, they deal with the importation of animals and animal by-products, the movement of animals, the inspection of livestock and vehicles, and allow for the Ministry of Agriculture to

Fig. 3.9 Tethered sows on slatted floors; a popular system but with risks of injury from bad flooring.

institute a large number of Orders relating essentially to specific diseases.

Under the Diseases of Animals Act certain specified diseases are designated notifiable. Those of current importance are:

Anthrax
Foot-and-Mouth Disease
Fowl Pest
Bovine Tuberculosis
Sheep Scab
Swine Vesicular Disease
Aujeszky's Disease
Enzootic Bovine Leucosis
Rabies
Warble Fly

There are also others, such as Swine Fever, which could well occur again as they are widespread not far from these shores.

The most important feature about the notifiable diseases is that the owner or person in charge of an animal suspected as affected by a notifiable disease must immediately report his suspicion to a police officer or an inspector of the Ministry of Agriculture. Once the owner has notified the Inspector or Police, then steps will be taken to diagnose the condition and measures may be taken to isolate the premises and treat, vaccinate or slaughter the stock. Different diseases have different procedures and these are dealt with later in the book under the respective diseases. Also, under the Zoonoses Order, the presence of conditions such as Salmonellosis and Brucellosis, which infect both animals and man, must be notified.

4 The Health of Cattle

Cattle have been as markedly affected by the trend to intensive methods as most other forms of livestock and this has produced its inevitable crop of problems. At the same time traditional practices still persist alongside the more modern methods, so health problems arising from these remain. In this chapter the health problems are dealt with on a life-cycle basis, dealing firstly with those health problems affecting the calf and continuing with growing stock and concluding with the mature beast and those diseases that have no special age incidence.

The health of the calf

Of the 5 to 10% mortality that occurs in calves, nearly two-thirds takes place in the first month of life and a large proportion of this is due to what is usually referred to as calf scours. This is a rather vague term which covers a number of digestive and more generalised upsets. The main cause is said to be the ubiquitous bacterium *Escherichia coli.*

Colostrum and protection against diseases in the calf
It is always considered essential that a calf should have a good drink of colostrum (see Table 4.1) shortly after birth. The importance of this cannot be stressed too greatly as it provides so many benefits. The calf — or indeed any young animal — is virtually free of disease-causing organisms at birth. Colostrum contains the immunoglobulins, the essential protection against infection. It also contains large quantities of Vitamin A (six times as much as in ordinary milk). Immunoglobulins are the proteins which contain the antibodies which protect the calf from disease organisms, whilst Vitamin A is the most important vitamin associated with the animal's resistance to infection.

The importance to the calf of having the colostrum is thus apparent but speed is of the essence for two reasons. Firstly, the production of

Table 4.1 Comparative levels of the main nutrients in colostrum as compared with ordinary cow's milk

	Colostrum	Milk
Fat (g/kg)	36	35
Solids not fat (g/kg)	185	86
Protein (g/kg)	143	32.5
Immunoglobulins (g/kg)	55–68	0.9
Lactose (g/kg)	31	46
Iron (mg/kg)	2.0	0.1–0.7
Vitamin A (μg/kg)	42–48	8
Vitamin D (μg/kg)	23–45	15
Vitamin E (μg/kg)	100–150	20

the best quality of colostrum is only a short-lived action and likewise so is the absorption and assimilation by the calf of the elements needed to counteract infection. Also, colostrum must be given before the calf gets a bad challenge of disease-producing organisms, so that antibodies *precede* the infectious pathogens. The aim is for the colostrum to be taken within one hour of birth and the consumption should be up to 2 kg.

Feeding systems for calves
There are a number of different systems for feeding calves, the choice is gradually increasing, and each has advantages and drawbacks. The main systems are:

- Bucket feeding twice daily.
- Bucket feeding once daily – warm.
- Bucket feeding once daily – cold.
- Unrestricted warm milk.
- Unrestricted cold acidified milk.

Then there are a number of different powders that can be used to constitute the milk. Milk may be acidified to a pH of about 5.2 which preserves the material in an unrestricted cold milk feeding regime using teat feeders. There are low fat milk replacers with 5–7% fat and up to 15–18% in the high fat materials. Whilst all these methods show different results there is no clear evidence that there are any strong differences in their effect on health, but methods simulating the natural sucking of the calf from the teat are less likely to cause digestive upsets.

It should be stressed that calf scours (often called 'white scour') does not appear to be a simple infection with strains of *E. coli*. There is abundant evidence inciting effects of more than one viral agent — reoviruses and coronaviruses being some of those implicated. Under these circumstances the use of specific vaccines and sera may have a limited chance of providing good treatment or prevention, though sometimes this can be the case. More often the disease must be treated with antibiotics with a broad range of activity, such as the synthetic penicillins, together with replacement therapy for the enormous fluid depletion that takes place. This will include electrolytes, glucose, minerals and vitamins in easily assimilated liquid form. Treatment is not something for the amateur to undertake, especially when it is realised that mortality in affected calves can easily reach within striking distance of 100%.

Salmonellosis
The salmonella group of bacteria is a very large one with hundreds of different types, all potentially pathogenic to man and animals but some more than others and many specific only to certain hosts. However, only relatively few are very harmful, most being exotic types that come in via the feed and are quickly eliminated. Specific salmonella diseases are described in the consideration of each species.

The two most important species in the condition in calves are *Salmonella typhimurium* and *Salmonella dublin*. The symptoms with either of these infections or indeed with other virulent salmonella can be largely similar. If a batch of calves is affected and there is close contact between them, then nearly all may be infected. A percentage may die so rapidly that no symptoms are seen; others scour profusely, with dysentery, pneumonia, arthritis, jaundice and nervous symptoms manifesting themselves in some cases. Extreme emaciation rapidly results if the calves live.

Treatment will be required urgently if the calves are to be saved and is likely to include antibiotics, e.g. ampicillin, chemotherapeutics and fluid therapy, isolation and general nursing, especially warmth. Thorough disinfection of the quarters will be essential and preventive measures may include vaccination and possibly preventive medication. However, the use of the last measure is hazardous as it may generate drug-resistance and encourage the establishment of the 'carrier' animal which can excrete salmonella organisms throughout its life.

Whilst salmonellosis is especially a disease of young stock, adult cattle do become infected and may not show symptoms, becoming carriers of great potential danger to man and other livestock. Abortions may be caused by salmonella and salmonella can be a source of infection via milk. In the main the biggest problems from salmonellosis arise from farms where the calves are brought in from outside and infection can easily spread back to the adults if they are on the same premises. A recent worrying means of infecting calves and cows with salmonella is through the spread of slurry on the land. Salmonella can persist in slurry for months. If it is then spread over pasture which is about to be grazed shortly it will be readily picked up by cattle, or indeed any animal that is on the ground.

In Great Britain salmonellosis is a notifiable infection and official measures can be taken to control the disease as appropriate. In the event of an outbreak in adult cattle, measures that may be taken will include laboratory testing of the cattle to identify the carriers, treatment of animals with antibiotics such as ampicillin and appropriate care of the milk to remove the risk of human infection.

Calf diphtheria

The bacterium associated with foul-in-the-foot in cattle, known as *Fusiformis* or *Actinomyces necrophorus*, is also capable of causing a serious disease in calves known as calf diphtheria. The infection attacks calves when very young, even as early as the third or fourth day of life, and causes inflammation within the mouth, leading to soreness, ulcers and ultimately necrosis. The calf becomes seriously ill, will not feed, salivates from the mouth and keeps on exhibiting swallowing movements. The course of the disease, if it is not checked at this stage, is progressive and the lesions will spread into the throat, necrosis will continue and there will be a characteristic foul smell. Without treatment most calves die.

The disease will respond very well to treatment. Sulphonamides are effective and also a wide range of broad spectrum antibiotics. It is a disease that is characteristic of bad hygiene so premises where this disease occurs should have a thoroughly good clean-up and thereafter management should be maintained at a higher standard.

Navel-ill or joint-ill

These two terms are used to describe jointly the diseases affecting calves where bacterial infection causes inflammation in the region of the navel, together with inflammation and lesions in the joints. The conditions that occur under this name are caused by a variety of bacterial organisms, common ones being *Corynebacterium pyogenes*, Staphylococci, *E. coli, A. necrophorus, Pasteurella septica* and haemolytic streptococci. The disease usually occurs because the calves are managed under dirty conditions and are challenged by a serious burden of bacteria before the navel has healed.

Treatment may be undertaken successfully in the early stages of the disease with sulphonamides or broad spectrum antibiotics; local application of dressings to the navel will help to prevent infection.

Some general points on the control of calf diseases

The moment a calf is born, or indeed even whilst it is being born, it will be subjected to 'challenge' from contagious or infectious disease. There are present in any local community of animals on a farm a large number of organisms which are potentially pathogenic but in the normal way these will not cause disease. Disease is only caused for a number of reasons as follows:

1. The calf may not have been born in the same environment as its dam was in during pregnancy so no immunity develops to local 'infections'.
2. The calf may not have received an adequate amount of the colostrum from its dam, the colostrum or first milk providing a major boost to the immunity of the calf to infections.
3. The premises may not have been cleaned and disinfected adequately so the calf will get an immediate and possibly overbearing contact with pathogenic micro-organisms.
4. If young calves are put into housing that already contains a substantial number of older and infected or 'carrier' calves, the challenge imposed on the younger calves from the old stock can cause very serious losses.

There are two main groups of diseases that affect calves – the enteric groups and the respiratory diseases. Management arrangements that avoid the stresses just listed will influence the likelihood of these two groups affecting the calves in a very real way. (See Fig. 4.1 and also under *Calf Tetany* in the section on metabolic diseases later in the chapter.) Table 4.2 sets out a 12-point plan for rearing healthier calves.

The health of growing cattle

Internal parasites

There are three major groups of diseases in cattle caused by parasitic worms. There is 'husk' or 'hoose', which is due to worms which live in the lungs; parasitic gastroenteritis, which is caused by roundworms

Table 4.2 A 12-point plan for rearing healthier calves

---

1. Place newborn calves in completely clean and disinfected pens.
2. Ensure they have colostrum immediately after birth and thereafter an adequate and balanced diet.
3. Isolate all calves moved on to the farm from outside for sufficient time to detect any disease.
4. Batch rear calves on the 'all-in, all-out' principle.
5. Small numbers should be kept in one common air space and with separation of dung between the small units.
6. Oppose movement and mixing of calves as far as economically possible.
7. Be generous with space allowances.
8. Provide free choice for the calves with a resting area warmer than the exercise and feeding area, as in 'kennel' housing.
9. Ventilation by natural methods is usually to be preferred if there is adequate air space. No draughts must be tolerated.
10. Provide enough insulation of the building surfaces to prevent condensation.
11. Separate different age groups wherever possible.
12. Remove sick calves and treat as speedily as possible.

---

which live in the abomasum and/or intestines of cattle, and finally liver fluke disease, caused by flatworms or flukes, which live in the liver.

As a preliminary comment it needs to be emphasised that parasitic worms do not multiply within the body of the animal in which they live as adults. The adults produce millions of eggs which each individual worm can lay, but none reaches maturity without first passing out of the animal with the faeces. They must then have a period of time outside the animal before they become infective, and this period varies from a few days to many weeks. Thus every worm in the animal has been picked up in the herbage while the animal was grazing. Their mode of multiplication is entirely different from bacteria and viruses which multiply within the body. The significance of this knowledge is that it provides for two ways of attack, one within the body and one without. Removal of contact of animals with their own faeces is a vital factor. If the husbandry is good, with clean environment and no over-crowding, the infestation may be so slight as to be unimportant. Mixed grazing is also useful since the parasitic worms are host-specific and infect only one species. It is

Fig. 4.1 Calf Housing (a) before and (b) after improvement. The first picture shows a dirty surface, where cleanliness is only obtained with great difficulty, and sagging moisture-laden roof insulation. The second picture is with a new lining of asbestos over Polyurethane board insulation (Purlboard, I.C.I.).

also important to know that it is chiefly the young and growing stock that are vulnerable to infection. Adults should have a naturally produced immunity due to earlier contact with the parasites.

Nevertheless, the adults do have a worm burden generally and will produce some eggs. And adults can become badly affected once again if they become stressed by poor conditions or nutrition.

The worm eggs once voided can remain viable for some time. Some can remain in an infective form for up to or even more than a year. Resting of infected pasture is a very successful means of reducing the worm burden, and even a short rest will help.

HUSK OR HOOSE

When certain forms of parasitic worms infest the bronchi in the lungs this is often called verminous bronchitis. It is at first an infection of the bronchial tubes and leads to the cough known as 'husk' or 'hoose'. This condition is caused by the lungworm, *Dictyocaulus viviparus*. These white worms are threadlike and up to 75 mm long. They live in the bronchial tubes of the lungs and the females lay vast numbers of eggs (see Fig. 4.2). After hatching, which soon takes place, they produce minute larvae which are carried in the mucus up the windpipe and to the mouth. They are then swallowed and pass

Fig. 4.2 Husk. A portion of a calf's lung showing adult lungworms 30 days after infection.

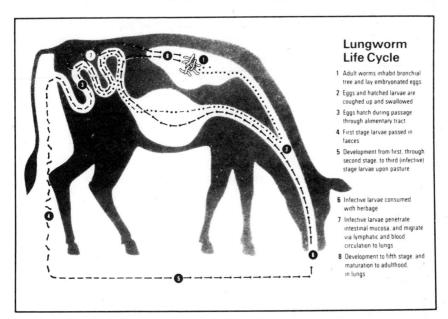

Lungworm Life Cycle

1 Adult worms inhabit bronchial tree and lay embryonated eggs

2 Eggs and hatched larvae are coughed up and swallowed

3 Eggs hatch during passage through alimentary tract

4 First stage larvae passed in faeces

5 Development from first, through second stage, to third (infective) stage larvae upon pasture

6 Infective larvae consumed with herbage

7 Infective larvae penetrate intestinal mucosa, and migrate via lymphatic and blood circulation to lungs

8 Development to fifth stage, and maturation to adulthood, in lungs

Fig. 4.3 The life cycle of the lungworm.

out onto the pasture with the dung. These larvae have to develop on the ground before they are able to infect cattle, who take them in with the grazing. The development takes about five days in warm, moist weather and over a month when the weather is cold. Whilst developing in the dung the larvae go through a series of changes and moult their skins twice. The larvae have little resistance to drying and can die off rapidly under these circumstances. Fig. 4.3 sets out the life cycle of the lungworm.

The season has a great effect on the infectivity of the larvae. In late spring, large concentrations of larvae may be found in the pasture but these generally die off quite rapidly. In summer, large concentrations are less likely to occur and equally unlikely to persist. Autumn conditions are ideal both for the creation of heavy infestations on the pasture and for their survival. In winter it is very difficult for new infestations to be formed on the pasture but existing infestations do persist. Pasture can become infested quickly but does not remain so for long. The weight of infestation depends partly on the number of worms being carried by the cattle that have grazed on it; the infestation in the herbage in turn determines how heavily calves grazing on it will become infested.

When the infective larvae are swallowed by grazing cattle they penetrate the intestinal wall and pass into the lymphatic system and by this route reach the blood stream and then pass to the lungs. Here they develop into the adult worms and begin to lay eggs after three weeks. These adults generally do not live long but small numbers may persist for a longer time and act as a continuing source of infection.

Cattle that have been exposed to lungworm infestation will in due course acquire a resistance; this resistance can develop quite rapidly but only as a result of sufficient infection. It thus follows that the number of lungworms which a susceptible calf picks up each day — depending on how heavily the herbage is infested — and the rate at which it increases, will determine whether the lungworm disease actually occurs.

If the level of pasture infestation rises at a moderate rate, the gradual and increasing resistance of the calf will enable it to reject the effect of the worms and no disease will actually occur. But if the pasture infestation rises rapidly, as it may do if the climatic conditions are favourable, disease may occur. The exposure of susceptible animals to a moderate uptake of larvae will produce symptoms of disease but will render the calves resistant so quickly that they are refractory to re-infestation. Exposing susceptible calves to a high rate of infestation will result in fatal disease. In all these cases the serious infection is acquired over a short space of time.

The situation in which a severe disease may appear can arise in a number of ways. The cattle may be insufficiently resistant either because (a) they have not had sufficient exposure, as in the examples given above, or (b) they have lost their earlier resistance, having for some time been withheld from contact with infection. It is in these cases that adult cattle can be infected.

High pasture infestation may occur in a number of circumstances. In early spring most pastures will be either clean or at least only very slightly infested. Contamination of the pasture by older animals, which have carried over some worms in their lungs from the previous season, may produce more significant levels of infestation on the herbage and may even give rise to dangerous infestation if the season and pasture conditions are suitable. Low levels of herbage infestation may be increased when susceptible calves become infected on the pasture and in consequence increased numbers of larvae are passed on to it in their dung.

Symptoms
The disease may be recognised, or at least suspected, if there is an increase in the respiratory rate, coughing especially when the animals

are moved, and some loss in body condition. If cases become severe then the coughing becomes louder, the respirations shallow with clear pain and distress, and the animal stands uncomfortably with head and neck outstretched and the tongue protruding. There is anorexia and the beast may die within a few days. Post mortem examination shows that parts of the lung have consolidated (liver-like in appearance) and the rest of the lungs seem water-logged and appear to be inflated with air and enlarged. The trachea and bronchial tubes are often filled with frothy mucus in which the worms can be seen. However, sometimes few adult worms are seen. Diagnosis may also be made in the absence of post mortems, since examination of the dung in the laboratory will show the presence of the larvae of the worms.

Control

The worms in the lung tend to be established in bronchial mucus or in the exudate caused by their presence. It is thus rather difficult for a drug to reach the worms because of the protection this mucus affords. There are, however, a number of useful drugs for lungworms, such as Levamisole (*Nemicide* by I.C.I.) and Fenbendazole (*Panacur* by Hoechst). However, it should be emphasised that removal of the worms by drugs does not necessarily cure the condition since it may take a long time and good nursing to effect recovery. The best procedure is really to remove the animals from the pasture altogether and house the cattle in warm, dry, well-ventilated buildings where they can be well fed.

Prevention

Obviously the important lesson to be learned from an outbreak is how to prevent the condition in the future. The control depends on establishing and maintaining a state of immunity in the animals and yet avoiding outbreaks of disease. It is, of course, difficult to get this controlled exposure without causing a disease, though modest rates of stocking are always likely to be of help. It is wise to keep animals grazing for their first year off pasture which has had animals on it recently. Strict systems of rotational grazing can always be of help since they will prevent heavy build-ups of disease. The calves should be moved twice a week on to ground which has not had calves on it for about four months, but even a shorter time would be of help in reducing infection. The vaccine which is available is also of great help in preventing the disease. This consists of infective-stage larvae which have been subjected to irradiation, a procedure that prevents the larvae from migrating into the lungs to produce disease but it does induce some immunological response. Thus it is an *adjunct* to good management but not a substitute.

LIVER FLUKE DISEASE
Liver fluke disease tends to go quite undetected or unsuspected until the animals start dying. It is admittedly more a disease of sheep than cattle but there is good evidence that liver fluke disease causes a very serious effect on growth and productivity. It can affect beasts outside at all ages and control should be taken very seriously. The liver fluke is a flat worm about the size and shape of a privet leaf. The worm lives and feeds on the liver of cattle. The flukes lay many thousands of eggs and they pass on to the pasture in the dung. The eggs hatch and produce a very small swimming creature but this, however, exists for no more than a day. If it is going to survive it must enter a particular type of snail and this snail must therefore be present for the disease to go on regenerating. The parasite grows in the liver of the snail and produces many young liver flukes. These look like the flukes which cause disease in the older stock, except that they are much smaller. These young flukes leave the snail when the snail is in water and encyst on any herbage which they contact. They lose their tails and surround themselves with a protective covering. There they remain as cysts but are inactive for long periods – up to months on occasion – until eaten by the grazing animal. When eaten the protective coat disappears and the fluke emerges and makes its way to the liver. During the next two to three months the fluke grows to maturity and then lays eggs (see Fig. 4.4).

Symptoms
There are two forms which are clinically differentiated. The acute disease occurs when the grazing animal picks up many flukes in a short time. These damage the liver seriously and this can lead to sudden death in the apparently healthy animal. A post mortem may show a liver which is actually ruptured and the surface pitted with white tracks. The chronic form is quite different and much more serious and common. It is due to the presence of flukes in the liver over a period of several months and affected animals waste during this time. If nothing is done to allay this state of affairs, the cattle will die. Post mortems show their livers to have a 'pipey' look due to the thickening of the bile ducts and they may contain hard and stony deposits.

Such symptoms can occur only if cattle have been grazing on

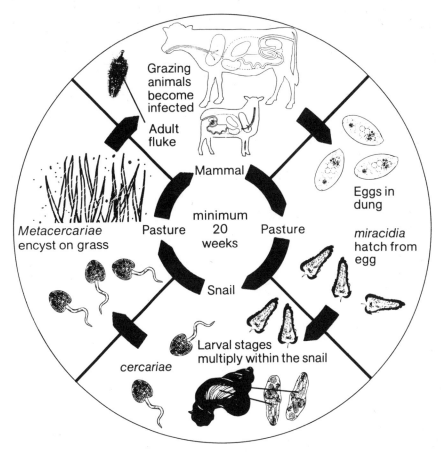

Fig. 4.4 The life cycle of the liver fluke parasite.

ground moist enough to support the snail. This will be badly drained ground. It tends to occur only in those years when the climatic conditions favour the secondary hosts.

Control

Certain drugs now exist for treatment *viz*. Oxyclozanide (*Zanil* by I.C.I) and Nitroxynil (*Trodax PML* by M. & B.). Also recommended is Albendazole (*Valbazen* by S.K.F.). Professional advice should generally be sought before use of these drugs in view of possible side-effects, contra-indications and withdrawal periods of milk for human consumption.

The disease can be effectively prevented by controlling the secondary hosts — the snails. Infestation in flukey areas is worse in the months of October to December and hence fluke-free pastures should be grazed in this period wherever possible. Badly drained areas should be properly drained. The snails may also be dealt with by treating the pasture with either copper sulphate at 12 kg/acre or sodium pentachlorphenate at 4 kg/acre. As these are dangerous materials they should be applied with care. However, a safer material is N-trityemorpholine which may be used much more safely.

PARASITIC GASTROENTERITIS

This is a disease, or infestation, caused by the presence in the abomasum or fourth stomach or the anterior part of the small intestine, of a group of small roundworms. Twenty-six species of roundworms have been identified in the alimentary tract of cattle in Great Britain. The most important species are *Ostertagia ostertagi* and *Trichostrongylus axei* in the abomasum; *Cooperia oncophora*, *C. punctata*, *T. vitrinus* and *T. colubriformis* in the small intestine and *Oesophagostomum radiatum* in the large intestine. There is every evidence that they are equally a problem in other countries. They cause considerable economic loss from both poor productivity and overt disease, chiefly in young animals but not excluding older ones. Some are large enough to be seen in the stomach contents with the naked eye whilst others are almost impossible to recognise in this way.

The life cycle of the worm is 'direct' — there being no intermediate hosts. Eggs are laid by the adult worms passing out with the dung on to the pasture where they can hatch within about 24 hours, producing minute larvae which feed on bacteria in the faeces. Within the next few days they moult twice and only then are they capable of infesting stock who ingest them in the herbage. In order to make the ingestion more certain they leave the dung and pass on to the grass, climbing upwards so that they will readily be consumed by the animals. All this can take no more than four days in warm, damp weather, but may take weeks in cool conditions. The infective larvae can resist adverse weather quite well though they 'like' cold and damp but perish fairly readily when the weather is hot and dry. Most larvae will live only 6—8 weeks but a few can survive even up to a year.

A limited number of worms do little or no harm to the beasts but a heavy infestation can be lethal. Thus infestation is assisted by overcrowding, moist, warm conditions and long grass in which moisture more readily persists. Adult cattle are generally resistant but this is only because they have normally been exposed to the worms early in life and have acquired an immunity.

Symptoms of parasitic gastroenteritis
These are nearly always indefinite and the usual signs are a progressive loss of condition — possibly leading eventually to emaciation and death. There is usually a severe scour but the animals continue to eat voraciously. The disease would be suspected from these signs when a substantial number in a herd was showing them. However, one should be aware of the fact that some animals will not scour and signs will be so indefinite as to go undetected. In every case it is wise to have positive indentification by examination of the faeces to determine the degree of infection.

Control
The first course of action is to consider medication, and there are a wide variety of materials that can be given. Organo-phosphorus compounds, such as fenbendazole (*Panacur* by Hoechst), parbendazole (*Helmatac* by S.K.F.) and thiabendazole (M.S. & D.); also levamisole (*Nilverm* by I.C.I.) and haloxon (*Loxon* by Cooper McDougall). These drugs can be given by injections or orally in several cases and a full course, as advised in the specific literature for the drug, should be given.

Preventive measures should consist of the following:

- Overcrowding of the young stock should be avoided.
- Grass should be kept short as larval worms tend to perish in such grass.
- Only adult stock should be put on badly infested land.
- Periodic treatment should be given to animals after laboratory examination of faeces has established the degree of infection.

Parasitic gastroenteritis in adult cattle
It has long been assumed that adult cattle are not affected to any extent with parasitic roundworms as they have developed an immunity during their rearing period. In recent years, however, evidence has accumulated to show that this is not necessarily so.

The symptoms of infestation with these parasites tend to be insidious and may be so slight as to go undetected. Trials have shown that after treatment of cows with anthelmintics milk yield may increase considerably.

The best methods of control integrate grassland management and chemotherapy. At present, herbage availability regulates grazing systems rather than helminthological considerations. In fact, because they have a low, faecal egg output, adult cattle are often used to reduce the level of pasture contamination prior to its being used by younger stock, which is a thoroughly dangerous arrangement.

Skin conditions and external parasites

RINGWORM

This is an extremely common skin disease of cattle which tends to be a problem in winter when the animals are housed. It is caused by fungi belonging to the genus *Trichophyton*, two species of which occur in cattle in this country and also attack horses, pigs, dogs and man. *Trichophyton verucosum* is the most common one and is responsible for most cases of ringworm in cattle, farmers, stock-keepers and their families, whilst *T. mentagrophytes* is very rare in cattle and occurs mostly in cats and dogs.

The fungi that cause ringworm are capable of surviving for very long periods in the farmyard, certainly for over a year and probably much longer. The spores that are picked up by the animals find their way into cracks on the skin and germinate to produce fine filaments which flourish in the surface of skin and hair. These fungal threads grow downwards inside the hair, keeping pace with its growth from the hair bulb and weakening it so that it snaps off at the surface of the skin producing the characteristic bald areas. The skin reacts to the infection by inflammation followed by the formation of a grey to yellow-white crust. The lesions of ringworm are most often seen on the head and neck, especially in calves, but in adults patches can occur on the flanks, back and rump, wherever rubbing takes place. Animals that are run-down are especially likely to suffer a severe infestation but ringworm itself does not seem to have a very harmful effect on animals. Also, recovery usually happens spontaneously, often taking place after winter housed animals are turned out to grass. Cattle that have recovered from ringworm are immune to further infection.

Control of ringworm

Whilst ringworm will disappear spontaneously in the course of time, it is never advisable to ignore treatment since the disease has a further debilitating effect on animals that may already be in low condition. Treatment may be done by dressing the affected areas with iso-quinolinium chloride lotion, handling with care, wearing rubber gloves and overalls. However, an antibiotic known as griseofulvin is now available for dosing animals with this condition. The drug is absorbed into the tissues of the body and is incorporated into newly formed skin and hair so that the growth of the fungus in these tissues is prevented.

The bald patches rapidly improve and new hair appears within 2–3 weeks of commencing treatment. Griseofulvin must be given every day for some three weeks to produce a cure. This is a considerable expense so that in general only the most valuable stock are dealt with in this way. A much more important and economic approach is to practise good hygienic measures by efficient cleansing and disinfection of the buildings and all objects that could harbour the fungal spores. In the same way, consideration should be given to anything capable of transmitting infection – such as grooming tools. It is noteworthy that most farmers do not bother to deal with this disease at all, accepting it as a normal happening in young housed cattle, but this ignores the debilitating effect of the infection which in trials has been shown to be harmful.

MANGE

Certain forms of mites infect cattle – these are *Sarcoptes scabei*, *Chorioptes bovis, Psoroptes communis* and *Demodex bovis*. All are extremely contagious conditions (sometimes called scabies). The result of the disease is to produce very patchy coats and areas of bare skin with an extreme amount of irritation.

The nature of the disease is as follows. The mites spend their whole lifetime on the animals and only survive a few weeks off them. The symptoms are always at their worst during the final winter months. Diagnosis is made by microscopic examination of skin scrapings. The mites are just visible to the naked eye.

The most severe form of mange is caused by sarcoptes. This mange parasite is a white, tortoise-shaped mite with eight stumpy legs (see Fig. 4.5). It burrows deeply into the outer layers of the skin setting

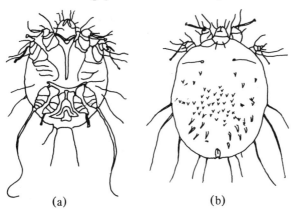

(a)   (b)

Fig. 4.5 Underside of (a) male and top side of (b) female *Sarcoptes scabei* mites (× 100) which cause mange in cattle.

up intense irritation while the mites form the tunnels in which the females lay their eggs. The larvae which hatch from the eggs resemble the adult but are smaller and have only six legs. These larvae moult and develop into eight-legged nymphs. Another moult takes place and within about 15 days from the laying of the egg a new generation of adults is produced. This species of mite spends nearly all its life under the skin of the animal so that it is difficult for insecticides to get to it.

The mites multiply very rapidly and spread out from the original area of infection. The most badly affected parts are often the groin and belly, whence it spreads to the head, neck and limbs. If the disease is allowed to spread it may affect all parts of the body. The burrowing of the mites and the bacterial invasion which accompanies it set up intense irritation and have a very serious debilitating effect. This type of mange also affects other animals and man − in the latter case the disease is called 'Dairyman's itch'.

Other types of mange are probably more widespread. *Chorioptic scabei* is a very widespread condition but does not burrow under the skin; it spends its whole existence among the scabs it produces on the surface of the skin. It does therefore tend to be much less irritating and harmful. Psoroptic mange is similar, being less severe than the sarcoptic form.

Control

Control is rather difficult and requires professional veterinary advice. Any incidence should firstly be identified and once this is done measures are advised to eradicate it from the herd. A traditional material is BHC (benzene hydrochloride) used as an emulsion. Amitraz (*Taktic* by F.B.C) is applied as a spray and Bromocycen (Hoechst) as a spray or suspension. All animals should be treated and in order to eradicate the condition it will be necessary to re-treat two or three times at 10-day intervals.

It is also necessary to keep the cattle away from those parts of the building that could harbour the mites and/or disinfect these areas as effectively as possible to prevent re-infestation.

Blackquarter (Blackleg)

The disease of blackquarter is similar to so-called blackleg of sheep. It is caused by a bacterium called *Clostridium chauvoei* the spores of which are common inhabitants of the soil in areas where sheep and cattle have long been grazed. It is equally common on permanent pasture as on uncultivated, low-lying damp soils. In general, drainage and cultivation will reduce or destroy the spores.

The disease occurs because the organism is able to multiply in the muscles of the leg. The symptoms are stiffness and lameness with swellings appearing in areas such as the loin, buttocks or shoulder. The swellings are hot and painful at first but later the swellings become cold and painless. The skin over the affected muscles will become hard and stiff and if pressure is applied there is a papery effect — a dry, crackling noise due to the stiffness of the skin and the movement of the gas underneath. In fatal cases the condition of the animal rapidly deteriorates and it will die quite quickly. So far as one can tell there is possibly initially some bruise or injury in the muscle and it is in this area that the clostridia can multiply in the absence of oxygen. Then they produce the toxins which have the serious destructive effect on tissues.

Animals affected with the disease can be treated successfully with antibiotics only if the disease is recognised very early on. Penicillin preparations are indicated. Prevention can be effected by using a vaccine but the best measures of prevention rely on good pasture management, avoiding areas of known susceptibility and draining or cultivating those that must be used.

Coccidiosis in cattle

Coccidiosis is a form of dysentery that primarily affects young stock in the summer and autumn months. It is caused by a microscopic unicellular parasitic organism known as a coccidium. The coccidial parasite forms spores that can live outside the animal for many months. Adults are frequently carriers of the coccidial parasites but show no symptoms yet spread the disease to younger animals. There are a large number of different species of coccidia, at least four types infecting cattle, and each causing rather different symptoms.

The adult coccidia produce masses of microscopic spores which are passed out in the dung and under favourable warm and wet conditions mature in a couple of days and can then infect other animals. The oocysts are very resistant to destruction and can often remain infective for a year. But if they are swallowed by a susceptible animal it hatches and the active forms of the coccidia are liberated. These penetrate the cells lining the intestine where they mature and multiply. Thus they affect a considerable amount of the intestinal wall and break down areas of the mucosa. This causes diarrhoea together with bleeding which is the characteristic symptom at this time. After some period of multiplication many oocysts are formed and are passed out with the faeces to infect the pasture or the bedding wherever the animals are housed.

Animals acquire a resistance to coccidiosis by receiving a light infestation early in life and developing an immunity. However, if the intake of oocysts is sudden and too great at one time before a resistance has been produced, then disease occurs. This is most liable to happen where animals are densely stocked and the weather conditions are warm and wet. Dirty walls of pens or boxes, as well as the floor, are common sources of infection. In addition to moisture and warmth, the oocysts also require air for their development in the dung so that small amounts of faeces on the wall of the pen are very dangerous because of the aeration they receive. Oocysts often ripen particularly well on the coats of cattle and can be readily licked off by calves.

Symptoms are of a bad diarrhoea with evidence of bleeding and strings of mucus in the dung. In severe cases the animal also strains with its back in a characteristic arched position. The affected animal usually develops a strong thirst and rapidly loses condition and becomes weak. Death can be all too common a sequel.

The disease is controlled in a number of ways. Affected animals should be treated with a suitable drug, such as a sulphonamide, plus plenty of really good nursing, especially fluids. It may also be necessary to consider carefully the hygienic standards of management, but it should not be the intention of management to try totally to prevent any access of oocysts — this would be impossible and potentially dangerous as the animals would have no resistance at all and would rapidly succumb when challenged with oocysts.

Over-stocking must be avoided; good bedding and cleanliness are important, and animals should be kept in good thriving conditions so that they can readily resist such infection that occurs.

Bovine virus diarrhoea (mucosal disease)

Bovine virus diarrhoea (BVD) or mucosal disease (MD) is an infectious disease of cattle caused by a virus. It was first recognised in the USA but in recent times has occurred in virtually all parts of the world. Originally the two diseases BVD and MD were distinguished but it is now clear they are caused by the same virus so the best term is probably the BVD-MD complex.

SYMPTOMS

The disease causes ulceration of the mouth and lips accompanied by foul smelling diarrhoea. There is often lameness and extreme scurfiness of the skin. By far the majority of cases occur in cattle between 4 and 18 months of age. Most cases can recover spontaneously and exceptionally if there are many young animals affected the death rate can be high.

TREATMENT AND CONTROL

There is no specific treatment but supportive therapy in the form of intestinal astringents and electrolytes can be of value. Vaccines are obtainable in some countries but are not evidently of very much use.

Infectious bovine rhinotracheitis (IBR)

This is an acute respiratory disease of cattle caused by a virus and is spread by contact or by the air-borne route. It is a very contagious disease and can spread through a herd within 7–10 days.

SYMPTOMS

The symptoms are of severe inflammation of the eyes and the upper respiratory tract. The disease can also cause a substantial fall in milk yield, abortion and infertility. There may be a fever, loss of appetite and drooling of the saliva. Sometimes there is a pronounced cough.

CONTROL

This is not too serious a disease in Great Britain. IBR is treated with broad spectrum antibiotics to help reduce pyrexia or the effect of secondary invaders. A vaccine is available to protect the herd.

Respiratory diseases in cattle

The dangers of disease inherent in intensive systems of housing cattle, which puts large numbers of beasts of all ages in very concentrated conditions, have already been alluded to in Chapter 1. The number of pathogenic organisms that can infect the respiratory system of cattle is enormous – there are some 20 bacteria, 6 fungi, 4 parasites that *commonly* infect them, not to mention the underlying primary damage that may be wrought by viruses. The wide involvement of so many agents has made the production of satisfactory vaccines most difficult and the use of drugs complicated and expensive. Thus the prime responsibility for dealing with such conditions rests with getting the environment correct.

Fig. 4.6 Typical features of naturally ventilated livestock buildings.

The general principles have already been given in Chapter 1. Specific advice for cattle may be summarised as follows:

1. Depopulate between batches and institute a rigid disinfection programme.
2. Reduce numbers in one environment to a minimum.

3. Keep different ages and sizes of animals separate.
4. Ensure copious ventilation without draught as cattle are hardy animals and do not require cosseting.

Good ventilation is particularly important and the diagrams in Fig. 4.6 illustrate the ways this is achieved using various forms of housing. Figs 4.7 and 4.8 show examples of well-ventilated cubicle houses.

Diagram A in Fig. 4.6 shows the type of ventilation suitable for a totally enclosed cattle building with chimney trunk ventilator on the roof and hopper air inlets. B shows the details of the trunk ventilator and regulating flap, which are important. C is a ventilating open ridge for all types of cattle yard, a vital component for proper air flow, whilst D is a detailed drawing of the hopper inlet. With mono-pitch buildings the best arrangement is a hopper inlet at the rear and a full width ventilating flap at the front (Diagram E). The yard should face south.

With cattle yards it is difficult to have too much ventilation but it must be without causing draughts and two excellent ways of assisting this is to use spaced boarding (Diagram G) and the breathing roof (F), the latter being an arrangement whereby the roof sheets are

Fig. 4.7 Well-ventilated and spacious cubicle house.

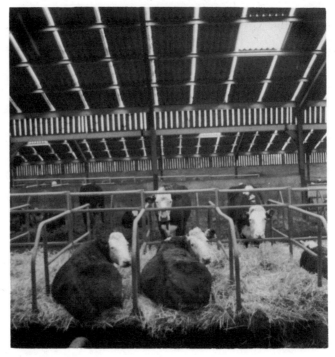

Fig. 4.8 A well-ventilated cubicle house with gaps between the roof sheets to give good air flow. The cattle shown are also well-bedded; without proper attention to the bed 'environmental' mastitis can be a major hazard.

placed upside down, with a 15 mm gap between them, thus giving ventilation all over the area of the yard. It is a very good system for wide yards with a shallow pitch on the roof. Table 4.3 provides dimensions essential for the provision of sufficient outlet area for cattle and includes other farm livestock for reference. Table 4.4 likewise gives the ventilation rates to be used wherever mechanical arrangements are used.

Table 4.3 Minimum area for the outlet of stale air in farm buildings

Type of building	Minimum outlet area m² per animal
Cows	0.09
Farrowing pigs	0.01
Fattening pigs	0.008
Calves	0.006
Laying birds	0.003
Broiler poultry	0.0015

Table 4.4 Ventilation rates for varying conditions in temperate climates for farm livestock

| Animal | (m³/hour per kg body weight) | |
	Maximum summer rate	Minimum winter rate
Adult cattle	0.75–1.4	0.19
Young calf	0.94–1.9	0.38
Sow and litter	0.94–1.9	0.38
Fattening pig	0.94–1.9	0.38
Broiler chicken	2.8 –4.7	0.75
Laying poultry	5.6 –9.4	1.50

A check list of essentials in countering respiratory disease outbreaks is given in Table 4.5.

Table 4.5 A check list of essentials in countering respiratory disease outbreaks in cattle

- Expert attention required for correct therapy.
- Improve ventilation – usually needed are more air flow and less draught.
- Check stocking density – are the cattle overcrowded?
- Is more bedding required?
- Separate and, if possible, isolate those cattle that are badly affected.
- Provide warmth for the very sick.
- Attempt separation of different ages.
- Reduce movement of animals to a minimum.
- Consider insulation and other essentials of construction relevant to the building.
- Can serum, vaccine or drugs be used to protect the unaffected animals?

Wooden tongue and lumpy jaw

These are two distinct diseases which have rather similar symptoms and are caused by unrelated organisms. They both run a slow course and are characterised by a steady enlargement of the tongue and swellings in various parts of the animal, but especially on the head and neck. Their presence may generally interfere with the normal functions of the animal – they can also ulcerate or burst an abscess, discharging into or outside the body. Untreated, they cause a steady wasting of the animal so that it becomes unproductive and will eventually die.

The cause of the two diseases are quite different. Actinomycosis is caused by a ray fungus known as *Actinomycetes bovis*, whereas actinobacillosis is caused by a bacterium *Actinobacillus ligneresi*. The main difference between the two diseases is that actinobacillosis tends to affect the soft tissues, such as the tongue, and actinomycosis usually causes diseases of the bones, especially those of the jaw.

SYMPTOMS

These depend on the organs affected and the seriousness of the disease depends largely on the importance of the affected part. Nodules of various sizes, usually hard to the touch, may form in the skin of the head and neck; at other times the skin becomes broken and the nodules are soft, yellow in colour and with a covering of crust.

The tongue is most commonly affected and becomes hard and rather rigid – thus the name 'wooden tongue'. There is a constant dribbling of saliva and food tends to be rejected. The tongue is also very sensitive and painful. The disease will also affect the glands of the neck and a swelling appears between the angles of the jaw. If this swelling is allowed to continue it will affect breathing and swallowing also becomes difficult. The lesions may burst and release a characteristic yellow and granular pus. In addition the bones of the jaw are often affected as a result of the fungus growing into the bone from the soft parts of the mouth, possibly through the sockets of the teeth. Pus forms within the bone and these diseased areas can eventually break through the skin to form an unpleasant discharging fistula.

These are, however, the external signs of the diseases. They may also affect the internal organs and will then cause a progressive wasting.

CONTROL AND TREATMENT

Other than in advanced cases, treatment can be very successful. If it does seem to have got a firm hold on the animal which is fast losing condition, it is probably best to cull it. Actinobacillus responds quite well to iodides and sulphonamides and actinomycosis will be suitably treated with penicillin or broad spectrum antibiotics. Very careful veterinary supervision will be needed if the measures chosen are to be satisfactory.

Prevention of the disease is best achieved by responding quickly to any wounds on the face of cattle and elsewhere by dressing with an appropriate antibacterial material. There is no preventive vaccine available.

Redwater

Redwater, also called bovine piroplasmosis or babesiasis, is a curious condition caused by the presence in the blood of minute parasites called piroplasms. These parasites live inside the red blood corpuscles where they can be seen in the early stages of the disease. It is a condition that tends to be found in certain well-defined areas; in the British Isles, for example, it occurs mostly in Wales and south west England and small areas of East Anglia.

Piroplasmosis is a much more serious disease in tropical countries than in the UK where only one species of the parasite is present. This is *Babesia divergens* and its presence is associated with rough scrubland or on heathland or woodlands where ticks are present. The condition is transmitted from animal to animal by the tick *Ixodes ricinus*, which acts as a carrier. The tick is infected by sucking the blood of an infected animal. Once the tick is engorged with blood it falls off and lies in the herbage. Later the tick may attach itself to other cattle and when it sucks from these, introduces the parasites into the blood. The ticks may be seen on the animals, often in considerable numbers. During the life cycle of the tick it feeds on three separate animals, first as a larva, than as a nymph and finally as an adult. At each stage it feeds on blood and when full falls to the ground in order to digest its meal and grow. It is probable that at each stage infection is transmitted. Infected adult ticks pass on infection through to the new generation via the egg. Thus an infection can remain within a tick population for a long while even in the absence of cattle.

SYMPTOMS

The two worst periods for redwater disease are from March to June and October to November. The main effects of the disease are to cause loss of condition and a very considerable loss of milk yield. The disease is characterised by the presence of the dark blood pigment in the urine of the affected animals, but this symptom is not invariably present. Sometimes there is very little discolouration or in others the urine may turn black. There is always an increase in urine.

Animals affected also show a high fever and diarrhoea and later constipation. The animal also often becomes jaundiced — the mucous membranes becoming yellow. The heart beat becomes very loud and there are tremors of the muscles of the shoulder and legs. Temperament also often changes for the worse. In the later stages of the disease the animal becomes dull and listless, anaemic, the urine darker and death may take place.

Many of the symptoms are induced by the destruction of the red blood corpuscles by the parasites and the release of the red colouring matter. Much of this escapes into the urine via the kidneys, causing the typical 'redwater' and damaging the kidneys thereby. The jaundice and the extra exertion of the heart are also associated with this same factor. It should be noted that young cattle are less susceptible than adults which have not previously been infected. If contracted early in life the disease is only mild and the animal is then immune against further infection. This indicates one of the great dangers; if adult cattle from a tick-free area are introduced into a red-water area, some of these may contract the infection and die quite rapidly without treatment.

CONTROL

Treatment of infected animals will be two-fold. Firstly, the animal will require injection with one of a number of chemotherapeutic agents that are lethal to the parasite, such as Piroparv. It is important that these are given to the animal early in the course of the infection. Secondly, careful nursing is perhaps even more important. Feed well, house comfortably, do not drive or excite for fear of heart failure and keep the animal warm.

The recovered animal usually retains the infection and thus is a carrier of the disease. This small degree of infection thereby protects the animal by ensuring that the body's immunological system is always 'alert'. Indeed, in redwater areas the usual thing to happen is for a young animal to contract the disease mildly and thus get a protection. This procedure is often good but there are certain inherent dangers in relying on this immunity. The resistance of these animals may be broken down by a sudden change of weather or any other circumstance that can lower the general condition of the animal. It is difficult to know which animals are protected and which remain fully susceptible. Thus if animals are newly introduced into a redwater area herd from outside then they must be very carefully watched for signs of redwater for several weeks.

PREVENTION

The disease could be eradicated if ticks were eliminated. The tick is extremely resistant to most measures of control. In addition it can feed off several species of animals and is not dependent on cattle alone. Sometimes sheep are put on pasture as 'tick collectors'. By placing them alone on the pasture at the worst tick seasons of the year and then adopting a heavy dipping programme, this will reduce numbers considerably. The only effective way of eliminating ticks is to clear the rough ground by cultivation and normal crop rotation.

Wherever this procedure is adopted and a part of the farm is freed from ticks, the importance of exposing young animals to tick infestation must be considered, otherwise they will be highly susceptible as adults to a first infection. Great care must be taken not to put them on to tick-infested ground for the first time in adulthood.

Diseases of mature cattle

Metabolic disorders

BLOAT

Bloat, also known as blown, hoven or tympanitis, is a common disorder of the rumen or first stomach and is one of several problems largely occurring from grazing. The rumen becomes distended with gas and the pressure from this on the diaphragm may lead to the animal dying from asphyxia or shock. Two types of bloat occur — the first is where the gases separate from the contents of the lower part of the rumen, and the second where the gases remain as small bubbles mixed with the contents in a foamy mass, giving rise to what is known as 'frothy bloat'.

Bloat most often occurs in the grazing of lush pastures which contain a high proportion of clover. It is likely to happen when the herbage is growing rapidly in the late spring or early summer but cases can occur throughout the whole of the grazing season and in some areas it has proved troublesome even where cattle are grazing on kale in the winter months. There are several possible explanations for this problem. It may be due to the fact that some kinds of herbage contain substances that may cause paralysis of the rumen muscles and of other organs concerned in the process of rumination. Or it may be due to the fact that more gas is produced than can be got rid of by eructation. It has also been suggested that bloat can be due to the result of foaming in the rumen caused by saponin and protein substances obtained from plants. Starches and sugars may also play a part and between them they produce a foam of great stability in the rumen.

Symptoms are obvious — distension of the abdomen which is particularly pronounced on the left flank between the last rib and hip bone. The swelling spreads as the attack becomes more severe and eventually the whole abdomen is swollen. In the early stages and sub-acute form, bloat is characterised by the animal's unusual behaviour; it becomes uneasy, moves from one foot to another, switches its tail, and occasionally kicks at the abdomen. Breathing becomes very distressed and rapid. If the attack is a severe one, any movement intensifies the discomfort and so the animal stands quietly with legs wide apart. If relief is not given very quickly, death from suffocation or exhaustion can follow rapidly.

Control
It is advisable to summon a veterinary surgeon as soon as possible. If time allows, a stomach tube may be inserted into the rumen to allow the gas out. In acute cases the only remedy is to puncture the rumen on the left flank with the surgical apparatus, the trocar and cannula. In an emergency, where death seems imminent and specialised assistance is not available, the only course of action is to puncture the area with a short pointed knife with a blade which is at least 6 inches long – the blade being plunged into the middle of the swelling on the left side and twisted at right angles to the cut to assist the gas to escape.

Although this treatment will serve to give immediate relief, more treatment is required if the case is one of frothy bloat. Drenching with one of the substances known as silicones, or with an ounce of oil of turpentine in a pint of linseed oil, often helps in the less severe cases and some gentle exercising may help to relieve the pressure of the gas in the rumen. There are also a number of drug treatments available, such as Avlinox, which is an ethylene oxide derivative of ricinoleic acid.

Prevention
A number of methods have been used to control bloat and in this way the incidence of the most serious cases can be reduced to negligible proportions. Efficient pasture management can help to avoid the trouble. After a pasture is closely grazed and then rested, the clover recovers more quickly than the grasses so that when pastures are used intensively the clover becomes dominant in the sward. It is not yet possible to assess the proportion of grass to clover needed to avoid the risk of bloat but it is generally considered that if there is less than 50% of clover present it is usually safe. A variety of seed mixtures has been tried to provide a suitable balance between clover and grass; one which has given promising results contains tall fescue. After it has been closely grazed this species of grass recovers almost as quickly as the clover and maintains a reasonably safe balance between grass and clover.

Another system which has been advocated is to allow the herd to graze a potentially dangerous herbage for a limited period and then turn it on to an old pasture for a time.

Controlled grazing can contribute to the prevention of bloat by ensuring that the grazing animal eats both leaf and stem, whether clover or grass, and that it cannot select clover or clover leaf which is thought to be the more dangerous. If an electric fence is moved forward so that the cows have access to a succession of narrow strips of pasture during the course of the day, bloat may be reduced or eliminated but it may reduce the intake of the feed and milk yield.

The second method of controlling grazing is to mow strips of herbage, then allow it to wilt and let the herd graze it as it lies on the ground. Alternatively, the wilted herbage can be carted to the cattle and fed indoors.

The feeding of roughage in the form of hay or oat straw shortly before the grazing of dangerous pasture has also been practised for many years. It is only completely reliable if the roughage is fed overnight.

It is also possible to feed anti-foaming agents, or even to spray the pasture with emulsified peanut oil. However, this is expensive and has to be done daily, so it is not a very practicable proposition.

MILK FEVER
Milk fever occurs in cows after calving, usually in dairy breeds of high milk yielding capacity. It is given various synonyms, such as hypocalcaemia, parturient hypocalcaemia, parturient paresis and parturient apoplexy. There is, in fact, no fever and indeed it is more usual for the cows to show subnormal temperatures.

Symptoms
The symptoms, which may not be noticed in the early stages, usually occur within 12–72 hours of calving though occasionally it occurs before calving and, in a few other cases, even months after calving. In its typical form, there is a short period of uneasiness with paddling of the hind legs, swishing of the tail and convulsive movements, but this is soon followed by depressed consciousness and paralysis. The animal usually falls on its side with its legs extended, rolling its eyes and breathing heavily. The characteristic picture is a twisting of the neck as it lies on one side, with spasm of the neck muscles, shallow laboured breathing, grunting, cessation of rumination and dryness of the muzzle. Bloat may occur and there is likely to be constipation. Other side effects can be pneumonia, inflammation of the uterus

(metritis), retained afterbirth and strained tendons and muscles. In straightforward milk fever, the calcium and phosphorus levels fall and the magnesium levels rise.

In practice it is quite difficult to distinguish between the simple hypocalcaemia and the more complicated metabolic disorder where there are a number of deficiencies which have to be corrected.

The background to occurrence

There does not appear to be any real breed incidence, but it is usually well-fed, high-yielding cows which are affected and the severity of the condition increases with age. It is very rare at the first calving. After one attack it is more likely to occur at future calvings. The cause is usually ascribed to a temporary failure in the physiological mechanism which controls calcium levels in the blood. The stress of calving and the physical adjustment necessary for lactation will upset the balance of chemical regulators (hormones) produced by various glands and if the cow does not adjust itself quickly enough she may suffer an attack of parturient hypocalcaemia. The sudden fall in the level of calcium in the blood is not due to any shortage of calcium in the food and cannot be prevented by feeding extra calcium compounds although it is of course essential there is adequate calcium always present.

Control

The immediate administration of a solution of calcium − calcium borogluconate is normally used − is highly effective in curing the simple uncomplicated milk fever. It may be given intravenously for a quick response, or subcutaneously for a slower effect. If the case is recognised earlier, the latter is usually effective and may be given by the stockman. Where a more immediate effect is required it must be given by the intravenous route.

In addition, the cow should be propped up in the box by means of straw bales on each side to prevent it from becoming 'blown', and to prevent regurgitation of ruminant contents. Further injection of calcium may be required and in addition, in complicated cases, there will be the need for administration of phosphorus injections and even other materials. Professional advice is certainly required for all but the simple case of hypocalcaemia.

One method frequently used in an attempt to prevent milk fever is to give the cow injections of Vitamin D. This vitamin increases the mobilisation of calcium in the body and thereby may help to prevent levels falling too low.

KETOSIS (ACETONAEMIA)

Ketosis is a disease involving ketones which are chemical compounds which may be produced during the metabolism of fat. This condition may occur when an animal's food intake is inadequate for its needs and it is drawing on its own reserves in considerable amounts to make good the deficiency. The usual form of ketosis is ketonaemia which includes an excess of ketones in the blood. Since acetone is the simplest and most characteristic of the ketones the disease is generally termed acetonaemia. It is also called 'post-parturient dyspepsia' as it often occurs soon after calving and is associated with indigestion. It often follows mild attacks of milk fever and almost appears to be a subnormally slow recovery — hence the traditional term for the disease of 'slow fever'.

Symptoms

The symptoms of ketosis are usually seen within two weeks of calving and in well-nourished stock of high milking capacity. But it may also occur much later than this — even several months after calving. It is most common during the tail-end of winter. In the mild form it may almost pass unnoticed and be over within a few days, but it is readily recognised in its more severe forms. The cow will appear listless, with a marked loss of condition, dull coat and a sickly sweet smell of acetone in the breath and also in the urine and milk. The milk production falls away quickly and the milk becomes tainted and undrinkable. There is also a failure to co-ordinate muscles and the cow so affected will find it difficult to walk straight so it tends to stand in one position with its back arched and with straightened hocks. Constipation with dark, mucus-covered dung is usual. The pulse is variable and the temperature is usually either normal or slightly down. Sometimes there is a licking mania, a rather wild looking appearance and champing of the jaws and salivation, and there may also be hyper-excitability.

The condition is rarely fatal but it may become chronic and resistant to treatment. Chronic acetonaemia can last for months during which the milk will be unsaleable and the animal's condition will deteriorate to such an extent that the only economic action to take is to cull her from the herd.

Control

Firstly, tests are carried out to confirm the presence of ketones in the blood. It will be usual for the blood sugar to be low and injections of glucose are an early procedure. Corticosteroids may be

administered to give a longer term beneficial effect. Other useful
treatments are glycerine and preparations containing sodium pro-
pionate. Molasses and/or molassine meal are also helpful.

Prevention will depend principally on skilful management. The
energy provided in the food must keep pace with the draining
demands of production — especially in early lactation. It is, however,
important not to increase concentrates too drastically or the cow
may be put off them just when she needs them. In late pregnancy the
cow should be kept in good condition but not over-fat. No excessive
steaming-up is called for. The roughage in the ration should also be
carefully selected and kept up to a good level or at least reduced
slowly if the cow's appetite and enthusiasm for a balanced diet are
to be maintained. Silage feeding can be a contributory factor to
ketosis due to the high level of butyric acid produced when
fermenting conditions are right. All changes in feed should be gradual
and carefully watched. If feeding is balanced in all items and a
sufficiency is always given, there is a minimum chance of ketosis
occurring.

HYPOMAGNESAEMIA

The amount of magnesium in the blood of normal animals keeps
within a fairly constant range. However, should the magnesium level
of the blood drop below this range, then the condition known as
hypomagnesaemia, or grass tetany, can result. The condition is
widespread throughout the world but occurs especially in areas of
cooler climate where the pasture has been improved and production
increased. In adult cattle it is called by various names, such as 'grass
tetany', 'grass staggers', 'lactation tetany' and 'Hereford disease',
whilst in calves it is known as 'milk tetany' or 'calf tetany'.

The underlying causes

Possibly the main period of occurrence of this disease is in the
period of sudden change of lactating cows from winter housed
conditions to those of the rapidly sown spring grass. But though the
occurrence of hypomagnesaemia does seem to be at its peak during
the spring flush, and the autumn one to a lesser extent, it is now
known to occur in cattle under most feeding and management
regimes, including winter feeding periods. For all these reasons and
confusions it seems fairly certain that the condition is not due to a
simple deficiency of magnesium, for sometimes the condition occurs
in cattle on pasture which has a very adequate magnesium content.
Underfeeding appears to be a predisposing cause, especially in out-

wintered beef cattle, but overall the disease seems to be due to physiological dysfunctioning that interferes with the absorption and utilisation of the magnesium which is in the food and causes sudden falls in blood magnesium levels.

Symptoms
Symptoms vary according to the intensity of the attack. The first signs are often nervousness, restlessness, loss of appetite, twitching of the muscles, especially of the face and eyes, grinding of the teeth and quite soon after, staggering. In less acute cases animals which are normally placid become nervous or even fierce. In severe cases paralysis and convulsions develop very soon after the onset of symptoms and if treatment is not given death will follow very quickly. In milking cows a sudden reduction in milk yield may occur just before an attack. Sometimes the attack comes on so rapidly that no symptoms are seen — merely a dead beast. Hypomagnesaemia often starts at milking times or during feeding when the animals are more excited or disturbed. There is also a chronic form of the disease in which cows show a gradual loss of condition although appetite and even the milk yield do not show any drop. This chronic state can last several weeks and then develop into the more acute condition.

In some cases where beef cattle are kept out all the year round, often without any shelter and under poor conditions, their blood magnesium levels 'cycle' in a regular seasonal way, being normal in summer, falling slowly in late autumn and winter, reaching a 'low' in early spring and then rising again to normal. In these cases there may be no clinical signs of abnormality but they can occur when calving or some other severe stress occurs during the periods of lower blood magnesium.

Hypomagnesaemia will sometimes occur at the same time as hypocalcaemia or acetonaemia. In these cases obviously the symptoms will be more complicated with some signs of all the diseases and only a blood examination will give the full picture.

Control
The moment signs are seen or suspected, veterinary advice should be sought. The veterinary surgeon may inject magnesium plus other solutions but it needs to be done by the qualified person for favourable results — haphazard use may kill the animal. Important measures need to be taken in an attempt to prevent the disease occurring. In most cases supplements of magnesium will prevent the condition. Two ounces of magnesium oxide per head per day has

been used for many years successfully in dosing adults to prevent the condition. The magnesium oxide is usually given as calcined magnesite in a granular form. This must be given daily to cattle under risk or blood magnesium levels can fall quickly.

Although it is thought that the disease is not caused by a shortage of magnesium in the diet, the use on pastures of magnesium-rich fertilisers has been quite successful in preventing the disease. On some soils, top dressing in January or February with 500 kg of calcined magnesite per acre can be a perfect preventative. Even 250 kg may be sufficient. Another method of preventing the disease is the magnesium 'bullet' in the reticulum with its slow release of magnesium and attempts have also been made to give multi-vitamin injections to increase the absorption and utilisation of magnesium. Such measures certainly help in preventing the disease but cannot replace the earlier methods given.

In out-wintered cattle where the condition occurs the incidence is highest during the coldest weather.

There appears to be no definite association with soil-type, nevertheless the condition does occur much more on some farms than others. It has also been shown that the liberal use of nitrogen and potash fertilisers, especially on young leys, may increase the incidence of hypomagnesaemia. But this also is by no means the whole story since the condition not infrequently occurs on old and new pastures at various stages of growth and after treatment with a variety of different fertilisers.

The condition occurs in all breeds but is very uncommon in Jersey cows. In contrast to milk fever, hypomagnesaemia is not particularly associated with cattle giving high yields and it occurs as frequently in beef cattle as well as dairy cattle.

CALF TETANY

Many years ago it was established that calves could not be reared to maturity on milk alone because of the onset of deficiency conditions — and in particular hypomagnesaemia or calf tetany during growth. But the condition does also occur under other conditions of feeding and it is an increasing problem in beef calves, especially if they are grazing at the time of the most active growth of spring grass.

The symptoms in calves are similar to those in older animals — hyperexcitability, irritableness and twitching of the muscle. The walk often becomes spastic, the feet being carried well above the usual height. Thereafter in the progress of the disease convulsions may follow and eventually death. Symptoms rarely occur before about six weeks of age and are often missed at first so that only the terminal convulsions are seen.

Treatment consists of immediate administration of suitable magnesium injections. Prevention is effected by administering about 15 g (½ oz) of calcined magnesite daily, or 30 g (1 oz) of magnesium carbonate daily.

Production diseases and the Metabolic Profile Test

High production in dairy cattle is being achieved in two principal ways – firstly by intensification and improvement of management and feeding and secondly by selecting and breeding animals which give the highest milk yields. Both trends have inherent dangers in that the animals may fail to withstand the combined strain of high production under the most intensive conditions. All production systems have three parts:

1. An input of the raw material – the feed.
2. An output of the finished product – in dairy cattle this being milk.
3. A processing system within the animal which is in fact extremely complex and under great strain in the high-producing animal.

The problem of production disease occurs when input rates fail to keep pace with the output rates, or when the processing system in the middle becomes overloaded. When the dairy cow is confronted with an input/output imbalance she tends to use her own tissues to make good the deficiency and will 'milk herself into the churn'. The cow can use up so much of her vital reserves of materials that she can kill herself in an effort to maintain production.

There are two types of metabolic disease that one can distinguish. The first are those when there are very sudden and severe demands on a cow which she fails to meet: for example, at the birth of her calf. The flow of milk demands a surge of energy requirements and food will be insufficient for this at once so the cow draws on her reserves. If too much is taken a condition such as hypocalcaemia develops because the high level of calcium in the milk seriously reduces the calcium in the blood. The more chronic metabolic disease occurs when there is a gradual depletion of the reserves over a lengthy period. The best example is when the dairy cow gradually depletes her reserves with a high output of milk and marginally inadequate feed intake. Calcium and phosphorus will be drained from the skeleton, leading to the so-called 'broken-down cow'. Ketosis is another major problem, due to insufficient carbohydrate for high production. The cow has to metabolise her body fat to make good the deficiency but if this goes too far there is collapse of carbohydrate metabolism followed by ketosis.

Another problem of a chronic nature is that due to trace element deficiency. Many pastures are deficient, for example, in iodine, sodium, manganese and copper.

Prevention of production diseases depends on balancing intake with output. Calculations based on a simple knowledge of the composition of the diet are not always sufficiently accurate. For instance, the maintenance part of the diet is impossible to assess. If the cows are at pasture and even on indoor rations, analyses of hay and silage can be misleading and the cows may not be consuming all their share of the food supplied. Some kind of measure of the state of balance within the cows themselves is needed — a test to show the nutritional and metabolic status of a dairy herd. Such a test gives a warning of an impending metabolic disease and is called the *Compton Metabolic Profile Test*. It is based on the blood chemistry of 21 cows whatever the size of the herd. Automatic analysers enable results to be obtained almost instantly. Tests for the following are usually done:

Glucose	Magnesium
Albumin ⎫	Copper
Globulin ⎭ Protein	Sodium
Urea	Potassium
Phosphate	Haemoglobin
Calcium	Packed Cell Volume

Samples are taken from 7 cows in each of the following groups:

Cows on high production.
Cows whose yield has dropped a good deal.
Dry cows.

Thus there is a total of 252 tests per herd.

The results throw light on causes of poor production or poor health, or indicate pointers to improvement in management or diet. They also show items of wastage in the diet and can lead to economies.

Mastitis

Mastitis means literally inflammation of the mammary gland or udder. It is, however, a term which is applied to all 'diseases' of the udder though most of these are caused by infectious agents of which there are a large number. It has always been an important disease of dairy cattle with potentially disastrous consequences but with the advent of antibiotic treatments there was a general optimism that the days of the disease were numbered. Regrettably this has not been the case, for a number of reasons. Organisms that cause mastitis have become increasingly resistant to the constant use, or perhaps more correctly misuse and abuse, of antibiotic therapy. Even with the introduction of an ever-increasing range of antibiotics, the disease has tended to outstrip the therapy.

Also there has been a growth of large dairy cattle units with the greater opportunity for disease build-up and cross infection. Cow cleanliness has become less satisfactory and some of the most modern practices lead to dirtier cows and udders — for example, with loose housing and cubicles. There has also been the emergence of different forms of mastitis, called environmental, because of their association with the newer forms of husbandry and rather different balance of organisms involved.

Thus a very worrying picture is presented that mastitis in the dairy cow may affect as many as 50% of the cows in the National Herd in one form or another, many cases being subclinical and so not readily recognisable. Since a cow with mastitis may *readily* lose a quarter of its milk output there is no doubt of the extreme economic importance of this condition. Whenever mastitis occurs it must be looked upon as a herd problem rather than a 'one-off' event and should be dealt with urgently and thoroughly. Even a single cow may be a warning of a managemental error and should be carefully considered in this respect.

Subclinical mastitis means that the udder is affected with a relatively mild bout of disease but it is not so apparent that the cow's health or even the milk yield is obviously affected. How can one know if this is the case? It can now be done most efficiently by *cell counts*. If an inflammatory process is proceeding, then the milk will contain more white blood cells than normal. The best way for the farmer to deal with this is to arrange for a regular monitoring of the cells in the milk. The range of 'counts', with the significance given, is as follows:

Cell count ranges (cells/ml)	Estimate of mastitis incidence in a herd	Estimate of milk (litres) production loss per cow
Below 250 000	Negligible	—
250 000 – 499 000	Slight	200 litres
500 000 – 749 000	Average	350
750 000 – 999 000	Bad	720
1 000 000 and over	Very bad	900

The cell count tests are an excellent procedure as they can act as warnings and enable preventive measures to be instituted.

THE MILKING MACHINE

A major predisposing cause of mastitis is the misapplication of milking machines, together with bad maintenance and poor hygiene routine during milking.

One of the most serious of these is over-milking, i.e. the milking machine is left on much longer than it should be. There has long been the traditional belief that it is critically necessary to extract the very last drop of milk. In many cases, too, the cowman has too much to do to give proper attention to each cow so that he is totally over-stretched. Over-milking tends to cause considerable damage to the very delicate mucous membranes lining the teat canal (see Fig. 4.9) and this then allows pathogenic micro-organisms to invade so that mastitis results. The cowman must see when the main flow of milk has stopped, then apply a mild pressure on the cluster to prevent it 'rising up' or enormous damage may be done since the force of the vacuum will grip the teat and a portion of the membrane of the cistern is sucked into it forming an obstruction so that the milk cannot flow. The cowman may either machine-strip the udder of milk by holding the cluster down for 15 seconds or so, or the remaining milk may be left in the udder. Either course is perfectly acceptable, but leaving the machine on for too long is disastrous.

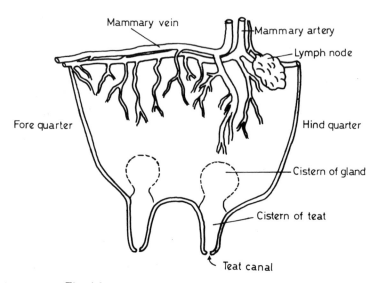

Fig. 4.9 Diagrammatic cross-section of cow's udder.

Other items in connection with machine milking have an important bearing on mastitis. Teat liners must be chosen of the right size and of gentle fit. They must never be slack and should be carefully maintained to prevent them from causing damage. Pulsations of the machine must be maintained between 40 and 60 a minute; if the rate increases squeezing may fail and mastitis is more likely to occur. The ratio between the release and squeeze phase should be between 2:1 and 1:1.

There are other vital parts and procedures. The pump needs to be maintained properly as it 'ages' or a surge of milk may result around the teat, such circumstances also being a predisposing cause of mastitis. The vacuum regulator prevents fluctuation in vacuum which can be very damaging to the udder and teats for, if it fails, a surge of milk results around the teat and clusters may fall off or, if it rises, it damages the teats causing extrusion of the lining of the teat canal.

No words here can over-emphasise the importance of having regular expert maintenance of the milking machine. A very substantial number of machines on farms are faulty in one respect or another and can take a large share of the blame in causing mastitis.

TYPES OF MASTITIS

There are various ways of classifying mastitis. It may be done on the basis of the *cause*, e.g. the type of bacteria or other pathogenic organisms that have invaded the udder, or it may be done on the basis of the symptoms of the disease. In the recognition and treatment of the disease both aspects are important.

The symptoms are probably the best starting point. There are the easily recognisable forms of clinical mastitis. In this category are the *acute, sub-acute* and *chronic* forms.

Acute mastitis

The cow is obviously ill — feverish, fast-breathing, depressed and there is no cudding. Examination of the udder will show that one or more quarters are tense, swollen and possibly discoloured (blue); the cow will usually object strongly to the examination due to the severe pain. It may be possible to withdraw from the affected quarter(s) a small quantity of fluid, looking not so much like milk but more akin to a yellow serum, or perhaps containing blood with a pus-like, foul-smelling exudate. In such cases gangrene of the udder may set in very quickly causing in effect the destruction of part of the udder around the base of the teat. This 'acute' mastitis, as it is clinically called, is often the same thing as the so-called 'summer mastitis' which, whilst it is most common in dry cows and heifers in the summer months, can occur in cows at other times. Such mastitis is caused primarily by a bacterium, *Corynebacterium pyogenes*, and may be treated with antibiotics and sulpha drugs. It is essential to treat it early if there is any hope of retaining the cow's milking ability, though this is never very likely in any case. Because of its common association with 'dry cows' its incidence *may* be reduced by using long-acting antibiotic therapy as soon as the cow is dried off.

Sub-acute mastitis

The symptoms are somewhat similar but milder and slower in their progress. The first sign of disease may be the appearance of small clots in the milk with some increased difficulty in extracting it. Pain also gradually increases and the affected quarter(s) swell. The milk eventually becomes yellowish and much decreased in amount. The cow does not usually become more than slightly ill, which clearly distinguishes it from the acute form.

Chronic mastitis

In this form of mastitis there is no pain, and any general sickness in the cow is unlikely, but there is a gradual hardening of the udder tissue, a decrease in the amount of milk and a progressive swelling of those quarters infected.

CAUSES OF MASTITIS

At one time the most frequently occurring bacteria was *Streptococcus agalactiae*, but this has generally decreased in incidence with the advent of successful antibiotic treatment. Other streptococci, *dysgalactia* and *uberis*, are common and also staphylococcus and corynebacterium, the latter already mentioned. There are, however, some serious new forms of mastitis that are of comparatively recent origin and are most difficult to treat.

Escherichia coli is usually associated with the so-called environmental mastitis. Also Pseudomonas is a common bacterial cause of mastitis, and *Corynebacterium bovis*. Mastitis may also be caused by micro-organisms other than bacteria, such as mycoplasma (*M. agalactiae*) and moulds, the latter being termed mycotic mastitis.

CONTROL OF MASTITIS

It is now accepted realistically that it is never going to be possible to eliminate mastitis by antibiotic treatment alone. This is because many preparations are not active against certain of the bacteria causing mastitis and also because so much infection remains sub-clinical and cannot therefore be recognised. Thus the view is now taken that the control of mastitis must depend largely on the application of hygienic criteria of the highest standard. In summary these methods are as follows:

Teat dipping
After milking, all teats should be dipped in antiseptic; this is usually based on an iodophor or chlorine solution which will not harm the tissue of the teat.

Cowman's hygiene
The cowman should wear smooth rubber gloves which can be dipped in the antiseptic before use.

Udder cleanliness
This is preferably achieved by using warm water sprays and then drying with disposable paper towels, which are much more effective than cloths which can cause cross-infection. If warm water cannot be used, cold water should be used first and then a good proprietary udder wash.

Good technique and equipment
The importance of this has been fully emphasised earlier.

Strip-cup
The routine use of the strip-cup where required is advisable. This device enables a little milk to be looked at from an udder and thus recognise the earliest appearance of mastitis.

Table 4.6 sets out a summary of preventive measures against mastitis.

Routine therapy
There is a vogue for the routine use of long-acting antibiotic intra-mammary treatments when cows are dried off. This is intended to get rid of any residual infection in the udder and also ensure that the cow does not have any infection when it calves down again. The theory is good but very careful professional advice on what should and should not be done is necessary; such routine use of antibiotics is liable to cause drug resistance.

Table 4.6 A summary of measures aimed to prevent mastitis in the dairy cow

---

- Basic design of cow accommodation must be right to ensure cow's bed is dry and clean and minimum chance of injury to udder.
- Replace fouled bedding frequently in stalls, yard or cubicles.
- Test milking machine regularly, check vacuum pressures, pulsation rates, air bleeds and liners daily.
- Monitor cell counts in milk. Keep detailed records for frequent reference.
- Teat-dip always to be used after milking. Use a sanitising mixture with an emollient such as lanolin.
- Wash udders before milking with clean running water and dry with disposable towels. Milker should preferably wear smooth rubber gloves.
- Ensure early diagnosis by use of 'fore-milk' cup.
- Treat all cases of mastitis promptly.
- Cull chronic cases of mastitis.
- Correct laboratory diagnosis of causal organisms assists in taking proper remedial measures.
- Treat cows as they dry off with a long-acting antibiotic.

Culling
Careful consideration should be given to culling from the herd all those cows which are a constant source of mastitis.

Treatment with antibiotics
Clinical cases need prompt treatment but measures should be taken to ensure the use of the correct antibiotic. As a routine, when a case occurs a sample of milk should go to the laboratory *before* any treatment is instituted. Treatment does not have to wait until after the report is back but it will enable confirmation that it is the right antibiotic. If the antibiotic used is insensitive the necessary change can be quickly made. It is also worth emphasising that the course of treatment must continue for the full time advised, that is, usually five days. One of the most serious errors of all is to administer the antibiotic for an insufficient period: this is one of the certain ways of producing resistant organisms.

Disease problems associated with breeding in cattle
Lowered fertility results in lowered production and causes great economic loss. However, infertility is not a disease as such, it is only the symptom of one. It may be due to any condition that prevents a vigorous sperm from fertilising a healthy ova to produce a robust calf. The process involved is complicated and the different causes of

fertility are numerous. Consider the whole physiological process. The bull must produce healthy sperm only, but the cow must not only produce a healthy egg but also provide the ideal condition for the fertilisation of the ova by the sperm and the establishment of the embryo in the uterus. The cow then has to provide the nutrients for the calf and then, when it is mature, she must expel the calf from the uterus.

Infertility has probably become more serious in recent years because it tends to be associated with cows giving an immensely good yield of milk.

CAUSES OF INFERTILITY

Fundamentally the breeding potential of an animal depends on certain inherited genetic tendencies and the presence of any inherited abnormalities. Such genes may either cause the animals to be infertile or produce faulty calves. However, some of the most important causes of infertility are bacterial or other infectious agents. Such an agent may be a specific organism producing a condition of which infertility is only one symptom. An example of this is contagious abortion (brucellosis), which is fully dealt with later in this chapter.

Another example is trichomoniasis, the causal organism being *Trichomonas foetus*, which is spread at service by infected bulls, which themselves show no obvious evidence of infection. A third example, vibriosis, is due to the organism *Vibrio foetus* and is carried and transmitted by apparently normal bulls. Both trichomonas and vibrio organisms multiply in the uterus and cause the death and abortion of the foetus. Infertility may also be caused by non-specific infections of the genital tract.

Control

When a cow or heifer fails to conceive to a second service it should be examined by a veterinary surgeon who, by carrying out tests, can establish if there is an infectious cause. If there is, it may well be treatable. Prevention depends on a number of factors. The herd should be kept as self-contained as possible and only maiden heifers and unused bulls should come into the herd. There should be no exchange of breeding animals. The diet must be adequate and balanced.

TRICHOMONIASIS

Trichomoniasis is a venereal disease which is spread by bulls. It can be one of the most important causes of infertility in cattle and has from time to time caused most serious losses to herds. Fortunately with the introduction and general adoption of artificial insemination in cattle the opportunity of cross-infection has greatly diminished.

The infective agent of Trichomoniasis is a small microscopic parasite called *Trichomonas foetus*. The bull becomes infected from an infected cow and the parasites live in the crevices of the moist skin covering the penis. When an infected bull serves a heifer or cow the parasites pass into the female tract, where they are able to multiply. Once infected, the bull may transmit the infection to all the females he serves for the rest of his life. The disease is exclusively venereal and this is the only way it can spread, i.e. via the genitalia. Infected cows cannot infect non-infected females and all danger of infection is removed when the infected bull is removed.

The first symptoms of trichonomiasis are usually a period of unsatisfactory breeding. The presence of the parasites in the uterus interfere with the progress of normal pregnancy and cows and heifers usually fail to hold to service and abortion will also occur.

There may be no other signs of infection and the disease may not be suspected for some time. Some small aborts may be seen from time to time; usually the abortions occur very early so that they are not seen and it is thought the animals have merely failed to hold to service. Sometimes a discharge occurs after the infection is established. Thus a suspicion of infection would be aroused when a number of animals fail to hold to repeated service and especially if the interval is in the period of two to four months.

Diagnosis of infection is made on a laboratory test of mucus collected from a number of females or, in the case of the bull which probably shows no symptoms, the parasites can be found in washings from the prepuce of the bull.

Control of this infection is done in two principal ways. Firstly, the use of a bull should be abandoned at least temporarily and replaced by artificial insemination. No bull should be used again on a cow in an 'infected' herd until after a normal calf has been produced by artificial insemination. The infection of a bull is sufficiently permanent and resistant to treatment to recommend that infected bulls are culled from the herd.

It is clear that it is possible to eradicate the disease from a herd by appropriate managemental techniques. The foregoing advice also stresses the importance of having good records at one's disposal since this is the only way the presence of a disease can be suspected early on, to achieve minimum loss and maximum results.

VIBRIOSIS

Vibriosis is a disease affecting the genital organs of cattle which leads to infertility and abortion. The symptoms are rather similar to those of trichomoniasis. The condition is caused by a bacterium, *Vibrio foetus*, which is also a true venereal infection spread during service. A bull may contract the disease initially by mating with an infected heifer or cow, or indeed by contracting the infection in unhygienic quarters. Fortunately the disease is of rather low incidence but when it arises the effects can be very serious.

Infertility and abortion are the only obvious symptoms. Cows and heifers return to service at irrrgular intervals — some may return after several months — so the economic loss is particularly serious. After a period of infection in a herd, the condition may tend to become less serious and it is very important under the rather vague and variable conditions of the disease to have laboratory examinations in order to see that it is properly diagnosed.

Control is dependent on a number of different procedures. The herd is best divided into two groups — one being the males and females which have not been exposed to infection, and the other consisting of all the other breeding animals which are or may have been infected. This group remains as a possible cause of infection and should have separate arrangements for service. It is possible to treat infected bulls with antibiotics to eliminate the disease though the safest way of stopping further infection is to use artificial insemination. This should enable elimination of infection altogether because the evidence suggests that cows clear the infection out after a pregnancy.

The following techniques to maintain freedom from infection also illustrate the general principles of preventing venereal diseases from being introduced into a herd:

- Only bulls which have never been mated, or have only been used with maiden heifers should be purchased.
- It is best to obtain bulls only from herds which are known to be free of infection.
- Females from other herds should never be brought into a herd for mating, and only maiden heifers or cows from herds known to be free should be brought in as replacements.

Diseases affecting cattle of all ages

Foot-and-mouth disease

Foot-and-mouth disease is an acutely contagious disease which causes fever in cattle and all cloven-hoofed animals, followed by the development of blisters or vesicles, which arise chiefly on the mouth and feet. The disease is an infection, world-wide in incidence, caused by at least seven major variants of the foot-and-mouth virus. Each type produces the same symptoms and they can only be identified by specialist examination. The disease is notoriously contagious, perhaps more so than any other disease, and it is known that it can spread some 50 miles down-wind from one outbreak to another. It has a fairly short incubation period of about 3–6 days so it can spread rapidly throughout a susceptible population.

The disease does not usually cause deaths, except in the young, but it leads to damaging after-effects. It will seriously lower productivity in all animals, especially the milking cow. Mastitis will possibly develop so milk production is permanently impaired and the infection of the hooves may lead to lameness that leads to secondary infections.

Infection with the virus of foot-and-mouth disease can occur in many ways, other than by wind-borne spread. People, lorries, markets, wild birds and other animals, wild-life such as hedgehogs and so on are just some of the ways in which the disease can spread. In addition, infective material can come in from abroad in imported substances, such as hay, and meat and bones which have not been sterilised.

In this country foot-and-mouth disease is a notifiable disease and has long been dealt with by immediate slaughter of infected animals. This has been a very successful policy and has meant there have been few outbreaks. In fact, the last big outbreak occurred in 1967 and there have been just two small infections since then. The important thing is to be sure of recognising a case as soon as possible so all the official measures can be taken to control the disease. Symptoms that would lead one to suspect foot-and-mouth disease are described below.

Infected cows suffer from fever and anorexia with a sudden drop in milk yield and there are blisters on the upper surface of the tongue and the balls of the heels of the feet. There may be profuse, frothy slobbering to be seen around the mouth, and falling to the ground. There is also a sucking sound produced by partial opening of the mouth. All this starts very early on in the period of infection and so too does the evidence of pain in the feet. Animals prefer to lie down but when they are forced to walk they move painfully, occasionally shaking their feet. The lameness then becomes worse so the animal can barely move. Because the animals cannot eat and with all the resultant discomfort they soon lose weight and condition and often blisters develop on the teats so that the cow cannot be milked. Blisters are present in the early stages on the dental pad inside the lips and on the muzzle; the blisters start as small white vesicles containing fluid, then quickly enlarge to the size of a walnut. Several blisters may join together to form a very large one. They burst and leave a raw area underneath. Much the same thing happens with the feet, leaving raw and sore areas.

THE CONTROL OF FOOT-AND-MOUTH DISEASE

The procedure in the UK, which is also used in many other countries, is to slaughter all the animals diagnosed as having the disease and all those in such close contact that they would almost certainly contract it. All examinations of the economics of the slaughter policy have shown it to be the least costly. The infected premises are then cleaned and disinfected and left empty for about six weeks before they can be re-stocked. Many restrictions are also imposed on the movement of susceptible animals within a 5–10 mile radius around the infected premises and no movement of animals is allowed out of this area. Restrictions may, if necessary, be imposed on an ever larger area. Recently in the UK a legal provision has been made for limited use, if felt desirable, for the vaccination of a ring of stock around infected premises in an endeavour to stop virtually any spread at all. One should also be aware of obligations as a stock owner. If there is any suspicion that the animals have foot-and-mouth disease, then the police or a veterinary surgeon should be informed. They will take the official action required though the premises should be isolated in the meantime. No one who has been in contact with the stock should go amongst other animals. No animals, vehicles, feed, milk, etc. should be moved from the suspected premises and so far as possible no person should leave, nor should anything be taken on to the premises. Thus with all these precautions and many others that can officially be brought into action, there is the maximum chance that the outbreak will be contained.

In certain other countries where the disease is endemic, vaccines alone are used to control the disease.

Rabies

Rabies is a notifiable virus disease which affects nearly all animals and is especially dangerous to man. It causes progressive paralysis and madness in most animals. The virus is present in the saliva so that the animals affected may bite one another, or man, and in this way cause infection to spread. It is nearly always fatal. The greatest danger represented by this disease is that infection becomes endemic — virtually permanent — in wild animals, particularly foxes but also in badgers, deer, vampire bats, and these infect dogs, cats and farm animals. Thus is the particular danger to man created.

The disease may be prevented in man and animals by vaccination, but it should be emphasised that no vaccinations are 100% effective and it is difficult to exaggerate the ghastly effects of this disease in the human.

One of the features of the virus is that after an animal becomes infected, perhaps via the saliva by being bitten by another rabid animal, several months may elapse before any signs of the disease are seen.

SYMPTOMS

Symptoms in animals may show great variation, ranging from the classical mad, biting, salivating beast, to 'dumb' forms in which the animals are incoordinate, progressively paralysed and make no noise. Usually the 'dumb' form follows the mad stage.

CONTROL

The British Isles have been free of rabies outside quarantine for sixty years, other than two cases in dogs which were quickly dealt with. Our rigid regulations prohibiting the importation of dogs and cats and certain other mammals without a six month quarantine period which includes vaccination is thoroughly justified. The fear remains that animals incubating the disease may be smuggled in — or could jump off a boat — and thereby rabies could become endemic in the wild animal population. This danger has increased with the spread of rabies in areas of the Continent near the United Kingdom. In those countries where the disease is endemic, great strides are now possible towards eradicating rabies with the aid of the greatly improved vaccines now available.

Brucellosis

This is a specific contagious disease of cattle widespread throughout the world, caused principally by a bacterium, *Brucella abortus*, though some other species of this bacterium occur in cows and other livestock. It is also known as contagious abortion or Bang's disease. *Brucella melitensis* infects principally goats but also infects cattle, while *Brucella abortus suis* causes abortion in pigs but may also infect cattle.

INFECTIVITY AND SYMPTOMS

Fortunately the disease is now virtually eradicated in cattle in this country so the danger is removed. Because the way in which its eradication has taken place is so valuable as a lesson in disease control it is worth looking at this briefly. Brucellosis infects both the bull and the cow and the organism has a predilection for the reproductive organs. In the bull it affects the genitalia; in the cow it causes a chronic inflammation of the uterus and usually, but not by any means always, causes abortion of the foetus between the fifth and sixth month of pregnancy. Infected cows that do not abort may be carriers of organisms. Infected animals do become immune but they may be carriers for an uncertain and lengthy period.

After abortion, or after the calf is born at full term, there will be a period during which the animal excretes large numbers of the brucella organisms. These can then infect other animals by any route — via ingestion or via service, or by the stockman who handles infected material.

CONTROL

There is no therapeutic cure for this condition that is effective enough to be advised. Control has therefore centred on testing for infected animals and slaughtering. In the meantime young stock are vaccinated with safe vaccines for a period of time and then, once the disease has been virtually eradicated, the vaccination can be stopped. However, testing must continue thereafter for a prolonged period.

Great Britain was declared free of brucellosis in cattle in 1981, and she joined, rather belatedly, several other European countries in virtually eliminating this condition. Other countries continue their efforts to the same end. Eradication is almost invariably achieved by a combination of agglutination and other testing procedures on sera and milk, the vaccination of young stock usually with the Strain 19 vaccine, and slaughter of adult reactors. Such measures are combined with good hygiene procedures and need to be supervised by Government Veterinary Services backed by legally enforced regulations.

Tuberculosis in cattle

Tuberculosis is a chronic infectious disease affecting virtually all species of animals and also man and birds and is due to a bacterium, *Mycobacterium tuberculosis*. There are three main strains of this organism. There is the human strain which affect primarily the human but can also affect cattle; the cattle (bovine) strain which is most prevalent in cattle but also affects man, pigs and certain types of wild life; and finally we must be aware of the avian strains which primarily affect birds but also cattle, pigs and other animals at times. All types of cattle may be affected but it is in the dairy cow that the main risk occurs. The milk from an infected dairy cow may contain the organisms that causes infection and this may affect calves or human subjects if the milk is not pasteurised or sterilised. Also, in advanced cases of tuberculosis, the uterus may become infected so that the calf is born with the disease.

Because the disease is usually chronic and the course of the disease slow it may be some time after the animal is infected that it will show any signs of the disease, but it is quite capable of causing infection in others long before this period occurs. Usually the first sign of any suspicion of disease is a lack of thrift and some progressive wasting of the animal. This will probably be accompanied by a cough – tuberculosis is essentially a disease of the lungs. In addition there may be an infection and hardening of the udder, and the milk that is produced contains tuberculous organisms and is thus highly dangerous. The milk may look quite normal until the later stages of the disease and eventually becomes watery and bluish in colour. Tuberculosis is essentially a slow, inflammatory action which produces almost any-where in the organs of the body nodular swellings, known as tubercules, which are of fibrous tissue with a core of pus-like, caseous (cheesy) material.

Fortunately it is possible to test an animal for the presence of the disease long before it has reached the contagious stage. This is done by injecting a preparation made from tuberculous organisms, known as Tuberculin. If an animal is infected this small injection of tuber-culin into the skin of the animal will cause a reaction, but not when it is completely healthy. In fact because the reaction could be due to a sensitivity to avian tuberculosis – and this is not a disease of any importance – an injection of avian tuberculin is also given and the difference between the two will be used to give the interpretation that is necessary. The conduct and interpretation of the test, known as the Intradermal Comparative Test, is a skilled operation and is conducted only by the veterinarian.

Tuberculosis has been virtually eradicated from the UK though testing continues and some cases do occur. Animals may be infected by man and wild-life – there is, for example, much concern about the infection of cattle by badgers which, in some areas, are serious reservoirs of the disease. Those same measures that have generally been successful in eliminating tuberculosis in the UK are also being applied in a similar fashion elsewhere.

Anthrax

Anthrax is a serious bacterial disease which infects cattle, other animals (see pig diseases) and man and tends to be fatal in both cattle and man. It is rare to see symptoms in cattle as infection is so acute that it usually causes sudden death. The cause of the disease is a bacterium, *Bacillus anthracis*, which may persist in the soil of a farm, once present, almost indefinitely. However, few cases occur in cattle in the UK — around 50 a year — because of the means taken to prevent its spread and re-infection. The means by which this is done are so important that I will draw attention to each facet as a useful example of disease control methods.

Anthrax should be suspected if an animal were found dead or there were a very high fever and a large swollen neck. At either point professional help should be sought. Diagnosis would be made by the veterinary surgeon taking a very small quantity of blood and examining this under the microscope. If the animal died from anthrax, or is infected with it, the blood will be teeming with the rod-shaped organisms that are distinctive features of this disease. *A major warning: do not allow the carcase to be cut or air to reach the blood since it is then that the organisms form spores which can survive for many years.* Some blood may be oozing from parts of the animal and this must be treated with disinfectant. Anthrax is a notifiable disease and measures that must be taken are mandatory. The carcase must be burned or buried deeply so that it is removed from any opportunity to cause re-infection, or for the organisms to form spores. The area around which the animal was found dead should be disinfected and isolated for a short while in case of spillage of the organisms. It is most likely that the source of infection is from a feedstuff — possibly meat or bone meal — which has come from imported infected material. Usually cases are isolated individual ones so it is not necessary to protect other animals but if there is a risk, then the animals can be given the hyperimmune antiserum or penicillin for immediate protection or relief, or longer-term protection by using vaccine. Anthrax is much more common in hot countries, particularly many parts of Africa where the climatic conditions favour its spread and where hygiene is noticeable by its absence.

Enzootic bovine leucosis (EBL)

This is a comparative newcomer to the list of notifiable diseases. It is a virus disease, slow and insidious in its effect, which may have been imported with Canadian Holstein cattle. It causes multiple tumours, known as lymphosarcomas, and whilst it is certainly not widely present in the United Kingdom, its presence has been confirmed. The symptoms in the live and adult animal are chronic ill-health, anaemia, weakness and inappetence – which are not diagnostic. Only special laboratory examinations will give a definite diagnosis.

External parasites

Insects of various types (see Fig. 4.10) which cause trouble to live-stock in various ways – by frightening them, by irritation, biting, blood sucking, or by damage by the maggots (larvae) on the skin or flesh. All insects can also act as vectors of disease.

The warble fly

There are two species of cattle warble fly that cause trouble – *Hypoderma lineatum* and *Hypoderma bovis*. Both are rather like

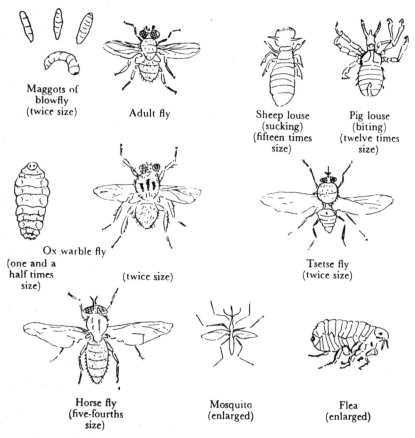

Maggots of
blowfly
(twice size)   Adult fly

Sheep louse   Pig louse
(sucking)   (biting)
(fifteen times   (twelve times
size)   size)

Ox warble fly
(one and a
half times   (twice size)
size)

Tsetse fly
(twice size)

Horse fly   Mosquito   Flea
(five-fourths   (enlarged)   (enlarged)
size)

Fig. 4.10 Some insect pests that affect farm animals (Wooldridge).

bumble bees in appearance as their dark bodies are covered with white, yellow and black hairs. They have no mouths and only live for a few days. They are found almost everywhere in the British Isles and most other parts of the world.

Adult female flies cause substantial losses to cattlemen, being responsible for 'gadding' during the spring and summer when the cattle can be so panicked by the approach of the flies that they may stampede in the fields. Such stampeding lowers milk yield and may cause serious injuries to the beasts and even broken limbs. There is also hide damage, and this is by far the worst loss. The maggots of the fly make breathing holes and these can ruin parts of the hide, even after the maggot has left the hide and the hole has healed over with fibrous tissue: this remains a weak area in the leather so that it has a much reduced value. It also damages the meat itself as a yellowish jelly-like substance forms around each maggot and spoils the appearance of the meat.

The life cycle of the warble fly is as follows. During the short life of the fly the female may lay some 500 or so eggs which are attached to hairs on the legs and bellies of cattle, those of *H. bovis* being laid singly (like louse eggs) and those of *H. lineatum* in rows of up to about 20. In 4—5 days the eggs hatch and tiny maggots emerge, crawl down the hair, and burrow through the skin of the beast by means of sharp mouth hooks.

The entry of the maggot causes some injury and it shows as a small pimple or scab. Under the skin the maggot moves along, feeding and growing. It takes 7—8 months to reach the skin of the back of the animal. When this point is reached the maggots make breathing holes and become isolated within a small abscess. It stays there for 5—7 weeks, casting its skin twice and growing to a length of about one inch. The full-grown maggot is dark brown, fleshy, barrel-shaped and covered with groups of tiny spines. When fully ripe they squeeze themselves out of their 'warbles' and fall to the ground. Here they slide into shallow crevices in the soil or pass underneath dead vegetation. The skin of the maggot darkens and it then becomes a puparium or chrysalis, inside which the warble fly is formed. This usually takes about four weeks.

Control must be achieved by dealing with the maggots. These can be destroyed by scrubbing derris into the warble holes and indirectly by treating the animal with one of the more recently produced systemic insecticides.

If derris is chosen, a mixture of derris and soap or detergent is used; it is compulsory to dress cattle in this way under the Warble

Fly (Dressing Order) in the UK and there are similar regulations in many other countries. It is a safe material to use but it cannot act properly unless the scab covering the warble hole is removed. The best method of application, therefore, is to scrub the derris wash well into the back of each animal after clipping the hair.

Because the maggots remain in their cysts for 5–7 weeks, monthly dressings from March until June are adequate to deal with the succession of maggots that appear. It is easy to deal with dairy cattle when they are brought in for milking but beef cattle – in which the condition is much more common – must be brought in for proper treatment.

Systemic insecticides are very effective in controlling the maggots before they can reach the back. All the preparations are organophosphorus compounds and are used either by scrubbing them on to the back or by dosing them by mouth. Normally this treatment will be effective in killing the maggots before they reach the backs of the animals, so preventing any damage to the hide or the muscle.

Lice

Lice infestation is a major problem only in cattle when they are housed. The thick winter coat, lack of sufficient air and sunlight and possibly poor nutrition can contribute to the occurrence of this problem. There are four species of lice infesting cattle – three being sucking lice and the fourth, which is also the commonest, a biting louse. The sucking lice are *Haematopinus eurysternus, Linognathus vituli* and *Solenoptes capillatus*, and the biting louse is *Damalinia bovis*. The sucking lice cause the greater damage and irritation as their sharp mouth parts pierce the skin to draw blood on which they feed. The biting louse, on the other hand, feeds on the scales of the skin and on the discharge from existing small wounds.

These four types of louse affect only cattle and cannot exist on other farm animals. The entire life cycle takes place on the skin of the animals where the females lay eggs on the skin in small groups. They are attached to the base of the hair by a sticky secretion. There the eggs remain for up to three weeks after which the young lice hatch out and very quickly start feeding and reproducing. Reproduction lasts for about five weeks; each female is able to lay about two dozen eggs and if conditions are favourable the number of lice can increase very rapidly. Lice cannot survive for more than 3–4 days away from cattle so that transfer of infection is largely by direct contact.

It is not too difficult to recognise an infestation with lice. They tend to congregate on the animal's shoulders, the base of the neck, head and root of the tail and examination of these areas will show them to be extremely scurfy and the lice should be obvious. As the infestation worsens more and more of the body can become affected. The affected animals rub and scratch themselves, greatly adding to the damage. The hair goes altogether in some areas. Rubbing thickens the skin which often breaks, so that bacterial infection gets in. All the effects of a bad infestation are ultimately to cause much loss of condition and production and should not be tolerated.

Insecticides must be applied to kill the lice, and materials that are satisfactory include organo-phosphorus and BHC preparations. Liquid preparations can be applied either under pressure or with a scrubbing brush. As these preparations have a reasonable residual effect, it is feasible for one good application to kill the lice and the larvae that hatch out after the application.

After treatment, measures must be taken to prevent reinfestation by contact with untreated animals and also by putting in fresh bedding and probably cleaning equipment. Never underestimate the damage that can be done by lice as mechanical irritators and as vectors of any livestock disease.

Minerals and health

Cattle suffer from all the problems associated with minerals, that is, too little, too much, or the unavailability to the animal of the mineral which is present in the feed in abundance. There are also problems with minerals being contained in the ration in sufficient amount but for some reason the mineral accumulates within the animal body in an abnormal amount. The first mineral we deal with, copper, provides a good example of all of these features.

Copper

Copper is an essential element in the metabolism of livestock. In the normal way copper is present in herbage at a level between 7 and 25 parts per million of dry matter. If, however, the copper content of the grass falls below 5 ppm there may be a copper deficiency in animals grazing the pastures.

This simple type of copper deficiency is not common and it is much more likely for a 'conditioned' deficiency to be produced due to an excess of molybdenum in the pasture. An excess in the grass can lead to reduced copper storage in the liver, but this is not the only conditioning factor because copper deficiency may also occur on pastures of normal molybdenum content. It thus seems impossible to predict the possible copper status of animals from chemical examination of feeding stuffs or soils in this country except in the case of obviously 'teart' pastures which are especially common in Somerset in the UK (see later).

Copper deficiency in soil is not confined to any particular soil type though it tends to be more common in peaty areas.

Symptoms are rather indefinite and not specific to this condition. The principal sign is a progressive loss of condition. The animals may scour badly; calves are more seriously affected than adults. First signs of the disease may appear after the animals have been at grass about a month; the calves appear stunted with the coat rough and discoloured. An almost diagnostic feature is that the hair round the eyes often changes colour or falls out, giving a spectacled appearance.

If copper deficiency is suspected then it is essential to have the blood analysed. If a deficiency is confirmed, then copper administration can be given as appropriate in the food, or as a drench or by injection.

Copper poisoning is not uncommon in cattle. Only very small amounts are needed. It usually occurs due to simple overdosing or over-enthusiastic correction of a shortage.

Cobalt

Cobalt is a further mineral that is needed in minute amounts by cattle and sheep and the common condition of 'pining' in sheep, due to a cobalt deficiency and fully described in Chapter 6, does also affect cattle in a lesser but nevertheless significant way. Deficiencies can cause unthriftiness, delayed puberty and infertility and arise in the UK in areas of the West Country, Ireland and Scotland due to pasture deficiency but more especially in North America, Australia and South Africa.

Molybdenosis (Teart)

Teart is the Somerset name for a scouring disease of cows and young cattle which has existed especially in certain local areas of Somerset. Such pastures are termed 'teart' as they produce the disease which is due to excessive amounts of the element molybdenum in the grass and soil. Pastures normally contain molybdenum at a level of 0.5 to 5.0 parts per million of the dry matter of the grass. At these levels there is no harm to the animals. But on teart pastures the level of molybdenum rises up to 100 ppm and 20–30 is very common. The chief areas of teart pastures are some 20 000 acres in Somerset but the problems do occur elsewhere. The severity of the disease depends essentially on the amount of soluble molybdenum in the herbage and this is at its maximum during periods of rapid growth in the spring. Symptoms shown, especially at this time, will include scour with yellow-green, evil-smelling dung. The animals become dirty, develop discoloured coats, lose condition rapidly and may eventually die.

The scour can be treated by the administration of copper supplements or injections. A daily amount of extra copper, about 1 gram, is all that is required. This can be given conveniently in the form of anti-teart cake or copperised dairy cubes or, if preferred, by the injection of a suitable copper preparation.

Lead poisoning

Lead poisoning is a very well-known and documented condition but in spite of this the inherent dangers of old paints and other compounds with lead in them are still not entirely appreciated. A large number of deaths still occur from this poison, especially in young calves, which tend to lick and chew all the fittings which in many cases may have residues of lead paint.

The symptoms of lead poisoning usually develop slowly. The first signs are dullness and loss of appetite, followed by signs of abdominal pain, grinding of the teeth, salivation and constipation. On other occasions there may be no symptoms at all until a few hours before death, when the animal abruptly starts bellowing, staggering and rolling eyes and frothing at the mouth before it collapses and dies. There are usually several intermittent convulsive phases during which the animal is very excitable and attempts to push against or climb walls. It appears to be blind and does not react to any outside stimulus but if the animal is not seen closely, these acute symptoms may be missed and it will be found dead because the phase of extreme excitation is often short.

Post mortem signs may include inflammation of the abomasum and the adjoining few feet of the small intestine, or sometimes very much further. Confirmation depends on the presence of abnormal amounts of lead in the liver and kidneys.

Lead poisoning usually arises from paint, woodwork, metal, tarpaulins, roofing felt, old paint tins and putty containing red or white lead: also old batteries and vegetation sprayed with lead arsenate. It is also possible for the calves to contract lead poisoning from lead derived from old lead pipes and cisterns. Lead poisoning is treated with magnesium preparations by the veterinary surgeon.

Table 4.7 The health of cattle: a summary of diseases, prevention and treatment

Disease	Prevention	Treatment
Anthrax	(Notifiable in UK). Vaccine. Antiserum.	Antiserum. Penicillin.
Blackquarter	Vaccine. Antiserum. Drain known infected land which is usually marshy.	Antiserum. Ampicillin or other broad spectrum antibiotics.
Bloat	Reduce intake of 'lush' material or other inciting food products.	Silicones. 'Oil of Turpentine'. Arachis oil. Avlinox.
Brucellosis	(Notifiable in UK). Vaccination. Removal of reactors. Improve hygiene.	Slaugher of infected animals advisable. Otherwise use broad spectrum antibiotics to assist recovery.
Calf diphtheria	Disinfection of utensils and accommodation.	Sulphonamides. Chlortetra-cycline. Oxytetracycline. Ampicillin.
Calf scour due primarily to *E. coli*	Colostrum. Regular and correct access to feed. Improve housing and hygiene.	Warmth. Antiserum. Vaccine. Supportive fluid therapy. Broad spectrum antibiotics, e.g. ampicillin, tetracyclines.
Coccidiosis	Cleanliness in rearing. Drain infected ground or remove cattle.	Potentiated or other sulpha drugs.
Foot-and-mouth disease	(Notifiable in UK). Vaccination if legally allowed.	Usually slaughter infected animals and in-contacts. Antibiotic therapy assists.
Husk	Use only clean and well drained land. Vaccine.	Diethylcarbamazine. Methyridine. Tetramisole. Antibiotics for 'secondaries'.
Hypomagnesaemia	Magnesium application to pasture or magnesium dosing or 'bullets'.	Intravenous magnesium solution.
Ketosis	Improve nutrition.	Inject glucose solutions. Sodium propionate. Corticosteroids. Glycerine. Molasses.
Lice	Improvement of hygiene and husbandry.	Organo-phosphorus compounds. Gamma benzene hexachloride.
Liver fluke	Avoid marshy land. Kill secondary hosts (snails) on pasture with chemicals.	Oxyclozanide. Nitroxynil. Albendazole.
Mange	Improve hygienic procedures around buildings and remove infected animals.	Gamma benzene hexachloride. Amitraz. Bromocyclen
Mastitis	Attend to milking procedures, equipment, housing and hygiene. Antibiotics as appropriate to infection.	Antibiotics via teat, single or in combination: sensitivity to be verified.

Disease	Prevention	Treatment
Milk fever	Improve nutrition. Inject Vitamin D.	Inject calcium borogluconate and Vitamin D and consider other mineral needs such as magnesium and phosphorus by injection.
Navel-ill (Joint-ill)	Improve hygiene. Dress navel with antiseptics.	Broad spectrum antibiotics, e.g. ampicillin, chlortetracycline. Oxytetracycline.
Parasitic gastro-enteritis	Revise husbandry methods to prevent infestation and its effects.	Fenbendazole. Parbendazole. Thiabendazole. Levamisole. Haloxon.
Rabies	Vaccination. (Notifiable in UK.)	Slaughter all infected animals.
Redwater	Vaccines. Imizal. Acoprin. Diampron. Gonacrine.	Use drugs listed under *Prevention.*
Respiratory disease of cattle	Improve environment especially ventilation. Increase space. Separate different ages. Judicious use of antiserum and vaccines.	Broad spectrum antibiotics, e.g. ampicillin, chlortetracycline. Sulphonamide.
Ringworm	Clean buildings, separate infected stock.	Local application of e.g. formalin, isoquinolinium or systemic treatment with griseo-fulvin.
Salmonellosis	(Notifiable under Zoonoses Order in UK.) Check feed to ensure freedom from sal-monella — also possible 'carriers', and destroy rodents. Vaccine.	Isolation. Ampicillin and other antibiotics. Supportive fluid therapy.
Tuberculosis	(Notifiable in UK.) Test for reactors and slaughter.	Usually none as infected animals should be removed and slaughtered.
Warble fly	(Notifiable in UK.) Systemic organo-phosphorus com-pounds, e.g. crufomate, trichlorphon.	As *Prevention.*
Wooden tongue and lumpy jaw	Disinfection and improved hygiene.	Sulphonamides. Iodides. Penicillin. Broad spectrum anti-biotics.

5 The Health of Pigs

As with most farm animals, there have been great changes in husbandry methods and the type of diseases in recent years. The well-known, traditional scourges of pigs, such as swine fever, foot-and-mouth disease and paratyphoid, have been eliminated in many countries or have been very well controlled. Instead, we are faced with extremely irksome, debilitating infections of the respiratory and enteric systems that are almost impossible to eliminate totally.

At present there is a great dependence in pig management on 'background' medication, usually given via the feed which is costly and never entirely satisfactory. Husbandry systems have developed without very much thought being given to disease control and the elimination of straw or other bedding in many modern systems. Improving the efficiency of muck handling has often caused welfare and additional disease problems and even a serious nuisance problem to the local population with offensive smells, nausea and enteritis.

Diseases of pigs are dealt with here on the same basis as the other livestock, considering the diseases on a life-cycle basis, starting with those diseases affecting the sow and piglet around farrowing and then tracing through the ages of the pig to maturity and into the breeding period. Sadly, in some ways, few pigs continue in a herd for long so that there are remarkably few pigs on the farm that may be deemed fully mature.

The health of the sow and piglet around farrowing

Losses in young piglets are considerable: 15% of those born alive die within the first few days of life.

Some years ago, when surveys indicated that losses were averaging about 20%, it was established that some 50% of these were due to 'mechanical' or physical causes. A high proportion of piglets died from cold and another high percentage from crushing by the sow when she lay on the piglets. The first problem has very largely been eliminated by the provision of heated nests, and the crushing has

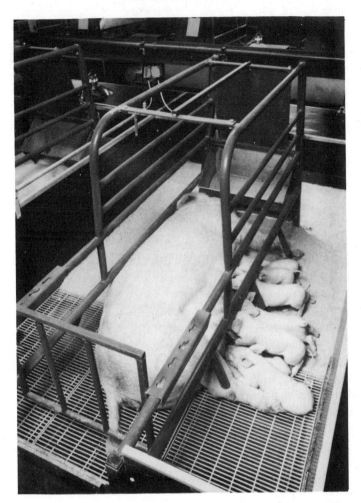

Fig. 5.1 Hygienically perfect farrowing accommodation with part-perforated floor.

been greatly reduced by the provision of various types of farrowing crates. But, in spite of this, losses, now largely due to disease, remain surprisingly high.

The underlying cause of the resurgence of disease in young piglets is probably due to increased concentration and size of units allied to an often pitiful neglect of hygiene in the maternity area. The fundamental importance of an all-in, all-out policy for the farrowing unit cannot be emphasised too strongly and allied to this should be a rigid disinfection of the building and cleaning of the sow herself, who often comes in dirty from the previous housing. Fig. 5.1 shows an example of hygienically excellent farrowing accommodation.

Emphasis must also be placed on the importance of good feeding of the sow during pregnancy. Sufficient feed of good quality is essential for the production of piglets that can withstand the stress of the early days. Many problems have arisen because there has been a tendency to feed too lightly during pregnancy; sows become thin and unable to provide either sufficient nourishment for the development of the piglets or for the production of milk to feed them.

'Farrowing fever' (metritis, mastitis, agalactia syndrome or MMA)

A complex condition may occur in sows during the period of farrowing which seriously affects the viability of the piglets and the health of the sows. In this disease the sow runs an elevated temperature, usually about 40.5–42°C (105–107°F), and is quite ill, refusing food. Her skin is usually inflamed and the udder is often hard and tender. There will be little or no milk 'let-down' ('agalactia'), and there is often inflammation of the uterus ('metritis'), which may be associated with retained afterbirths.

It is usually possible to cure the disease by immediate administration of broad spectrum antibiotic injections such as tetracyclines or ampicillin, and posterior pituitary hormone (oxytocin) to 'let down' the milk. It should be stressed that when 'farrowing fever' occurs it is clear warning that certain changes in husbandry are required to try and prevent its recurrence. It is not usual for any specific infectious organism to be so involved that it can be said to be the certain cause. It is essentially a case that the animal's resistance is in some way lowered so that such organisms that are normally present become invaders. These include bacteria, such as *E. coli, Corynebacterium pyogenes*, staphylococci, streptococci and clostridia.

What are these factors? It is necessary to list a number, one or all of which may be involved. Some are easy to deal with, but others are more difficult. Bad hygiene, overfeeding — giving rise to fat sows, inactivity during pregnancy, and immaturity of the breeding herd may all play a part. Moving of pigs between herds can be an inciting cause, and assuredly the size and concentration of the unit will always tend to add to the problem. In many cases sows may be affected with some of the symptoms of the disease and then only relatively mildly. For example, it may be the agalactia alone or the mastitis that is 'seen'.

Farrowing fever is a syndrome often associated with undue pressure on space. Some farmers in desperation have put their sows to farrow in simple outdoor accommodation. This usually does the trick and yet no one is really the wiser as to why. However, in diseases which are not caused by one factor but by several the aim is to *reduce* the challenge as far as practicable as it is rarely possible to do it completely under the restrictions of commercial farming.

It is essential with farrowing fever to ensure the quickest possible treatment of the sow so that she not only recovers but also provides the essential milk for the piglets. If she fails to make a quick response then it will be necessary either to foster her piglets or rear them artificially.

Diseases of young piglets

Escherichia coli infection
There are various ways in which this ubiquitous cause of trouble on the livestock farm can do damage. In the young pig, within the first few days of life, *E. coli* may be a cause of an acute septicaemic condition. Within only a few days of birth a number of pigs in the litter can become very ill with no particular symptoms except extreme illness leading to death.

NEONATAL DIARRHOEA
Those pigs that are infected with *E. coli* but less seriously than are the piglets killed with the septicaemic form of the disease show a most serious profuse watery diarrhoea. The piglets affected, whilst reasonably active and able to feed, nevertheless rapidly waste, have a staring coat and sunken eyes.

MILK SCOURS AND POST-WEANING DIARRHOEA
Another form of diarrhoea due to *E. coli* but occurring later is that known as 'milk scours'. A pale, greyish scours affects piglets in the period between 1–3 weeks of age and is very often associated with a change in the diet. Whilst under many circumstances the condition is quite transitory it may unfortunately become persistent and need treatment. Much the same can be said for post-weaning diarrhoea which affects pigs some ten days after weaning. This is obviously induced by the changes in husbandry, housing and management, often exacerbated by bad hygiene and the mixing of too many piglets from too many different sources.

There are many strains of *E. coli* that cause these symptoms and almost certainly many of these strains will be living in perfect harmony within the intestines of the pig and will generally be present around the pigs' quarters. The *E. coli* appear to be able to multiply if there are certain stresses in the management and in the piglets' early life there are very many of these. The first necessity in reducing the likelihood of infection with *E. coli* is to ensure that the piglets have sufficient supply of colostrum. Thereafter changes should be as gradual or gentle as possible and this is often most difficult to achieve at or around the time of weaning. *E. coli* often follows the occurrence of virus infections − the many kinds of which are discussed throughout this chapter.

TREATMENT AND PREVENTION OF *E.COLI* INFECTION

The treatment of *E. coli* infections is best achieved either by injections or medication incorporated in the feed or water. There are many antibiotics that can be used for this purpose, such as chlortetracycline, oxytetracycline, streptomycin, ampicillin, amoxycillin, Lincospectin or the chemotherapeutic Trimethoprim sulphonamide. Nitrofurans, Framomycin or neomycin may be given orally. The recovery of pigs suffering with *E. coli* diarrhoea will also be helped by administering fluids fortified with minerals, electrolytes and vitamins.

Prevention may be achieved by using certain antibiotics in the feed. There are a number of alternatives to choose from, including furazolidone, organic arsenicals, chlortetracycline or carbadox. An alternative approach is to attempt to create an active or passive immunity by the use of serum or vaccine. The former course makes use of *E. coli* hyperimmune sera. In the case of vaccines, *E. coli* vaccine may be given to the sow during pregnancy or even to the piglets if there is adequate time before the problem would normally occur. In both cases at least two injections would be needed some 14 days apart.

A more recent approach has been to incorporate mixed strains of killed *E. coli* in the feed to the sow ('Intagen'). In many cases this method, as with the use of all vaccines, has been most successful but considerable variations are reported in its efficacy, due to the great variation in strains of bacteria that occur. It may be truly emphasised again that the eventual approach must always be to 'root out' the cause rather than 'add a vaccine' to the trouble.

Diseases of young and growing pigs

Transmissible gastroenteritis (TGE)

This is an alarming disease of pigs caused by a virus which is a comparative newcomer in the piglet field. When it strikes it tends to do so suddenly and will probably kill most of the piglets in a herd under three weeks of age. The symptoms in the piglets are a very severe diarrhoea, the piglets really dying of dehydration. Some piglets vomit; all tend to have a very inflamed stomach and intestines. The sows may also be ill and have little milk. Pigs older than 3 weeks will also be affected to varying degrees and for a period will scour and make little progress. However, the symptoms in growing pigs may be so slight as to go unnoticed.

The disease appears to have occurred with the growth of large herds. The virus sweeps across the whole area like a bush fire and there is virtually nothing a farmer can do to protect his pigs. No vaccines are licensed for use in the UK though they are available in some countries but are not of great value. However, once the disease has swept through the herd, it may be resistant for some years. Even this statement, however, is not entirely true since the nature of the virus seems to be constantly changing and variants may affect a herd soon after recovery from a previous attack, and sometimes in a rather different way. For example, a variant may affect sows rather than piglets, the older the pig the worse being the effect.

In a large herd, virus infections like this may be rather slow to infect the herd and it is important to make every endeavour to get all the stock infected as quickly as possible to produce an immunity. This is most important with the young breeders since they can then later produce viable litters. Ways of achieving this are to spread infected material — such as intestinal contents or even feeding homogenised piglets that have died from the disease. It seems a rather offensive method, and it has the danger of spreading other infections, but it works. It is, of course, in essence a crude way of live-vaccination and if it can be done some time before the sow is due to farrow it should save the litter. Some attempts have also been made to give passive immunities by the use of serum from recovered pigs.

A good deal may be done to save piglets and lessen the effects in older pigs by feeding-up and nursing them by providing highly nutritious extra feed and additional comfort and warmth in the piggery.

Piglet anaemia

It can be said that every pig which is born in intensive housing requires some extra administration of iron if it is to be ensured that it does not become anaemic. It is interesting to study the reason for this. The piglet is born with limited reserves of iron in its liver, iron being an essential constituent of haemoglobin, the oxygen-carrying element in the red blood cells. There is also little iron in the sow's milk so the piglet will not get its requirement this way. Under natural conditions, however, the piglet would be outside on pasture and would gain vital and sufficient quantities of iron from this source. But no such source is available to the intensively housed pig and in any case modern pigs grow so quickly they more rapidly outstrip their limited reserve, so some supplementary source of assimilable iron must be given. There are several ways of doing this. It may be given by mouth — by solution, tablet, capsule or paste — or it is feasible to provide sods of grass or earth fortified with iron which the piglets can take in themselves. But these are rather inexact ways of giving iron, so now it is almost always preferred to give the iron as an injection. It is usual to inject 200 mg of a soluble iron preparation at not more than 3 days of age and this is sufficient to carry the piglet through to the time it is eating solid food which should be liberally supplemented with iron.

Piglet anaemia may be recognised by pale, dull and hairy skins, scouring and exaggerated noisy heart beats — as the heart is overtaxed in an endeavour to increase the oxygen supply to the tissues. Diagnosis is confirmed by laboratory examination of the blood. Haemoglobin levels should be about 12 g/100 ml blood, but in anaemia the levels fall to 6 or less.

Bowel oedema

This is an interesting disease of pigs, once extremely common but now rarely seen, and caused by certain strains of *E. coli* in the intestine. The condition almost invariably occurs about ten days after weaning. First indication of an outbreak is usually the appearance in a pen of weaners of one dead pig — often the biggest of the bunch. Close observation of others in the group may show they are suffering from various degrees of 'nervous trouble' — staggering, incoordination, blindness, loss of balance, falling about when roused. As the disease progresses in these pigs they will lie on their side and paddle their legs and they then go into a coma and die within a day. In bowel oedema, such pigs usually show swollen (oedematous) eyelids, nose and ears and may have a moist squeal resembling a gurgle. A post mortem, if carried out speedily, shows oedema of the stomach and in the folds of the colon and in the larynx.

The occurrence of this disease seems to be associated with the stress of weaning, with the addition of *ad lib* dry feeding when pigs may tend to eat too much, perhaps drink too little and become constipated with their intestines engorged with high quality diet.

Under these circumstances it seems that certain strains of *E. coli* can multiply in the small intestine and produce toxins which do the damage.

Treatment is rarely successful but measures can be taken to prevent the spread of the disease, probably with success. All dry foods should be withdrawn and replaced with a limited wet diet. Pigs may be injected with broad spectrum antibiotics, antihistamines and *E. coli* antiserum, and a saline purgative given. Consideration should be given to some change in the husbandry system that prevents pigs getting so much food at weaning – the ideal, at least for a time, would be to give a restricted wet feed.

Streptococcal infections

In recent years streptococcal infections of young piglets have become very common. The *Streptococcus suis Type 1* infects the sow and she then transfers the infection to the piglets soon after birth. The organisms, after getting into the piglet, may cause a general infection (a septicaemia) which may cause immediate hyper-acute infection and death or may be less acute and cause an endocarditis, meningitis and arthritis.

The disease usually occurs at about 10 days of age. Affected pigs run a temperature, show painful arthritis, have muscular tremors, appear blind, and cannot coordinate their movements. Some die suddenly with heart inflammation. Typically, some 20–30% of a litter are affected.

Affected pigs may be treated successfully with injections of suitable antibiotics such as penicillin or with sulphonamides such as trimethoprim. The disease tends to be a very tiresome herd problem and is often tackled by providing the sow with medicated feed. But this is a very expensive way of dealing with the disease and good hygiene; 'isolation' farrowing and rearing are better.

A similar organism, *Streptococcus suis Type 2*, can also cause serious disease in older pigs. Here, what seems to happen is that young pigs, already carriers of the disease, are mixed with older pigs around the early fattening stages, say 8–12 weeks. The carriers infect the pigs they are mixed with and after a few days of incubation the affected pigs show a high temperature, nervous signs such as 'staggering', paralysis, arthritis and tetanic spasms: in other words, much the same signs as the younger pigs. Treatment is with penicillin or other antibiotics, but the main need is to make sure that the cycle of infection is broken so infections do not take place.

Clostridial infections in pigs

Whilst the effects of clostridial infections on pigs are in no way comparable with those which affect sheep or even cattle, there are problems from time to time, particularly in outdoor-reared pigs on 'pig-sick' land.

For example, *Clostridium welchii* (*perfringens*) can produce a fatal haemorrhagic enteritis in pigs up to about a week old. The disease has a very dramatic effect, with profuse dysentery, becoming dark from the profusion of blood within it. Usually pigs so affected die very rapidly though a few take a more chronic turn. Most die within 24 hours of the symptoms being noted. The litter affected should be treated with an antibiotic, such as ampicillin, and those under risk of infection can be given lamb dysentery antiserum. A more permanent answer may be needed and the sows can be given a vaccine for the infection — this being administered twice during pregnancy.

Piglets are also infected with *Clostridium tetani* in the same way as lambs by penetration of the organism from dirty conditions, possibly through the navel or by the injury caused during castration or even by bad techniques in injection, such as for anaemia. The signs are of stiffness and then tetanic spasms and death after lying on their side with the limbs held out stiffly. It may be of some use to treat the affected piglet, though it usually dies, so the best course is to protect the other piglets and improve the hygiene of the pens and the techniques.

Infections also occur with *Clostridium oedematiens*, which causes sudden death in breeding and fattening pigs, the latter usually in the later stages of growth. It usually affects pigs which are otherwise in very good health. The organism that causes the disease multiplies in the liver and produces the toxin that does the damage. It would seem that, with the liver active and vascular, the opportunity is provided for these organisms to invade the liver and multiply. If the problem threatens to be severe the antiserum may be used for immediate protection, and the vaccine can be used thereafter for long term protection.

Greasy pig disease (exudative epidermitis; Marmite disease)

This is an acute skin inflammation of piglets with the production of excessive amounts of sebaceous secretion and exudation from the skin which does not cause irritation. It tends to be most common in hot weather. If it is severe, it leads to dehydration of the pig to such an extent that it dies. The actual cause of the disease is a bacterium,

Fig. 5.2 Pigs on flat deck housing. Such systems are basically healthy but have hazards, one of which is 'tail biting'. Two of the tails seen here have been savaged.

Staphylococcus hyicus but it is unlikely that it can produce this condition without prior injury in at least some of the piglets from, for example, abrasions from bad flooring, or fittings and equipment, but it could arise after a good deal of fighting and biting.

The condition usually occurs in piglets of about 2–8 weeks of age, and shows as a covering of the skin with an exudate of a greasy nature which mats the hair. The skin soon gets very dark, thickened and wrinkled and pigs lose weight and die. The number affected in a pig herd varies tremendously but normally only a modest number is affected. The best procedure after recognition of the condition is to inject a broad spectrum antibiotic, such as ampicillin or lincomycin.

It is vital then to make sure that the cause is removed: in particular, the best procedure is to provide plenty of soft bedding. It is also believed that fortification of the feed with additional vitamins may assist in the ability of pigs to resist this condition.

Swine influenza

The swine influenza virus which causes serious losses amongst pigs in the USA and elsewhere in the world does not appear to be present in the UK. In the normal way, if the animals are well-housed and are not infected with other respiratory invaders, the course of the disease is acute but the animals quickly recover. Symptoms include accelerated breathing, fever and lethargy. It infects all animals in a group and most appear to be affected but after 4–5 days they recover unless secondary invaders do further damage.

Swine pox

This is a mild disease of world-wide incidence caused by a virus. It shows as red pimples (papules) over the abdomen at first, and then they become brown scabs which soon turn black. They will spread from the abdomen to other parts of the body and cause a slight general illness in the animal with a rise in temperature. The disease tends to occur in successive litters of young piglets but they normally recover quickly and are then immune to any further infection. The disease is mild so usually little is done to treat or prevent it but it is good to practise better disinfection to try and eliminate it.

Atrophic rhinitis (AR)

Atrophic rhinitis (see Fig. 5.3) is a respiratory disease caused principally by a bacterium *Bordetella bronchiseptica* and other organisms, notably a virus — the Inclusion Body Rhinitis virus. Atrophic rhinitis

(a)   (b)   (c)

Fig. 5.3 Cross section of pig's snout showing both normal and diseased turbinate bones after infection with atrophic rhinitis. (a) No atrophy of nasal turbinates. (b) Typical atrophy of nasal turbinates. (c) Severe atrophy of nasal turbinates.

affects primarily the membranes lining the delicate bones of the nose and leads to inflammation, nose bleeding, sneezing and eventually general degeneration of the bones of the snout. This does profound damage to the growth of the pig and it also makes the animal more susceptible to enzootic pneumonia and any infections of the respiratory tract.

This disease has become much more prevalent recently. It usually occurs in the early days of the pig's life and the increase in its occurrence has coincided with the advent of early weaning. This is not difficult to understand since pigs at this time are often kept in very close confinement in kennels and other poorly ventilated accommodation at a time when their immunity to infection is at a minimum. Atrophic rhinitis may start a chain reaction with enzootic pneumonia in the fattening house as the final, economically disastrous outcome (see later in this chapter).

In order to prevent the condition a vaccine may be used, or continuous preventive medication may be instituted with a suitable antibiotic, such as Tylan, or a chemotherapeutic drug such as a sulphonamide. It is essentially better to improve the environment and management than to rely on measures of vaccination and medication. The procedures listed under enzootic pneumonia are equally applicable to AR.

Diseases largely of fatteners

Salmonellosis

All forms of salmonellosis can occur in pigs but there are a number of serious ones which are a matter of great practical concern, especially because of the dangers of contamination of the human food supply. *Salmonella typhimurium*, for example, is a virulent salmonella to all livestock and man and is common enough to warrant especial care. On the other hand, the purely pig pathogen *S. cholerae suis*, which was once a frequent problem, is now quite rare. There are a great number of salmonellae of 'exotic' type which come from the pigs' feed but these do not tend to cause serious difficulties for long.

Symptoms vary tremendously, depending on the type and virulence of the salmonellae. All ages can be affected but the worst outbreaks seem to be after weaning, in large groups of 'stores'. This often shows itself in the septicaemic form, causing sudden death or acute fever with blue (cyanotic) discolouration of the ears and limbs. Another form of disease shows itself as acute diarrhoea, also with a fever, but these are not all the signs. Pneumonia may occur with abnormal breathing, and also nervous abnormalities, such as incoordination and paralysis. Also the skin is often affected and parts may even 'slough-off' later in the disease. In more chronic forms, pigs may be in a state of almost perpetual diarrhoea, eating yet still wasting. A very high proportion of a group or pen may be affected so the economic effects are very serious.

Diagnosis by an expert is essential and the laboratory can arrange for 'typing' of the organism. This is often important if the cause of the infection is to be traced.

In order to deal with the disease, a number of measures are advised. It is such a serious infection that it is vital that *all* those advised are taken.

Firstly, it is necessary to treat infected animals. This will require drugs or antibiotics with known activity against salmonella, such as sulphonamides, tetracyclines, ampicillin, lincospectin, furazolidone or streptomycin. The alternative methods of application are by injection or in the water or feed, depending on the product. The best technique is to give an initial injection to each pig individually and then follow with medication in the drinking water.

The only form of salmonella that can be prevented by vaccination is *S. cholerae suis*. A general preventive measure is to isolate the pigs from their own excreta, so far as possible, and also to prevent cross-infection of excreta from pen to pen. Feedstuffs may be monitored by a laboratory for salmonella, but the pelleting process itself goes far to limit the possibilities of infection. If rats or other rodents could be the cause, a 'blitz' on their presence is called for. It may also be necessary to carry out more careful isolation of pigs that are possibly carriers. It would certainly be advisable to take the greatest care in disinfecting all contaminated areas and to institute a more thorough process than hitherto. With salmonella it may also be necessary to consider the testing of staff because on several occasions in the author's experience it has been carriers amongst the stockmen who have been the cause of the infection. Salmonellosis is a notifiable disease under the Zoonoses Order in the UK (see also Chapter 3).

Enzootic pneumonia

One of the most serious scourges and causes of economic loss on the pig farm is the disease of pneumonia caused by a species of myco-plasma — *M. hyopneumoniae*. Though this is recognised as the principal cause of the disease, other organisms are commonly secondary invaders, including other types of mycoplasma and bacteria, such as *Pasteurella multicoida* and *Bordetella bronchiseptica*.

The lesions of enzootic pneumonia tend to be in the anterior lobes of the lungs which become consolidated (solid) and grey in colour.

Treatment with drugs should be instituted in pigs showing serious clinical signs. Broad spectrum antibiotics, such as chlortetracycline and oxytetracycline, may be injected but may not have a permanent beneficial effect as no immunity follows an attack.

Whilst the final effects of this disease may be to kill a proportion of pigs, chiefly in the fattening house, its most serious effect is to lower the growth rate and food conversion efficiency of nearly all the animals in the building. In addition, badly infected stock may require constant treatment, so that considerable costs have to be faced with medication. The disease is readily recognised by the constant harsh coughing of pigs in the fattening house.

There is no doubt that it is ideal to have stock that are entirely free of the infectious agent that is primarily responsible. Such animals are available and a very small proportion of herds maintain this status. In total, however, they are a minute percentage of the national herd and many herds that were free have broken down. Thus it is pertinent to consider how one deals with this problem environmentally in an infected herd. This is the surest way of minimising the effects.

The first essential is to start, if possible, in a building which is free of all stock and then 'batch' the groups of fatteners through the building. If this is impossible, the next best thing is to sub-divide the building so that each section can be dealt with in this way.

There is, in any case, considerable virtue in limiting the number of pigs on one air space since it makes a build-up of infection less likely and enables the environment to be more satisfactorily maintained. Ventilation is easier, draughts are less likely and heat is better conserved.

Virtually all these factors which enable good ventilation will assist in reducing the effects of enzootic pneumonia. Ventilation must never be sacrificed in order to maintain temperature. Air flow must be arranged so that it takes fresh air to the pigs before it moves over dung or slurry. All gases that emanate from the slurry channels must be taken immediately out of the house. Condensation must be prevented and this is often only achieved by good thermal insulation of the surfaces. Cold and damp are the most lethal combinations; insulation assists the maintenance of good temperature.

It is also important to stock the house as lightly as is compatible with good economy and also sub-divide the unit into as small pen sizes as possible. This will help to ensure a fairly uniform distribution of the pigs through the house and prevent overcrowding in limited areas which thereby become overstocked.

Swine dysentery ('bloody scours')

This is an infection which has probably affected pigs at least in a limited way for as long as pigs have been raised intensively but has only recently come into major prominence. It is a disease largely of fattening pigs and the infection causes inflammation of the intestines which leads to dysentery (diarrhoea together with some bloody effusions), with a general debilitation of the pigs. It is highly contagious, being spread via contact with infected faeces. It is of course readily understandable that it has become a more common disease in recent years since modern intensification has brought much larger numbers of pigs together and there is a greater opportunity for the spread of infection. Furthermore certain changes in husbandry practices have apparently contributed to the increased incidence of infection. The absence of bedding to absorb or dilute the pig's faeces and urine has made for closer contact between the pig and its excreta. The use of slatted floors of imperfect design often leads to a build-up of faeces in dark and ill-ventilated corners where it may almost never be cleaned out. Another major contributory cause has been the practice of feeding on the floor. This is a good procedure if the floor conditions are good and the pigs are thus eating off a clean surface. If, however, the floor is contaminated with excreta and the food is thrown on top of this, it needs little imagination to realise the easy way in which infection can be spread and it becomes an appalling arrangement.

The main causal organism involved in swine dysentery is a bacterium, *Treponema hyodysenteriae*, though it is not the only one involved and others such as *Vibrio coli, E. coli* and salmonellae of various species may always be present as secondaries.

Early recognition of the disease is important. Affected pigs swish their tails; at the same time there may be diarrhoea and if this is examined more closely there will be streaks of blood, mucus, and some pieces of the lining of the intestine which have come away (necrotic material). The faeces have a characteristically unpleasant smell. As the condition progresses the affected pigs gradually waste and may show a capricious appetite but they still drink freely. Swine dysentery affects primarily the large intestine which, on post mortem, shows degenerative changes.

TREATMENT

There are a number of useful drugs which may be given via the food or water — the latter route being preferable since sick pigs will drink but may not eat. The range of drugs used includes organic arsenicals such as sodium arsanilate, or macralides, in the form of Tylosin, Erythromycin or Spiramycin or Tylosin in combination with a sulphonamide. A further excellent drug is Lincomycin which may be used as a feed additive or in combination with spectinomycin may be given in water. Further effective drugs are Tiamulin and Dimetridiazole. Most drugs also have forms which can be given by individual injection if preferred.

Pigs under threat of swine dysentery can be treated 'in feed' with the drugs already mentioned for treatment being used at a lower level. A popular preventive is Carbadox with sulphonamide.

It can be seen that the range of drugs is very extensive but it is regrettable if complete reliance is to be placed on medication. Systems of husbandry which tend to produce swine dysentery should be modified to reduce the danger by disinfection, isolation and improvement in dung disposal arrangements.

The intestinal haemorrhage syndrome ('bloody gut')

This condition, often known as 'bloody gut', affects fatteners in the later stages of their growth and after a short period of depression, with an appearance of paleness and an enlarged abdomen, they die rapidly. Post mortem shows the small intestine full of blood-stained fluid and also gas in the large intestine. There may also be a twisting of the gut.

The condition is more particularly common in whey-fed pigs, but not exclusively so, yet its cause remains a mystery.

Mulberry heart disease

This is a rather curious disease mostly of fatteners over the weight of about 45 kg (100 lb). The symptoms are either sudden death or the pigs become depressed and weak and collapse and die within about 24 hours of the onset of the disease. Few pigs ever recover. On post mortem examination the signs are of an enlarged and mottled liver and the surface of the heart is streaked with haemorrhages running longitudinally and also occurring in the endocardium. The cause is not really known but there is a suggestion that a deficiency of vitamin E or selenium may be involved. There is little evidence that treatment does much good but the use of multi-vitamin injections and broad spectrum antibiotics may be of some benefit.

Diseases of pigs largely without age incidence

Swine erysipelas ('The diamonds')

A bacterium — known as *Erysipelothrix insidiosa* or *E. rhusiopathiae* — is one of the most common causes of disease in pigs. Most pigs are under risk of this disease because the organism can live in and around piggeries and 'pig-sick' land for very many years in the sporulated form. It is found mostly in breeding pigs but it can occur in pigs of all ages. It manifests itself in a number of entirely different ways. In the peracute form of the disease there may be hardly any signs at all, and the pig may be found dead after a very brief period of severe illness. In the acute form the pig is also ill, has a high temperature and the skin is inflamed. It will not eat. Then there is a sub-acute form which is the more typical disease, showing characteristic discolouration of the skin with raised purplish areas (said to be roughly diamond-shaped) throughout the back and on the flanks and belly. Finally, there are two 'chronic' forms of the disease. In one the joints are affected, which causes the pig severe lameness, whilst in the other the organism causes erosion of the valves of the heart, leading to cauliflower-like growths, so that the pig will often show signs of heart dysfunction or even heart failure and death. If pregnant sows are affected they will almost certainly abort. A feature of swine erysipelas is that it tends to affect pigs during hot and muggy weather conditions; for some reason such stressful conditions favour the multiplication of the organisms and the infection of the pigs. Indeed, any stressful conditions will increase the risk.

It is clear that there are very serious effects on pigs of all ages and a programme of protection is necessary on farms where the trouble commonly occurs.

There are good vaccines available which will protect a pig for about one year. Affected pigs can be treated with the hyper-immune antiserum or an antibiotic, penicillin being totally effective. In-contact pigs may be protected with the antiserum or penicillin. When the condition arises in a herd it is usual for it to have quite a limited effect in the first instance but gradually rise in severity as the disease progresses. Thus it is vital to deal with the condition at once. Vaccines protect for about six months and it is usually only the breeder pigs which require protection, on an annual basis, before the summer weather.

Heat stroke

Many pigs are lost from this cause — certainly many more than are really suspected. It happens under almost any circumstances when pigs are kept in a temperature of above about 32°C if the air circulation is bad and the pig has no way of cooling itself by 'wallowing'. The pig is virtually without sweat glands so it can keep cool only by increasing respirations (panting) or by wallowing in water and allowing evaporation of the water to cool it. Wallowing is virtually never possible under intensive conditions of husbandry and indeed when it does happen it is usually done in the dunging passage in a mixture of the pigs' urine, faeces and drinking water. Such a procedure represents a possible disaster area in attempts at disease control!

If pigs are found suffering with heat stroke, immediate cooling with cold water as rapidly as possible, with good air movement created around, is an absolute necessity and is often much more successful than appears likely. It is also useful to spray water in the building as an emergency measure using, if possible, a horticultural type of spray applicator. It is also a good policy to drip water over the roof or walls of the building and in mechanically ventilated buildings it is useful to trickle water over the inlets. Some mention should be made of the so-called 'sweat box' system of rearing fatteners in accommodation that is kept at a deliberately high temperature and humidity. Apart from the fact that this contravenes the pigs' welfare code in the UK, it is noteworthy that it may also cause heat stroke because the margin between a high figure which is safe (about 28°C) and one which is lethal (say 32°C) is a rather thin one. Also, whilst the system appears to be tolerated by pigs if the humidity is high and the floor wet, no such tolerance is apparent if the air becomes dry and the pigs cannot wallow to keep cool.

Swine fever (hog cholera)
This is a virus disease of pigs formerly of world-wide incidence. It is still probably the most serious of all pig diseases though it has now been eliminated from many countries, including the UK. Swine fever affects pigs of all ages. When it first affects a herd it is more likely to occur in the acute form with the pigs showing a very high temperature, great depression and discolouration of the skin. Less acute cases may occur at the same time – in these cases pigs have a fever and usually diarrhoea of a particularly foetid type. Pigs also have a depraved appetite and thirst. This highly contagious disease will also manifest itself in other forms – the pneumonic form characterised by respiratory illness, skin form showing itself as ulcers and plaques on the skin, and the nervous type leading to incoordination, paralysis and

death. The most likely outcome of infection of a herd with swine fever if it is allowed to run on is to find a considerable proportion of pigs with a chronic scour which hardly responds at all to any treatment so the pigs continue to lose weight.

In this country swine fever has been controlled for many years by a slaughter policy. Elsewhere it may be controlled by vaccination, but there is little doubt that the slaughter policy, if it can be achieved to eliminate the disease altogether, is by far the most economic method.

There is also a highly virulent disease, with symptoms rather like swine fever, known as African swine fever. However, though the symptoms are much the same, it is caused by a completely different virus. It has a devastating effect and may kill 90% of the pigs in a herd or even more. Until recent years it only occurred in Africa but recently it has occurred in parts of southern Europe. It has been eliminated from France and Italy. Should it occur in the UK it would undoubtedly be dealt with by a slaughter policy. There are import restrictions on pigs or pig products from areas where African swine fever is present.

Aujeszky's disease
This is currently of much concern as a disease in certain areas of the UK and indeed in many other parts of the world. It is an infection caused by a herpes virus which leads to nervous and respiratory symptoms with a fever. Death often occurs in young pigs. In adults there may be few, if any, signs but sows will often abort or their litters are stillborn, if they are affected. It is a notifiable disease in the UK.

Infection with Aujeszky's disease virus occurs in the epithelium of the upper respiratory tract and multiplication of the virus here is followed by its spread into the nervous system – but some strains of the virus also produce pneumonia. The virus also invades the uterus to cause abortions, stillbirths, mummification and foetal resorption.

The mortality in the piglet affected up to about four weeks of age may reach 100% but in the older piglet it is likely to be below 50% – up to about 8 weeks. Above this age range the effects are much more slight or animals may even be symptomless carriers.

In young animals such clinical signs as may be seen are vomiting, diarrhoea, trembling, incoordination, muscular spasms and convulsions. A certain diagnosis can only be made by serological tests in the laboratory.

The disease is very widespread in some countries and 'carrier' pigs easily spread this very contagious disease. It is much more likely to be of economic importance with the big herd of 250 sows and above.

There is no treatment of any use. Prevention is achieved by the use of live attenuated and dead virus vaccines in many countries, including the USA, Europe and Northern Ireland, but no licence has yet been given for its use in the UK. It is possible to test, remove reactors and possibly eliminate the disease, but there is no agreement whether to use vaccine as the best control method, or test and slaughter.

Leptospirosis

There are two species of the bacteria leptospira (*L. canicola* and *L. icterohaemorrhagiae*) which affect pigs. The disease it causes varies in its symptoms depending upon the acuteness of the infection. In young pigs there is usually some fever (temperature about 40°C: 106°F) and diarrhoea and jaundice (yellowing). In breeding pigs the disease will often cause abortion and stillbirths together with sickness in the sow. Post mortem lesions tend to be largely confined to the kidney — a greyish-white lesion in the cortex of the kidney. Diagnosis is made certainly by isolation of the organism from the pig, especially the urine. Many pigs may be symptomless carriers of the disease.

The disease is picked up from carrier pigs or from rodents which frequently carry the disease under rather unsanitary conditions. In overtly sick animals antibiotics, such as streptomycin, may be used successfully. Rodents should be eliminated as far as possible and disinfection programmes improved.

Anthrax

The bacterium, *Bacillus anthracis*, which is so serious a cause of sudden death in cattle, also infects pigs but causes different symptoms. Infection usually comes into the herd via infected animal products in the feed, the organism entering through the throat glands. A common symptom is oedema and swelling of the neck region, with difficult breathing and a very high temperature — up to 40.5°C (107°F). In younger pigs it may just cause sudden death without any symptoms showing at all.

Penicillin is the most effective treatment and this or the specific antiserum can be used to treat and prevent infection in the contact pigs. Anthrax is a notifiable disease and has great potential danger to the human subject. Thus the diagnosis should be undertaken by a veterinarian if the disease is suspected and thereafter, if confirmed, appropriate official action will be advised and taken (see also the section on anthrax in Chapter 4).

Tuberculosis in pigs

Three forms of tuberculosis can infect the pig — the bovine, avian and human forms. Because of the much reduced incidence of tuberculosis in cattle and man, there is now very little in pigs but it does still exist as a clinical entity. Of the cases that occur, most are of the avian type doubtless infected from wild birds since tuberculosis is virtually non-existent in the domestic fowl.

The symptoms are rather non-specific and would rarely be suspected by the pigman. Loss of weight, coughing and discharge from the nose will hardly lead to suspicion so that it is unusual for the disease to be recognised before it is seen in the slaughterhouse by the occurrence of swollen and infected lymph nodes in the throat, chest and abdomen. If samples are taken the disease can then be diagnosed positively.

Treatment is rarely called for but careful note should be given to any lessons there may be in isolating stock from sources of infection and also in improving hygiene of the premises. The organisms that cause tuberculosis in all species are very persistent and resist destruction by most means; it is therefore very important to take such measures that eliminate them. It is also pertinent to stress the risk to the human population and whilst it is not a highly contagious agent of disease, it could represent a very undesirable challenge to man if the infection became widespread in a pig herd.

Mycotoxicosis

Pigs, like all farm animals, have been affected with these poisonous substances — mycotoxins — in the feed as a result of the growth of fungi. Results will vary, depending on the fungi involved and the toxins produced, from abortion and stillbirths to a condition in which there is no more than reduced growth, weight loss, jaundice and undersized pigs. The former is often caused by fusarium poisoning, the latter by *Aspergillus flavus* (aflatoxicosis). This organism is a common contaminant of groundnuts which, because of this problem, are rarely used now for feeding to livestock. Ergot poisoning also occurs occasionally when grain contaminated with ergot, another fungus, is fed to pigs. It causes agalactia and the birth of small or weak piglets.

There is no effective treatment for poisoning by mycotoxins. Diagnosis is sometimes quite difficult and depends on specialist laboratory examination. Obviously prevention lies in removing the contaminated feedstuffs from the animals. There is also a number of chemicals now available that can be placed in the food to inhibit fungal growth.

The farmer can do little or nothing about cereals imported on to his premises but it is known that one of the problems that arise is due to the growth of fungus in the bulk bin and these should receive periodical clean-outs and then treatment with anti-fungal agents to take care of the next batch of bulk food.

Gas poisoning

There have been many cases of serious losses in pigs, and even danger to the pigmen, from toxic gases. Whilst these mostly arise from the slurry under slatted floor channels, sometimes there occurs carbon monoxide from incomplete or inefficient combustion of gas in gas heaters. The result may be death in the young piglet or the sow may abort her litter (see Chapter 1).

Foot-and-mouth disease

This notifiable disease in the UK and its importance is discussed fully in Chapter 4. Three special points may, however, be made with regard to the disease in pigs. Firstly, symptoms of lameness are more often the first signs of illness, whereas in cattle the vesicles on the mouth are usually the first symptoms. Secondly, primary outbreaks can well occur in pigs fed infected meat products that have been improperly sterilised.

The final point is that the symptoms are largely indistinguishable from swine vesicular disease which is also a viral and notifiable disease, but this affects only pigs. It is described below.

Swine vesicular disease (SVD)

This is another condition caused by an enterovirus and was first recognised in the UK in 1972. Since then it has been a sporadically occurring infection. Clinical signs are similar to foot-and-mouth disease, including lameness due to inflammation and vesicles developing on the foot and also on the mouth, tongue and areas of the skin over the legs. Affected pigs may also show some nervous symptoms.

SVD is a highly contagious infection but the effect on pigs is relatively mild. Nevertheless, in view of its similarity to foot-and-mouth disease, a positive diagnosis only being possible at a specialist laboratory, the two diseases are dealt with in exactly the same way by slaughtering all infected and in-contact stock.

Rabies

The virus that affects all mammals (see Chapter 4) may very rarely affect pigs in rabies-infected areas. It will cause much the same symptoms of incoordination, salivation, muscular spasms, paralysis and death within about 3—4 days from the onset of the symptoms.

A group of important virus infections affecting pigs of various ages

Pig enterovirus infections, including 'SMEDI'

A popular discussion point by pig farmers is the condition known as SMEDI — the initials of Stillbirth, Mummification, Embryonic Death and Infertility. The condition is caused by various enteroviruses. Suspicion of this condition will be aroused when the various symptoms listed occur, and it is important for the farmer to obtain a specialist diagnosis before appropriate control measures are taken, which will have to be on the same lines as the parvovirus problem (see later in this chapter). The process of 'feeding-back' infected material, however, is very risky because it may spread diseases other than the particular infection which is causing concern; a laboratory diagnosis can help to reduce this risk by establishing that the pigs are not otherwise diseased.

Pig enteroviruses may also be associated with nervous symptoms not dissimilar to poliomyelitis in man. Affected animals run a high temperature and show incoordination, followed by stiffness, tremors, convulsions and then most pigs die within a week of infection. This condition will occur in all pigs in herds which are non-immune and where the disease is enzootic. It may also occur in a mild, less serious form in which the pigs have fever and show some incoordination which is often followed by recovery, though some become paralysed and have to be culled.

The acute form of this disease, known as Teschen disease, is probably not present in the UK but it is a notifiable disease and would be dealt with by a slaughter policy to attempt to eradicate it. The mild form, known as Talfan disease, is certainly present in the UK but no special control policies are instituted and reliance is made on the pigs developing a natural immunity, as with many other virus diseases of rather mild and uncertain symptoms. Vaccines are made though none is licensed in the UK (see earlier in this chapter under TGE).

Rotavirus infection

Rotavirus infection causes very severe scouring in piglets which can lead to quite a heavy mortality. The symptoms are anorexia, vomiting, diarrhoea — yellow or dark grey in colour and very profuse. The diarrhoea causes rapid dehydration, which can kill, otherwise the pigs can recover in about a week to ten days.

These clinical signs are very similar to other conditions of young pigs causing profuse diarrhoea, such as TGE and *E. coli* infection and only a laboratory diagnosis which identifies the virus will confirm the cause. There are no specific control measures and reliance will have to be placed on endeavouring to provide good nursing for the affected piglets with generalised treatment to deal with secondaries.

Vomiting and wasting disease
This is a disease of the newborn pig caused by a coronavirus similar to the TGE virus. Affected pigs firstly vomit, huddle together with general illness, are depressed, run a high temperature and show little interest in suckling. Only a proportion of piglets in a litter are affected and only a proportion of all litters may be affected at all.

Parvovirus infection
Parvovirus infection of pigs is a cause of infertility, stillbirths, small litters and mummification. It is a relatively new condition that has been recognised in a number of large units. It tends to be most commonly seen in young gilts or newly introduced pigs which have no resistance to the 'local' infection. It may also infect boars which then act as spreaders of infection. It appears to be far more of a problem in those housing systems where the sows are kept as individuals (as in tethering or sow stalls) and where the lack of contact fails to produce a passing infection and then resistance. In this type of condition there is no treatment that is of any real use. No licensed vaccines have been produced in the UK but none is really recommended anywhere. One procedure is to 'infect' a young gilt before service and the most effective way is to 'feed' homogenised placenta from known infected cases.

Epidemic diarrhoea
This is a very contagious disease of pigs caused by a virus which produces a profuse diarrhoea, vomiting, wasting and inappetance. The disease is similar to TGE but affects largely the older pigs; younger pigs are affected either very much less or not at all. The effects of the virus vary a great deal but generally they are most

serious and many piglets die due to the inability of the sow to suckle them. Also, quite a number of sows will show such wasting that they may never breed again and have to be culled. There is little that can be done. It is suggested that all sows within about two weeks of farrowing are isolated. On the other hand, those that are in earlier stages of pregnancy than this should be deliberately infected with the virus by mixing of pigs, dung, and pathological material. It is yet another of the infections of a viral origin which seem to pass by the smaller herds and yet have a devastating effect on the larger ones. One of the greatest difficulties is to obtain a reasonably speedy total infection and consequent immunity in the herd but the crude measures that seem necessary to accelerate the build-up of immunity may be quite harmful in other respects by spreading other infections. This is a further argument in favour of establishing and maintaining breeding herds of a modest size where such problems do not occur or, if they do, have minimal effects.

General control measures for virus infections when no vaccines are available

The upsurge in the number of virus infections in pig herds in recent years is worrying and provides us with lessons of great importance. They appear to be very similar to those conditions that have affected poultry but the pig industry is much more vulnerable. It tends to be more careless about hygiene, has no general policy of depopulation of sites and moves pigs around during their lifetime much more generally than is the case with poultry.

To minimise the effects, the following preventive measures should be considered:

1. Introduce a minimum of new stock from outside the unit.
2. Depopulate the housing of young pigs as frequently as possible.
3. Keep adult breeders closely but cleanly housed.
4. Do not use sow stalls or tethers but use kennels or yards which group the gilts, sows and boars.
5. Limit the size of each self-contained unit to a minimum. This will ensure speedy effects of any virulent viruses in the area.
6. Practise careful isolation of the site in terms of feed deliveries, visitors, collecting lorries for fat pigs and any other potential danger.

External parasites

Pigs may be quite badly infected with lice (*Haematopinus suis*), the mange mite (*Sarcoptes scabei var. suis*) and the stable fly (*Stomoxys calcitrans*).

Lice

Lice tend to be most common in the folds of the skin of the neck, around the base of the ears, on the insides of the legs and on the flanks. The louse is quite large — about 0.5 mm long — and can be seen moving amongst the hairs on the pig's skin. The constant irritation causes the pig to rub and scratch and this reduces growth and food conversion efficiency. Also, the lice may be vectors of other disease agents.

Knowledge of the life cycle of the pig louse assists in effecting the control measures. The lice lay their eggs on the bristles and can be seen as a yellow crust. The eggs hatch into a nymph in 10–20 days, then after two further nymphal stages the life cycle is completed in about 30 days. The lice can only live away from the host for 2–3 days and the pig is the only host.

Because lice cause considerable economic loss it is unwise to tolerate an infection. The best way of dealing with the problem is to treat all sows just before they enter farrowing accommodation. Suitable preparations are washes of diazinon (Fison's lice and mange powder) and gamma benzene hexachloride (I.C.I.'s louse and insect powder). It is quite feasible to eliminate infection altogether by improved attention to hygiene and a number of washes.

Mange

Mange is an infinitely more worrying problem than lice. The parasite which is most common in the pig (*Sarcoptes scabei var suis*) burrows in the skin and lives in so-called 'galleries'. The mange parasites are about 0.5 mm long and lay their eggs in the galleries and develop through larval and two nymphal stages to adults within a period of about 15 days. Whilst the parasites can only multiply on the pig, the mites can survive up to 2–3 weeks in piggeries.

The burrowing and feeding of the mites cause considerable damage to the skin and intense irritation. Fluid exudate oozes from the lesions and dries and causes crusts on the skin. The skin becomes grossly thickened and keratinised and may also become infected with bacteria. In the final stages of the disease the skin resembles more that of an elephant than a pig.

The disease has important economic considerations and must be eliminated if pigs are to thrive. It can be treated with a number of different washes, such as gamma benzene hexachloride, diazinon, bromocyclen and sulphur and amitraz. Two applications at intervals of ten days may be fully successful. If such pigs are then put into completely clean accommodation it is feasible to eliminate the disease or at least reduce it to a very low level.

Internal parasites

Not many years ago the various internal parasites of pigs constituted a major problem in pig husbandry but that situation is largely over. For one thing, the adoption of more intensive systems has tended to eliminate the secondary hosts which have an essential role in the life cycles of some parasites. And for another, modern anthelmintics are so effective that treatment and prevention enable the problem to be readily resolved. The main concern to the pig farmer is of sub-clinical infection which may go undetected while in reality doing great harm. It is also pertinent to observe that as there is some return to less intensive methods, with pigs grazing outdoors, there may be a resurgence of internal parasites. The important ones are:

Ascariasis

Ascaris lumbricoides is the common large roundworm that lives in the small intestine. Some can achieve a length of up to a foot and a half (450 mm). Infection can be so bad that the intestines are literally blocked with large numbers of these worms. In any event, the presence of worms invariably leads to some deterioration in the food conversion and growth efficiency. But these are not really the worst effects of this particular infection. The life cycle is direct — no inter-mediate host is involved — and after the eggs are laid and ingested by pigs kept under unhygienic conditions, the eggs hatch out and the larvae, in their development to the adult stage, which is always in the intestine, actually pass through the lungs and liver. The effect on the liver appears to be slight because the pigs usually show no symptoms. However, so far as the lungs are concerned, it is a different story. Coughing and pneumonia result from the migration of the larvae in the lungs, and the damage by the larvae almost certainly allows bacteria to invade and cause secondary symptoms. The tracking of the larvae through the liver does some damage, however, and leaves small white areas known as 'milk spots', so it is possible to tell, at post mortem, or at the slaughterhouse, that the worms are doing their damage. These signs provide a good warning to the pig farmer. In addition the livers may be condemned as being unfit for human consumption.

Control can be relatively easy as the life cycle is a direct one. If pigs can be prevented from reinfesting themselves by ingesting any-thing which is contaminated with their faeces the life cycle can be broken. One must beware of dirty pens, floor feeding, dirty troughs, contaminated drinking water or 'pig sick' land. Good disinfectants will kill the eggs or larvae. Treatment of the pigs with anthelmintics will eliminate the worms. The condition should not be tolerated and a plan of campaign to eliminate the worms will have beneficial effects, not only by eliminating these worms but also other susceptible types.

Other intestinal worms of pigs occur in various parts of the intestine. There are the two stomach worms *Ostertagia* and *Hyostronglyus rubidus*. These are small reddish worms about 10 mm long which infect the stomach lining chiefly affecting and causing damage to sows. Clinically it causes weight loss and anaemia in sows, mainly after weaning. It is most likely to arise when the sows are put on to pasture after weaning for service with the boar. Also, most common in breeding pigs is the worm *Oesophagostomum*. This is a worm of about 15 mm in length which is found in the caecum and colon. Again, it is a direct life cycle and it causes diarrhoea and weight loss. It is also associated with dirty paddocks.

Finally, there is a lungworm of importance known as *Metastrongylus*. The adult worm lives in the bronchioles of the lungs. In this case the life cycle is indirect, infection being caused by ingestion of the earthworm which is the intermediate host of the larvae of the Metastrongylus. The lungworms undoubtedly cause damage to the lungs and pneumonia, but it is chiefly in the younger pigs that the symptoms are serious. Older pigs are not usually adversely affected but do remain as carriers of the infection.

Control of the endoparasites

Symptoms such as those described may enable at least a suspicion of infection to be made but it will be on proper laboratory examination by the expert parasitologist that a definite diagnosis will be made. It is important to do this. Usually treatments are carried out by in-feed medication of suitable products such as:

Fenbendazole (*Panacur* by Hoechst),
Tetramisole (*Nilverm* by I.C.I.),
Thiabendazole and Piperazine (*Thyrazole* by M.S.D.), and
Dichlorvos (*Atgard*, Squibb, M.S.D.).

Regular programmes should be instituted where problems exist, according to the direction of the manufacturers.

Deficiency diseases

Because pigs are usually fed efficiently calculated and mixed rations, deficiencies of vitamins, minerals and other food substances are uncommon. Nevertheless, one still has to be closely aware of the possibility of deficiencies arising. Sometimes the essentials are missing due to error, but more often deficiencies arise because the element is not available. For example, *Parakeratosis* is an absolute or conditioned deficiency of zinc which causes poor growth and hyperkeratosis — the latter being a proliferation of the epidermis causing scaly, crusty skin, especially on the abdomen and legs. It is readily dealt with by ensuring a level of 100 ppm of zinc in the ration.

As a second example, the B group vitamin Biotin may need extra supplementation. Deficiencies cause scaly skin and lameness due to cracking of the horn of the feet (see Fig. 5.4). Levels up to 220 micrograms per kilogram are required in the diet. High energy feeds with a cereal basis of only wheat and barley, but no maize, appear to be the cause of the trouble.

Foot and leg lesions in pigs

Warning must be given that many pigs, especially young piglets, suffer damage to their feet and legs due to unsatisfactory flooring.

Fig. 5.4 Biotin deficiency in a boar. The hooves of the hind feet are painful as a result of the damaged soft horn. The pig stands uncomfortably to relieve the weight on them with typical hunched back stance. Poor, dirty skin is also seen.

Rough concrete floors cause sore feet and serious abrasions on the knees and legs. In addition slatted or slotted flooring can cause even more serious and penetrating damage due to poor design and sharp edges. Parts of the foot can be literally torn off. Apart from the immediate damage and pain caused in all these cases, secondary infection can readily set in to cause highly destructive damage to the tissue.

Lameness in older pigs may be caused by Foot Rot, an infection affecting the claws of the feet and causing penetrating damage and erosion. The primary cause is probably an injury. Then comes secondary infection with bacteria, such as *Fusiformis necrophorus* (see Chapters 4 and 6). The lameness created can be serious and the lesions so penetrating that no treatment can arrest the process of destruction of tissues. Lameness is also caused by abnormal or excess growth of the claws. All these conditions may be caused by keeping pigs on soft and wet flooring, with insufficient exercise. Good clean straw bedding can be a perfect surface but if it is not renewed frequently it can be disastrous.

It is estimated that foot and leg lesions together are responsible for about *one third* of the culling in breeding pigs. Apart from the conditions drawn to the reader's attention in this section, there are other reasons for lameness, such as general infections like swine erysipelas (see earlier in this chapter), and the inherited susceptibility of certain strains. It has long been apparent that an obsessive concentration by the geneticist on the growth and carcase quality of the pig in his selection programme can jeopardise the health and vigour of pigs, the strength of the feet and legs being a critical part of this.

Table 5.1 The health of pigs: a summary of diseases, prevention and treatment

Disease	Prevention	Treatment
Anthrax	(Notifiable in UK). Vaccine. Antiserum.	Antiserum. Penicillin.
Atrophic rhinitis	Improve environment, especially ventilation. Vaccine. Tylosin. Sulpha drugs.	Tylosin. Sulpha drugs.
Aujeszky's disease	(Notifiable in UK). Vaccines.	None.
Bowel oedema	Avoid over-feeding after weaning. Ensure ready access to drinking water or feed wet.	Antihistamines. *E. coli* antiserum. Broad spectrum antibiotics.

Disease	Prevention	Treatment
Clostridial infections	Vaccine. Antiserum.	Antiserum. Penicillin. Ampicillin. Broad spectrum antibiotics.
E. coli infections	Serum. Vaccines (e.g. Intagen). Nitrofurans. Organic arsenicals. Chlortetracyclines. Carbadox.	A wide range of antibiotics by injection and oral route, such as Amoxycillin, Linco-spectin, Trimethoprim sulphonamides. Framomycin. Neomycin and supportive therapy using minerals, electrolytes and vitamins.
Enzootic pneumonia	Consider: improve ventilation and reduce numbers of pigs and their stocking density.	Broad spectrum antibiotics in general.
Farrowing fever (metritis, mastitis, agalactia syndrome (MMA))	Improve hygiene of sow and her quarters before and during farrowing.	Oxytocin. Oxytetracycline. Chlortetracycline. Ampicillin.
Greasy pig disease	Ensure soft bedding is provided or good flooring. Fortify vitamin content of rations.	Broad spectrum antibiotics, e.g. Linco-spectin. Ampicillin.
Leptospirosis	Antiserum. Vaccines. Attend to hygiene and destroy any rodents.	Antiserum. Ampicillin. Tetracyclines. Streptomycin.
Lice	Clean pens and equipment using disinfectant with insecticides.	Diazinon. Gamma benzene hexachloride.
Mange	Clean accommodation and remove badly infected pigs.	Diazinon. Bromocyclen and sulphur. Gamma benzene hexachloride. Amitraz.
Mulberry heart disease	Increase selenium and vitamin content of ration, especially Vitamin E and fat-soluble vitamins.	None.
Mycotoxicosis	Avoid feed or litter that may contain moulds. Check any doubtful samples.	Supportive therapy of vitamins, minerals and electrolytes and antibiotics to prevent secondary infections.
Parakeratosis	Zinc must be in the ration at least to a level of 100 ppm.	Add zinc sulphate as in *Prevention*.
Piglet anaemia	Iron Dextran injections or iron by oral route using pastes, solutions or tablets, or by natural access to pasture.	Injection of Iron Dextran solutions and Vitamin B_{12}.
Roundworm infestation	Enable pigs to be reared without close contact with their dung.	Fenbendazole. Tetramisole. Thiabendazole. Piperazine. Dichlorvos.

Disease	Prevention	Treatment
Salmonellosis	(Notifiable in UK). Improve system of management and possibly use vaccines and drugs similar to those given under *Treatment*.	Sulphonamides. Tetracyclines. Ampicillin. Linco-spectin. Furazolidone. Streptomycin.
'SMEDI' and related virus infections	Often prevented by deliberate early exposure of breeders to infection in a controlled way.	Supportive therapy including injection of vitamins, liquids by mouth with electrolytes and broad spectrum antibiotics to reduce secondary infections.
Streptococcal infections	In-feed medication with penicillin.	Penicillin. Trimethoprim. Broad spectrum antibiotics.
Swine dysentery	Improve husbandry and management to separate pigs from contact with infected dung. Drugs listed under *Treatment* may also be used for prevention.	Organic arsenicals. Tylosin. Erythromycin. Spiramycin. Tylosin + sulpha drugs. Linco-mycin. Linco-spectin. Tiamulin. Dimetradiazole. Carbadox + Sulphonamide.
Swine erysipelas	Vaccine. Antiserum.	Antiserum. Penicillin.
Transmissible gastro-enteritis (TGE)	Vaccines available in certain countries.	Non-specific supportive therapy and broad spectrum antibiotics.

6 The Health of Sheep

Health problems at or near lambing

The health of sheep is dealt with in the same way as has been done with cattle and pigs, that is, on a life cycle basis and commencing with disease conditions and the maintenance of health around the time of lambing. The first point to stress is the essential need for the highest standard of hygiene at all times. Lambing is the period of greatest risk from infection, transcending all other periods in the life of sheep. There is almost equal danger to the ewes and their lambs.

Ewes must be carefully observed during lambing to reduce losses due to difficulties in the birth of the lamb (dystocia). Up to 4% of ewes may experience difficulties and if assistance is given the loss can be reduced to about 1%.

It is always difficult to decide when assistance should be given but the general advice is that if no progress is made within 3 hours of the start of lambing the competent shepherd should carry out an examination. He may then find he can readily correct any mal-presentation or may decide to call in a veterinary surgeon according to his judgement of the position.

E. coli infection (Colibacillosis)

This is perhaps the most serious disease. There are essentially two different types — the enteric and septicaemic forms. Symptoms in the enteric form usually manifest themselves at 1 to 4 days of age and the lamb becomes depressed, shows profuse diarrhoea or dysentery and dies, usually within 24 to 36 hours of the onset of symptoms. Those affected with the septicaemic form are usually 2 to 6 weeks old. Affected lambs have a fever and become stiff and unco-ordinated in their movements; later they lie down, paddle with their legs and become comatose.

The disease usually occurs after a period of lambing due to the 'build-up' of infection that tends to occur during the intensive use of an area. Lambing quarters should not be over-used; it is asking for all manner of problems. Nevertheless, it may be possible to prevent the trouble from occurring by injecting a vaccine into the ewes during pregnancy so that the lambs acquire some passive immunity to protect them from the disease during the earlier days of their life. When an outbreak of *E. coli* occurs then a number of treatments can be considered. It is possible to give an antiserum if desired but it is more usual to use broad spectrum antibiotics by injection to treat lambs with this worrying condition. If there is evidence of intestinal infection it is also advisable to treat the lambs with an oral dose of antibiotics.

Navel-ill

This is virtually the same in sheep as in other species. Dirty environmental conditions cause an absence of healing of the navel and the infection that may penetrate this point — bacterial in nature — can kill the lamb either in a septicaemic acute way, or more often by leading to general infection of the organs and certain parts of the body, especially the joints. There is only one answer — cleanse the quarters, clean the navel with antiseptic and a dusting of antibiotic and the troubles should be over. Affected lambs may respond to antibiotic injections if they are administered very quickly after the symptoms are observed.

Mastitis

It is usual for a number of ewes to develop an infection of one or other of the halves of the udder. This is a very damaging disease in ewes which often leads to the complete destruction of the parts affected. It is difficult to know why this condition occurs, though bad hygiene apparently plays its part, but quick treatment with a broad spectrum antibiotic, given both locally into the teat and by injection, may save the udder and the ewe. Staphylococcal, pasteurella and clostridial organisms are frequently involved so that gangrene and general tissue destruction can be severe if the disease goes unchecked.

From young lambs to mature sheep

The clostridial diseases

The group of bacteria known as clostridia are spore-forming organisms to be found almost universally wherever sheep are kept. As soon as the bacteria pass out of the animal's body they form the tough spores (or capsules) which make them extremely resistant to destruction. In the normal way they may live in the soil for many years. And though we associate the main diseases they cause with sheep, where they tend to transcend all others in importance, they can affect most other livestock including, in some cases, man. Their mode of action is to manufacture toxins which make the animal ill or kill it. Under certain circumstances favourable to the bacteria they can and do multiply in large numbers; otherwise the organisms may be present in small numbers and cause no trouble. Clostridia will multiply only in areas where there is no oxygen and they do this in wounds, especially deep ones, in the intestines of animals, or in organs within the body such as the liver. Rather strangely, clostridial diseases tend most seriously to affect animals in very good, thriving condition. Below are listed the main clostridial diseases of sheep with their symptoms briefly described.

LAMB DYSENTERY
This is caused by a form of clostridium known as *Clostridium welchii, Type B*. This organism is widespread, like most clostridia, but still tends to be localised in certain areas. The disease occurs in lambs in the first few weeks of life but displays itself in a number of different ways — acute, sub-acute, and chronic forms are described. Whilst the principal symptoms are of bloody diarrhoea (dysentery), the disease may start in a fairly mild way in a flock in the lambing season but gradually increases in severity and intensity as the season continues and will quickly cause many deaths — up to 30% of the flock if it is unchecked.

The first lambs affected may be several weeks old but as the season advances the lambs are affected earlier and eventually as soon as they are born. In many cases no symptoms are seen, the lamb or lambs being found dead, usually overnight. Post mortem examination shows a very dehydrated carcase, and inflamed and ulcerated small intestine.

Control
As soon as an outbreak occurs, treatment and prevention are achieved successfully by the immediate application of the hyperimmune anti-serum. But for the prevention of attacks in the future it is much better to vaccinate the ewes. If they are given two vaccinations, the last one being about one month before lambing, they will transfer a strong immunity to the lambs and they will be safely protected in this way. In succeeding years ewes will only need one additional 'booster' injection.

PULPY KIDNEY DISEASE

The second of the clostridial diseases that is common in sheep is caused by *Clostridium welchii, Type D.* Symptoms may not be seen — the first sign is often the sudden occurrence of a number of deaths in really good lambs at 2–3 months of age. However, it does not only occur at that age, it may also happen in older sheep (see enterotoxaemia). For example, it may occur when store lambs and ewes are put on good pasture in the autumn. It will tend to affect only the best lambs and will also be more likely when animals go on to a better plane of nutrition. The name 'pulpy kidney' is given because on post mortem the kidneys show a high degree of destruction.

Control

As with lamb dysentery the disease can be treated or instant protection is achieved with the antiserum, whilst vaccination of the ewe during pregnancy will give the necessary protection to the lambs for the first weeks of life. However, because a major predisposing cause is when sheep are placed on rather too good a pasture, much can be done to prevent trouble by watching their condition and regulating their nutrition.

BLACKLEG

In this case the clostridia (*Clostridium chauvoei*) do not infect the intestine but the muscles, usually those of the limbs. It appears that after some injury to the body the organisms gain entry and then multiply. The symptoms are caused by the toxins destroying muscles and generating gas which causes swelling of the area and a general discolouration and darkening of the skin. It is, in effect, the condition known as *gas gangrene*. It also tends to affect the best sheep and it is the younger that are at risk as they have little natural immunity. It is similar in nature to blackquarter in cattle (see Chapter 4).

Control

As with other clostridial diseases, vaccines can be given to prevent it. Treatment of affected animals or immediate protection is effective using penicillin injections and/or, the specific antiserum.

BRAXY

Braxy is caused by *Clostridium septique*. Usually the first sign is the sudden death of some young sheep in good condition on frosty autumn mornings. The predisposing cause is the eating of frosty food which damages the wall of the abomasum and allows the invasion of the clostridial organisms. Post mortem signs are of a very inflamed and degenerate abomasal wall. Sometimes some symptoms are seen before death but these are not diagnostic, being those of dullness, inappetance, diarrhoea and incoordination. The most likely age incidence is from 6 to 16 months. The disease tends to be confined to certain areas, especially northern hilly regions. Vaccination is totally effective as a preventive.

BLACK DISEASE

The symptoms again are sudden death, usually in adult sheep. The organism, *Clostridium oedematiens*, invades the liver after damage by the liver fluke. It usually occurs in the autumn and early winter when flukes migrate in their largest numbers from the intestine to the liver.

Post mortem signs are of general degeneration of the body's organs but in particular of the liver which shows characteristic foci of necrosis.

Control

The same measures are used as in other clostridial diseases. It will also help to prevent black disease if the fluke infestation is controlled.

TETANUS

Tetanus, or lockjaw, caused by *Clostridium tetani*, is not the same as other diseases since it does not cause sudden death. In this case the organism finds entry through a wound, which may be an accidental wound, or a deliberate one such as castration. The wound heals over and the organism multiplies within this anaerobic atmosphere producing the toxin which causes nervous symptoms – spasms of muscular contraction, stiffening of the limbs and eventually death.

Control

Control and prevention is on the same lines as other clostridial diseases. It may also be pointed out that proper attention to injuries with cleansing and treatment will greatly reduce the likelihood of tetanus infection in sheep. It will also help with this disease, as with other of the clostridial diseases, if the sheep are not kept on the same land for too long. Whilst it is true that the sporulating bacteria can exist for a very long time in the soil, resting and cultivation will reduce the numbers and also the risk.

THE USE OF VACCINES AND SERA WITH CLOSTRIDIAL INFECTIONS

All the clostridial diseases can be countered by the use of sera and vaccines – sera for immediate prevention or treatment or vaccines to

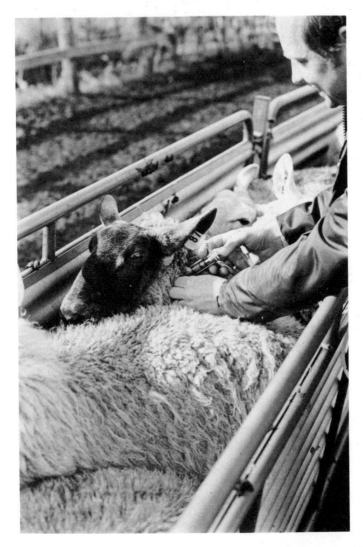

Fig. 6.1 A ewe being vaccinated with a multivalent clostridial infection. Note the way in which the ewes are well controlled in the crush so that the operator carries out the injection easily and without risk of injury to the animals.

build up an immunity over a period of weeks (see Fig. 6.1). In order to assist the use of the vaccines the pharmaceutical companies have prepared preparations that combine several vaccines together – up to at least eight covering all the common sheep diseases – are now available. However, it is best not to use these all regardless of need but to choose only those that are entirely necessary.

Wellcome manufacture two vaccines, 'Covexin 8', which is an

aqueous preparation for subcutaneous use and 'Omnivax', a similar vaccine which is prepared with an oily adjuvant which is administered intraperitoneally. Booster doses for the latter are achieved by 'Omnivax CVA' administered subcutaneously. The programme to be used is summarised below:

Covexin 8 (Wellcome)

First dose	5 ml subcutaneously
Second dose 6 weeks later	2 ml subcutaneously
Booster dose	2 ml subcutaneously

For lambs which have been passively protected the first dose should be given at about 3–4 months of age. The booster dose is advocated at 6 month intervals or annually if the risk is low. The booster dose should be given 2 weeks before lambing to achieve maximum colostrum antibody levels.

Omnivax (Wellcome)

First and only dose (protection for 2 years)	2 ml intraperitoneally
Booster dose	2 ml Omnivax CVA subcutaneously

Respiratory conditions

PNEUMONIA

Many losses occur from acute pneumonia in sheep and these have undoubtedly been more frequent and more serious in their incidence with the advent of more intensive methods. But in recent years it is significant that it is *both the acute and chronic* forms which have been increasing.

Acute pneumonia infections, which are especially serious in winter and autumn, are caused by infection with pasteurella bacteria. These organisms are, however, common and normal inhabitants of the respiratory system but manage to generate disease under certain stressful conditions. Such 'triggers' to acute pasteurella infection can be intensification, harmful weather conditions, transportation under less than ideal conditions, and infestation of the lungs with parasites.

Treatment of pneumonia is best undertaken by the use of antibiotics such as ampicillin, which have a good activity against pasteurella. Sulphonamide administration is also satisfactory. If problems are anticipated then pasteurella vaccine may be administered and is a wise precaution, particularly in housed sheep where the risk is really very great. It may be emphasised that the environment in housed sheep is nearly always wrong because it is under-ventilated. I have never seen a sheep house with too much air! The reader is referred to the section on pneumonia in Chapter 4 and in particular the details given of good ventilating practice.

PULMONARY ADENOMATOSIS (JAAGSIEKTE)
This is a contagious neoplastic (tumour-forming) disease of the lungs of adult sheep of insidious but continuous development, accompanied by weakness, nasal discharge, laboured breathing and invariably death. It is caused by a slow-acting herpes virus. The only control is by slaughtering infected animals. It does not occur frequently in the United Kingdom but is quite common world-wide.

Orf (contagious pustular dermatitis)
Orf, or contagious pustular dermatitis, is a virus infection of sheep which affects the skin, causing vesicles and scabs, especially on the mouth and legs. It may even spread to the inside of the mouth and the genital organs. It can also cause an unpleasant disease in those handling sheep.

It is caused by a virus and older animals develop an immunity after infection. Thus the infection is found mostly in young stock. It can have only a mild effect in the older lamb but is extremely serious in the younger animal and can even cause death. A good live virus vaccine is available and, if orf is a common and serious problem in a flock, is best used in an attempt not only to control but eventually to eliminate the trouble altogether.

Deficiency conditions

SWAYBACK (ENZOOTIC ATAXIA)
Swayback is one of the best known mineral deficiency diseases. It affects the nervous system of young lambs either at birth or a week or two thereafter. The symptoms are of incoordination and paralysis of the limbs of the body due to a degeneration of the nerve cells in the brain and spinal column; it is associated with a low level of copper in the blood and tissues of the lambs and ewes. The basic cause of the disease is a deficiency of copper, this element being

essential in the formation of enzymes for the construction of nervous tissue. The critical level of copper necessary for the proper development of nervous tissue is 5 ppm. In swayback areas levels of copper are generally well below this. The disease also tends to occur at its worst when the pasture is very lush and weather conditions have been particularly favourable to good growth.

Blood copper levels in swayback-affected lambs are very low, as indeed they are in the ewes, but the strange fact is that only a proportion of lambs born to ewes with low levels of copper actually have swayback. Thus the whole reason for this disease is not fully understood. However, in order to prevent the disease, it is necessary to supplement the copper intake of the pregnant ewe. Mineral mixtures need to be given by some means or another. Individual dosing or the use of long-acting injectables are further ways of providing the copper and have the merit that they do provide a known dose to every ewe. Adult ewes require an average daily intake of 5–10 mg of copper as an adequate allowance. Mineral block mixtures containing 0.5% copper sulphate are satisfactory, or diet supplementation with 0.2 g of copper sulphate fed weekly to each sheep would be adequate.

Top dressing of the pasture is not advised as it is wasteful, inexact and may give rise to toxicity. Copper toxicity is a very serious condition and sheep are the most susceptible of farm animals to this condition; they accumulate copper quite slowly before symptoms appear. Cases have always tended to occur in housed sheep fed diets that are too rich in copper.

PINE (PINING)

Pine is a disease of sheep which leads to wasting and is caused by a deficiency of cobalmin, alternatively known as vitamin B_{12}. However the deficiency is not a straightforward deficiency. Cobalmin is an essential vitamin which is synthesised by the bacteria which are present in the sheep's stomach, but in order that this can take place there must be sufficient cobalt in the diet as cobalt is an essential constituent of this vitamin.

Lack of cobalt may be a simple deficiency of the element or there may be such a preponderance of calcium that the cobalt is chemically tied to this and is not available in sufficient amount for absorption. In either case it is a disease of great economic importance. A simple way of preventing pining is to add a supplement which has been enriched with cobalt to the normal concentrate feed. Animals may also be dosed individually but this is rather tiresome because it must be done on several occasions and indeed once weekly is necessary. The cobalt 'bullet' is thus the best treatment since it is released gradually over a long period (see also Chapter 4). One 'bullet' is usually sufficient for twelve months and each 5 gram 'bullet' contains 90% cobalt oxide. Some 'bullets' are eliminated by the sheep so it is still necessary to watch their condition closely and re-dose as soon as this is apparent. The pasture may also be treated and this is done quite easily by giving about 2 kg of cobalt sulphate per acre about every five years.

RICKETS
Rickets — a condition of poor bone construction when the calcification fails to take place efficiently — is sometimes seen in lambs. Proper formation of bones is due to a sufficient quantity and balance of the minerals calcium and phosphorus, together with the Vitamin D. Unless all these minerals are adequately provided, rickets occurs. It is not easy to explain how lambs can suffer from serious deficiencies under normal husbandry conditions but usually injections of Vitamin D are successful in arresting the problem.

Internal parasites of sheep
The three main types of internal parasites that infest sheep are tapeworms, the flatworms represented by the liver fluke, and the roundworms, which infest both the intestines and the lungs.

TAPEWORMS
Tapeworms require an intermediate host, as well as sheep, for their existence. The adult tapeworm lives in the sheep's intestines where it lays eggs which pass out in the dung on to the pasture and further development can occur only if it is picked up by the intermediate host. The sheep is host to only one adult tapeworm, the 'milkworm' which largely infests suckling lambs and the secondary host is a small pasture mite; lambs become infested when they consume the mites accidentally when grazing.

It is thought improbable that these tapeworms do very much harm unless the infestation is a very heavy one in which case it is necessary to treat the lambs. There is no way of effectively getting rid of the secondary host.

Sheep may also be infested with a number of bladder worms, infestation being picked up on grazing contaminated with the droppings of dogs and foxes which carry the adult tapeworms in their intestines. These bladder worms occur as thinly-walled, fluid-filled bladders, usually up to two inches in diameter and are found among the intestines, in the lung and liver and in the nervous system. Although of little harm to sheep, two are also found in man and are of public health concern. Whilst they are relatively uncommon, all raw sheep offal and carcases should be carefully disposed of to prevent infestation of dogs and foxes.

LIVER FLUKE

Liver fluke is a serious problem in many parts of the world in wet years and infestations in Great Britain are most serious in the wetter parts of the country. It has a two host life-cycle, the adults living in the bile ducts of the liver in sheep, cattle and other animals and the intermediate younger stages in a snail. The snail can exist only in areas where the soil is saturated with moisture for considerable periods though it is not found naturally in running water or ponds. In dry periods or in winter it tends to burrow into the mud and can survive in the inactive state for a considerable time.

Hatching and development of fluke eggs is restricted by the climatic temperature and humidity requirements to the period of May to September, coinciding with the season of activity of the snail. The larvae when hatched must find and penetrate a snail within about 24 hours. Within the snail a number of developmental stages occur, the final form leaving the snail and attaching to vegetation and forming a protective capsule. This stage is infective to sheep and if eaten is liberated in the intestine, burrows into the abdomen and attacks the liver, where it wanders in the tissue for 2—3 months and then settles into the bile ducts. Acute fluke disease occurs during the migration of the larvae in the liver in heavy infestation and the chronic disease occurs some months later as the adult flukes cause thickening of the bile ducts and they also interfere with normal liver function. The total period from egg to adult is five to six months, producing one generation of flukes each year, thus explaining the incidence of the acute disease in the spring and chronic disease in the autumn. The economic importance of fluke losses varies considerably from year to year but it is important to institute some control measures in areas where the disease is common. The first thing to do is to treat the sheep with appropriate drugs, such as diamphenethide; secondly measures should be taken to prevent the sheep becoming infected by either isolating them from the area of the snails or by destroying the snails. If the area can be drained more efficiently, that will also serve a very useful purpose. Treatment of land to rid it of snails includes the use of copper sulphate solution and sodium pentachlorophenate.

One of the difficulties with fluke control has been that it is difficult to justify taking expensive control measures when the likelihood of infection only occurs every few years. But now it is known that an infection can be predicted, depending on the rainfall that occurred in late winter and spring. Thus control can be put in operation just at the time it is appropriate.

ROUNDWORMS OF SHEEP

At least ten species of roundworms (nematodes) cause parasitic gastroenteritis (or nematode gastroenteritis), which is considered the most economically serious cause of loss in sheep. Heavy infestations are disastrous but even light ones can cause great loss of productivity. Principal worms are: *Haemonchus contortus; Ostertagia circumcincta; Trichostrongylus axei; Nematodirus spathiger; Trichuris ovis; Oesophagostomum columbianum.*

In the control measures, attention is directed principally to animals in the first year of life as this is the time when they are severely affected. The older sheep usually develop a degree of resistance to infection.

The parasitic roundworms do not multiply in the sheep, and their numbers are increased only by the intake of fresh infection. The degree of infection therefore depends on the build-up of the worm burden in the pasture with the eggs of the worms and the frequency of the contact between the grazing animal and this contaminated pasture. Control is tackled in two ways — firstly, by treatment of the animal to eliminate the worm burden, and secondly by pasture and flock management to minimise infection.

Drugs that are used to control the infection must have a wide spectrum of safety and yet be highly effective. Recently there have emerged some very good products, which are basically thiabendazole, levamisole hydrochloride and organo-phosphorus preparations. They are effective against all intestinal stages of the worm. They clear out the worms effectively but of course do not prevent re-infestation. This is done by suitable pasture management which is based on rotational grazing allowing up to a week on pasture then closing it for three weeks. This is because eggs take about a week to become infective, and if they do not find a host they largely perish within four weeks.

Sheep may also be affected by lungworms and the reader is referred to Chapter 4 for the description of the similar condition in cattle.

External parasites

It is difficult to exaggerate the danger to sheep of the various species of external parasites. These include insects, mites and ticks which show considerable similarities in their physiology and susceptibility to chemicals and can really be treated as a group. These parasites can only be effectively dealt with when they are actually on the animal. The easiest to kill are those which spend their whole time on the sheep — the mites, lice and keds — and which cannot survive off the host for more than a couple of weeks. This group is effectively controlled by a single whole-body treatment with a preparation which is lethal to adults and young stages and persistent enough to kill the larvae as they hatch from resistant eggs, or by repeated use of a material which kills the adult only. This was the basis for the traditional double-dipping and single-dipping regulations which controlled sheep scab, which is caused by the psoroptic mange parasite.

The compulsory treatment of all suspected cases led at one time to the eradication of sheep scab in the British Isles once the highly effective DDT and BHC preparations became available. The sheep scab treatment also effectively controlled lice and keds, but now lice are frequently resistant to the common insecticides. The *blowfly*, in comparison with the other external parasites, completes only one fairly short stage of its development on the sheep and is thus open to attack by an insecticide for only a short time. Larvae hatch rapidly and feed on the skin and tissues for several days, then they fall on to the herbage and form the resting stage, known as the pupa, from which the adult fly emerges several weeks later. The flies' breeding activity extends from about May to September and several generations will emerge during that time.

Thus the problem of blowfly control is the short period in which it is possible to attack the problem on the animal, the repeated infestation and the very severe damage done by the larvae. However, modern organo-phosphorus compounds and carbamate mixtures are quite effective if properly applied. Whole body dipping is really the most satisfactory method; it is better than spraying, which is not so thorough in its penetration.

The problem of fly-strike requires additional measures to be effective. All cases of scour should be treated and wounds should be dressed immediately. Any weakness of an area attracts the flies and can be a contributing cause of breakdown of a control programme.

In the north of England and in Scotland a very nasty problem, the 'headfly', has recently emerged. This fly, which is closely similar to the house fly, feeds on the fluid from the eyes, nose and mouth of sheep. As a result of the irritation the sheep rub their heads against fences and walls causing wounds which make them even more attractive to the unwelcome attention of the headfly. The result of this disturbance is a very restless animal and considerable economic loss.

The *sheep tick* spends even less of its life actually on the animal. It attaches itself only for a relatively few days during its three year cycle of development, the rest of the time being spent on the pasture where it requires a high moisture level for prolonged survival and so infestation is common in rough pasture, particularly woodland. The principal active time is in the spring and early summer, with another period of activity in the moist time of autumn. Most ticks, therefore, are only capable of being destroyed over these two relatively short periods, each of about three weeks' duration. The preparation that is used must therefore be highly active against all the developmental stages and should protect the sheep over a period of about two months. Organo-phosphorus compounds are probably the best. Some note should be given to the other methods of control involving the improvement of pasture so that it is less attractive to the tick.

Sheep scab, the commonly used name for a mange in sheep caused by the psoroptic mange parasite, is a notifiable disease in the UK. This mange parasite can invade all parts of the body that are covered with wool, and also the ears. The total effect is extremely damaging, which is the reason for the disease being notifiable. Although at one time it was eliminated from the sheep in the UK it has now returned.

The mite in its progress in the skin causes injuries and serum oozes out on which it feeds; the wounds develop scabs after a time, hence the name 'sheep scab'. The poison produced by the mite causes intense irritation so the sheep rubs and scratches itself endlessly, the skin becomes thickened and ulcerated and the wool is detached and the sheep looks increasingly ill.

Treatment is instituted by a dipping of the sheep with approved materials. Prevention is also by a regular dipping procedure. Excellent dips are produced which in one treatment give a long-term, persistent (residual) effect. For example, Wellcome's Border Winter Dip, containing gamma BHC, dichlorfenthion and phenols control scab, keds and lice in one dipping and give as much as five months' protection against reinfestation with keds and lice.

Other forms of mange do occur in sheep, for example, sarcoptic mange, but this is usually only on the head, and chorioptic mange, which is in the pastern and interdigital space of the feet. But none is as bad as the psoroptic mange mite.

Infections of mature sheep

Scrapie

Scrapie is believed to be a virus disease which occurs naturally only in sheep and goats. It is nevertheless a strange virus, if such it be, as it is very resistant to the normal methods of destruction. The disease has an immensely protracted incubation period and even after the symptoms develop it may take as much as six months for death — which is inevitable — to take place.

The organism affects the nervous system, causing alternating periods of lethargy and excitability. As the disease progresses the sheep become unable to control their hindquarters and then develop a severe itchiness which makes the sheep bite frantically at the area of irritation, or rub furiously against posts or other protuberances, which can then result in a very bedraggled fleece and sore, raw places. The disease affects some breeds more than others; indeed some strains seem to be completely resistant to the disease so that breeding from resistant strains offers a method of eliminating infection.

The long incubation period of up to 3 years has made research a problem but generally the condition occurs sporadically with just a limited proportion of the sheep being affected. Control is also difficult. No treatment is of any use and all sheep that are infected will die.

All infected sheep should be slaughtered; in fact, to deal with the disease correctly the ancestors and progeny should be slaughtered as well. A technique that has been used successfully to eliminate scrapie from a flock is to slaughter all the infected animals and then to take replacement ewe lambs only from mature mothers at their third or later lambings. Scrapie is rarely seen in sheep over 5 years of age. Unfortunately, because of the long incubation period it is very difficult ever to know when or if a flock is free of the disease; this makes it difficult to see how the disease can ever be completely eradicated.

Johne's disease

This condition in sheep is similar to that in cattle (see Chapter 4). The disease organism, *Mycobacterium johnei*, causes a chronic wasting condition of older sheep accompanied by a characteristically foetid form of scour. Lambs pick up the infection when they are very young from infected pasture. No symptoms are seen at this time but later in the sheep's life, and it may be very much later — even three years — under the stress of poor management, nutrition or housing, that the condition becomes apparent. There is no cure and affected sheep must be culled. It is possible to protect sheep with a vaccine but it is more important to try to remove the opportunities for infection of the young lambs.

Foot rot

This remains one of the biggest causes of serious economic loss in sheep everywhere. It is primarily caused by a bacterium *Fusiformis nodosus* and still occurs widely if not properly controlled. It spreads from sheep to sheep via infected soil, but the bacteria do not live many days in the soil. The harbourers of infection are, in fact, the sheep with bad feet in which the organism can survive indefinitely. The conditions that favour the spread of infection are wet weather and soil when the feet are softened and the organisms released to invade other feet through any injured part.

Control of foot rot

Control programmes must be instituted because it has been well established that infection has a profound effect on profitability. A suitable programme will make use of the following facts:

- The organism infects only sheep.
- It can only survive outside the sheep for about two weeks.
- It is very vulnerable to treatment provided the areas of the feet which harbour infection are exposed.

Firstly, all feet must be inspected and trimmed and all bad cases showing inflamed areas should be separated. Those with very badly shaped feet may be symptomless carriers and should also be separated. All healthy sheep are then walked through a foot bath which contains a 5–10% solution of formalin. Contact with the formalin should last at least one minute. After this they are put on to clean concrete for an hour or so then on to pasture which has had no sheep on it for some weeks.

Secondly, those with affected feet are individually handled. All the damaged separated horn is carefully pared away so that the inflamed and infected tissue is exposed to the air and to treatment. Great care must be taken not to damage the feet by this paring with no cutting of living tissue.

The foot, having been prepared in this way, is then treated with a suitable preparation. This may be 10% formalin, but suitable antibiotic preparations are to be preferred as they have a gentle, more specific action. Then, the treated group should be kept entirely separate from the healthy animals so that the former can be handled and re-treated at something like weekly intervals. After this period the sheep can then rejoin the main flock, but any that seem incurable are best culled as they may be a constant source of re-infection and very costly to maintain. It is as well to try and choose a suitable period to carry out this eradication programme and the driest summer weather is best.

The metabolic diseases of sheep

There are three most important metabolic diseases of sheep — *pregnancy toxaemia* (or twin lamb disease), *milk fever* (lambing sickness) and *hypomagnesaemia* (grass staggers).

Pregnancy toxaemia (twin lamb disease)
This is a disease of ewes which affects them in the last few weeks of pregnancy and nearly always in ewes which are carrying more than one lamb. First symptoms are of incoordination but the affected ewes quickly become totally recumbent and comatose and will invariably die unless treated.

The condition to some extent is due to excessive demands being made on the ewes' metabolism when associated with insufficient nutrition. Affected ewes may have injections of intravenous glucose solution together with dosing with glycerine and/or glucose solutions. However, most of the effort should go into prevention. The important and indeed essential requirement is that during the last six weeks of pregnancy the ewe is given a diet which is low in fibre, nutritious and easily digested. The nutritional problem is often exacerbated by the bad conditions which may face the ewes in the winter months, diverting the feed being given from building up strength, to keeping the ewe alive in the face of the cold. As with most metabolic disorders, the condition is not simply a deficiency and it appears to be especially likely to occur if there is some stress, be it environmental or nutritional, late in pregnancy (see also Chapter 4).

Milk fever (lambing sickness)
This is virtually the same as in the dairy cow with a serious fall of blood calcium occurring soon after lambing and associated with the rapid production of milk by the ewe. The symptoms are depression and coma. Treatment is an immediate injection of calcium borogluconate given either intravenously or subcutaneously.

Hypomagnesaemia (grass staggers)

This is caused by a low level of magnesium in the blood, the effect being usually sudden death without any symptoms. Alternatively there may be some symptoms of hyper-excitability which eventually lead to coma and death. The problem usually occurs soon after lambing. The highest incidence is in ewes on chalk soil and during cold and wet weather. It is a condition associated with intensive husbandry and with rather excessively lush pasture. The treatment is to administer as quickly as possible an injection of a magnesium solution.

Prevention is not easy. The cause of the problem is, as with cattle, a shortage of magnesium. In one way or another this has to be provided. Supplementary feeding with a mixture of molasses and magnesium, using a special feeder is good, the molasses making an unpalatable magnesium mixture into a palatable one. The best method, however, is to use a magnesium 'bullet'. This consists of a heavy magnesium rich ball or 'bullet' which is given to the ewe and which lodges in the reticulum. The magnesium is absorbed over a number of weeks and will safely carry the ewe over the danger period.

Diseases causing abortions

There are several diseases that lead to abortions – viral, bacterial and parasitic – and their economic importance can be very great. It should also be noted that in sheep, as in all animals, any disease that has a serious generalised effect during pregnancy can lead to abortion.

Enzootic abortion

This is caused by a chlamydial organism and tends to be common in certain well-defined areas; in the UK it is especially prevalent in N.E. England and S.E. Scotland. The infection is usually introduced into a flock by a 'carrier' which releases a great amount of infected material when it aborts. This infects the ewe lambs which will not abort the first season but will abort in the second. After abortion they are then immune but young sheep and bought-in animals will continue to become infected.

There is no specific treatment for infected animals but it is good policy to isolate the ewes which have aborted for the period when they may be discharging infected material. Thereafter a policy of vaccination may need to be instituted. Good vaccines are available and will protect the non-infected animals satisfactorily – one administration being sufficient for life.

Salmonellosis

Salmonella abortion is an acute and contagious condition caused by the bacteria *Salmonella abortus ovis,* and can also be caused by the non-specific salmonellae, such as *S. typhimurium* and *S. dublin.* It is a condition that is present in virtually all sheep-rearing countries and tends to cause abortions late in pregnancy. The disease does not give rise to specific symptoms – clinically it can be indistinguishable from other causes of abortion – and it is thus imperative to seek professional advice, including a laboratory examination, to be certain of the agent. Once the cause is known measures of control can be instituted, including antibiotics or chemotherapy, vaccination and hygienic measures.

Vibriosis

Vibrionic abortion, caused by *Vibrio foetus var. intestinalis,* is another bacterial cause of abortion which, like salmonella infections, causes late abortions. There is no specific treatment but vaccines are available to control the condition.

Brucella

The Brucella species of bacteria can also cause abortion in sheep, the effects being the same as in cattle. *Brucella abortus, Brucella mellitensis* and *Brucella ovis* are all capable of causing the problems. After positive diagnosis, control relies on hygiene and vaccination.

Toxoplasmosis

There is also a parasitic cause of abortion in sheep which is due to a toxoplasma – *Toxoplasma gondii.* With this disease it is suggested the best course in an infected flock is to mix infested ewes with non-pregnant ones to stimulate natural immunity before pregnancy, but this is only a partially satisfactory approach.

The notifiable diseases of anthrax and foot and mouth disease also occur in sheep and the reader is referred to Chapter 3.

Table 6.1 The health of sheep: a summary of diseases, prevention and treatment

Disease	Prevention	Treatment
Black disease	Specific antiserum and vaccine. Avoid fluke-infested pastures.	Antibiotics, e.g. penicillin preparations.

Disease	Prevention	Treatment
Blackleg	Specific antiserum and vaccines.	Penicillin, ampicillin and antiserum.
Braxy	Specific antiserum and vaccines. Frosted food predisposes to infection.	Penicillin, ampicillin and antiserum.
Brucellosis	Specific vaccines.	Remove all infected animals from the flock.
E. coli (Colibacillosis)	Improved hygiene or new quarters. Antiserum or vaccines.	Antiserum. Broad spectrum antibiotics, e.g. clamoxyl. Supportive fluid therapy.
Enzootic abortion	Vaccination with oil-based vaccine.	Broad spectrum antibiotics will limit secondary infection if necessary.
Foot rot	Careful attention to feet by trimming, and foot baths of copper sulphate or formalin.	As *Prevention*, together with local antibiotic preparations, such as oxytetracycline.
Hypomagnesaemia	Magnesium preparations in food or 'licks'. Magnesium 'bullets'.	Intravenous magnesium solution.
Lamb dysentery	Specific antisera and vaccines.	Antiserum, supportive fluid therapy and antibiotics, such as clamoxyl.
Liver fluke	Attention to land drainage; destroy snails, the secondary hosts.	Diamphenethide.
Mastitis	Improve hygiene.	Inject antibiotic appropriate to infection and also administer via teat.
Milk fever	Administration of minerals including calcium by oral route or vitamin D by injection.	Calcium borogluconate injections.
Navel-ill	Improve hygiene of lambing quarters. Dress navel with antiseptic at birth.	Inject antibiotics with a broad spectrum of activity.
Orf	Specific vaccine.	Isolate and treat affected areas with antiseptics and antibiotics.
Pining	Dressing pasture with cobalt salt.	Dosing with cobalt chloride or administration of cobalt 'bullet'.
Pneumonia	Improve environment in housed sheep. Improve nutrition in all cases.	Antisera; vaccines; sulpha drugs; antibiotics, e.g. ampicillin.
Pregnancy toxaemia	Improved nutrition in pregnancy.	Glycerine; glucose; molasses.
Pulpy kidney disease	Antiserum and vaccines.	Antiserum and penicillin preparations by injection.

Disease	Prevention	Treatment
Rickets	Improved provision of minerals and vitamins.	Vitamin D by injection and minerals.
Roundworms	Improved pasture management to prevent infection and especially removal of lambs from contact with infected ground.	Thiabendazole; levamisole; organo-phosphorus compounds.
Salmonellosis	Vaccination where appropriate. Rigid hygiene.	Antibiotics, e.g. ampicillin.
Sheep scab	Rigid dipping of all sheep and following statutory obligations.	Dips include organo-phosphorus compounds, carbamates, gamma BHC.
Swayback	Administration of copper preparations to ewes in pregnancy.	None.
Tetanus	Antitoxin. Vaccine.	Antiserum; antitoxin; hexamine.
Vibriosis	Vaccination.	Broad spectrum antibiotics.

7 The Health of Poultry

The chick

The day-old chick is especially susceptible to every form of stress and the environmental conditions must be accurately maintained to avoid either chilling or overheating. Since most birds are now kept together in substantial numbers, unless sophisticated environmental control systems (see Figs 7.1 and 7.2) are used it is almost impossible to provide an optimal and uniform environment and whilst the conditions required by the chick are well-known, the ability of the housing to provide them properly is often lacking. Thus there may be almost immediate losses from chilling in certain areas of a house, but in

Fig. 7.1 Interior of controlled environment poultry house showing plenty of space, good lighting and clean, dry litter.

Fig. 7.2 It is important to give all young animals and birds plenty of space from as early an age as possible.

general the losses in the chicks in the first four or five days of life are after-effects of the management and health of the breeders or the management and hygiene of the hatchery.

Yolk-sac infection

This is also called 'mushy chick' disease, omphalitis or navel infection, and is undoubtedly the commonest of all conditions causing early mortality. The signs soon show themselves — the chicks so affected are usually normal when placed in the brooder house but make no progress and die mostly from about 36–72 hours after placement. Examination of the chick shows a 'blown-up' abdomen, a wet or scabby navel and a very offensive odour which is virtually diagnostic. If the abdomen is opened, it will be seen that the yolk sac is not absorbed but is filled with discoloured fluid, often brown and infection may have spread throughout the abdominal cavity. The infective agents that cause the disease are bacteria and *Escherichia coli* is frequently the main one involved.

The disease may be due to many different reasons, ranging from mismanagement or bad hygiene in the breeder flocks, to poor hatchery standards and inefficiency in the control of the incubator or hatchery.

There is usually a much bigger incidence in chicks hatched towards the end of winter or in early spring when the health and condition of the breeding flocks are usually at their poorest. No treatment will save those chicks affected but it is advisable to treat affected flocks since it may help to limit the spread of infection. The infected birds may release into the environment enormous numbers of pathogenic organisms so the following measures may be logically applied. The warmth of the house should be increased to assist the birds' resistance to infection and help to prevent huddling. Tests should be carried out in the laboratory to establish which organisms are involved and which treatment would be most appropriate. Then, medicate the drinking water with a vitamin and antibiotic mixture. All abnormal chicks should be culled. Careful investigation should be made of the hatchery or breeding organisation as to the likely cause. It is of great importance to do this and trace the source of the disease; if the breeding management is not informed it may be unaware of the problem and obviously no measures will be taken to stop it.

Aspergillosis (or brooder pneumonia)
This is the most important but by no means the only disease of poultry caused by a fungus and leads to early death in chicks. The fungus, usually *Aspergillus fumigatus*, is one which occurs widely on farms and in the countryside and can therefore readily contaminate hatching eggs. The fungus in natural conditions needs mouldy, damp conditions in which the moisture content is more than 20% — so it can be common, for example, if breeders are kept on damp litter or there is damp and dirty material in the nests. Hatching eggs can pick up the fungus in the nests or on the litter itself quite readily and the pathogen will then be taken through to the hatchery. If infection enters the hatchery and the fungus is not destroyed by fumigation, an almost explosive incidence can occur in the chicks and mortalities in the first few days of life may vary from a few up to 50% or even more on occasion. Alternatively the chicks can themselves pick up infection from damp and mouldy litter used as their bedding.

The signs of infection are of pneumonia, the chicks gasping and struggling for breath with their mouths open. Post mortem findings are of tiny yellowish-green nodules with a green furry extrusion in the lungs, bronchi, trachea and viscera, whilst the air sacs may be covered with thick yellow exudate. A laboratory will identify the fungus definitely; a sure diagnosis cannot be made by the naked eye or by the symptoms, which may be similar to other diseases.

There is no specific treatment. If outbreaks occur in chicks they provide an important warning that there are serious errors in hygiene and/or management, and it is vital that the areas of infection are located so that remedial steps can be taken. Control measures will include a culling of affected chicks, a more thorough disinfection of housing and equipment, removal of unsuitable litter or nesting material, and better cleaning and fumigation of hatching eggs and equipment and the hatchery. There has been a recent upsurge in aspergillosis due to the more frequent use of chopped straw as the litter in broiler and other poultry houses. The danger is present only if the straw becomes wet, with a more than 20% moisture content.

Salmonellosis

The group of bacteria known as salmonella is world-wide and one of the greatest causes of losses in poultry on a world scale. In many countries, including the UK, prolonged control measures have led to few losses nowadays in poultry due to salmonellosis. It must be stressed that overriding emphasis is now attached to an attempt — which we may well achieve before long — to eradicate salmonella diseases altogether from our birds because certain members of the species of bacteria are a principal cause of food poisoning in man. It will be appreciated that under intensive conditions there is an extra risk of contagion taking hold of many birds at one time, so it is highly desirable that all possible sources of infection are removed. A few areas of the world — notably in Scandinavia — have been able to rid themselves of salmonella infections in animals and man.

TYPES OF SALMONELLA INFECTION

There are two forms of the salmonella species which are specific to poultry; these are *Salmonella pullorum* and *Salmonella gallinarum*. The former, perhaps the oldest of all diseases diagnosed in poultry, used to be called bacillary white diarrhoea (BWD), whilst *S. gallinarum* is commonly called fowl typhoid. In addition there are those diseases in poultry caused by other salmonella and coming under the general title of salmonellosis or sometimes termed avian paratyphoid. There are many different forms — at least 200 types of salmonella have been found in poultry — but the most important is *S. typhimurium*, which can be a virulent killer of chicks in particular.

SYMPTOMS

The symptoms of the various forms of salmonella infection vary considerably. Mortalities are extremely variable, ranging from no more than 1 or 2% up to as much as 50% or even more. If chicks, for example, are infected with pullorum disease via the infected hen and thereby spread through the hatchery, signs of illness will occur within a matter of hours of hatching. In cases where the infection is light and the environment and husbandry good, the losses can be modest but early losses from salmonella infection more usually run at between 10 and 20% and may extend over two weeks. Chicks dying early on in life usually die quickly with few symptoms but as the disease proceeds, symptoms progressively appear of huddling, inappetance, constant cheeping, a swollen abdomen, and white diarrhoea. There are also chronic cases in which numbers of chicks are stunted, scour, and experience lameness due to swollen joints. These symptoms are much the same for all forms of salmonella infection in chicks and growing birds and it is quite impossible from these symptoms to distinguish either which form of salmonella is present or indeed whether it is a salmonella disease at all.

In the adult, acute salmonella infection is typically that known as *fowl typhoid*, due to *Salmonella gallinarum*. Signs that would lead to suspecting an attack would be when a number of birds scour with greenish-yellow and evil smelling droppings, have a greatly increased thirst, show very pale (anaemic) head parts and there are also a number of sudden deaths. As mortality may go as high as 75%, with 50% being common, this is a disease which is hardly likely to be missed.

Post mortem signs in the chick are not diagnostic but are at least strongly suspicious. If the bird dies at the hyper-acute stage the signs are few, apart from congestion of internal organs, especially the liver and lungs. In later cases, where the infection is not acute or sub-acute, the liver and other internal organs show characteristic yellowish nodules and the caecal tubes often contain semi-solid yellow 'casts'. The yolk sac may likewise be filled with a pus-like 'sludge'. In the adult, the post mortem signs in pullorum or gallinarum infection are similar and especially associated with the ovary in which the ovules are grossly misshapen and the contents are also abnormal. Other internal organs may be infected, including the heart which shows inflammation of the membranes around it (pericarditis). These generally diagnostic symptoms in the adult are only rarely seen with the other forms of salmonella.

THE CONTROL OF SALMONELLA INFECTIONS

With pullorum and gallinarum infections, simple and rapid on-the-spot blood tests have been in use for many years and can detect carriers with great accuracy. These tests have been enormously successful since they enable immediate removal of the carrier birds from a flock. Thus the two diseases caused by *Salmonella pullorum* and *S. gallinarum* have been controlled with great success in many countries, including the United Kingdom. Under these circumstances only few isolated cases turn up from time to time detected by the blood tests and regular testing may be necessary only on the foundation breeding stock.

Unfortunately the position with regard to other types of salmonella is entirely different and somewhat confusing. There are some 200 different serotypes that have been isolated from poultry. A few can be quite devastating in their effect, such as *Salmonella typhimurium*; others are mild or cause no symptoms at all. In every case infection may spread to other livestock or man. It is probable, however, that the main risk is not that the poultry will infect other forms of life, but that other livestock will infect poultry!

In general the symptoms of salmonella infection in chicks are similar to those seen in pullorum disease and indeed it is possible only to distinguish the cause by laboratory examination. Post mortem lesions do not enable more than suspicions to be raised though there is always the likely involvement of the liver, which is usually enlarged and congested.

Because of the great value in attempting to eliminate salmonellosis from poultry, many countries including the UK have legislation that requires compulsory notification of salmonella infections to the authorities. Unfortunately there is no simple serological or plate test for the detection of the salmonella species other than the host-specific pullorum and gallinarum. Detection depends on isolation and identification of the causal organism and this is often a laborious procedure.

Salmonella eradication is important for several reasons. A number of the salmonellae which infect poultry can be serious causes of food poisoning in man and it is therefore of great public health importance that birds entering the processing plant, in particular, are clear of salmonella either from obvious clinical infections or as symptomless carriers of the disease organisms.

Salmonella in poultry flocks originates from a number of sources. It may come from foodstuffs, especially the animal protein element. In order to control the entry of salmonella infection via foodstuffs, it is necessary for all protein foods of animal source and used in feed-stuffs to be heat-treated before they are used. All foodstuffs, how-ever, may be polluted with the infected droppings of birds or vermin. Infection may also originate from other livestock but nowadays it is general to avoid keeping at least large flocks and especially breeders in the presence of other animals.

It is laudable and by no means too ambitious an aim to eliminate the main pathogenic salmonellae from poultry flocks. A programme for eradication would include monitoring breeder flocks for sal-monella bacteria in birds and litter, and also monitor food and probably pelleting the food, since the heat in the process reduces the infectivity rate. Special care would be taken of the hygiene in the hatchery and sampling of danger areas, together with appropriate hygienic steps in the processing plant. No use would be made of treated birds for breeding. Certain drugs, such as the nitrofurans, are very effective in treating the disease but leave 'carriers', so it is unsafe to keep treated birds once infected other than for slaughter for food. In the latter case suitable precautions must be taken to eliminate risks in the processing plant.

Gumboro disease (infectious bursal disease)

This is an extremely serious virus infection which occurs in most areas of the world. It was first reported in 1962 in the USA and very soon afterwards appeared in the UK and Western Europe. The symptoms of the disease generally first show as an acute infection of sudden onset in young chicks, mostly broilers, then a quick peak of mortality — followed by a return to normality which leaves a sub-stantial number of birds stunted in their growth and very unproductive. Affected chicks show anorexia, depression, huddling, ruffled feathers, vent pecking, diarrhoea, trembling and incoordination. The most significant post mortem sign is an extreme inflammation of the bursa of Fabricius (see Fig. 7.3) which will be greatly enlarged and oedematous — subsequently, after the inflammatory period, becoming small and shrivelled. Haemorrhages may be seen here and in the muscles of the body and the kidneys will be swollen, pale and contain urate deposits.

Whilst the disease may not cause a high mortality — usually in the region of 5% — the other effects of the disease can be even more serious. The virus, by adversely affecting the bursa of Fabricius, causes profound damage to the whole immunological system of the chicken. The chick may suffer in consequence from other diseases, especially as it may now be unable to get proper protection from

Fig. 7.3 Gumboro disease (IBD). The bursa of Fabricius on the left is normal; that on the right has almost disappeared after infection with Gumboro disease.

vaccines. In many ways it is this last effect which is the most serious one and will be considered further in this chapter.

There are a number of live and inactivated vaccines available throughout the world but only a limited number may be licensed for use in some countries. For example, in the UK only two are currently licensed. This is because it is extremely unwise to use a vaccine which causes such a strong reaction which, whilst it will protect against Gumboro disease, will also cause damage to the immunity system of the bird (termed immuno-suppression). The vaccines currently in use in the UK appear capable of controlling infection in young birds, and when given to adults enable a passive immunity to be passed to the chick to last several weeks after hatching. One live and two inactivated vaccines are available.

The infectious stunting syndrome

A new and rather alarming condition was recognised in broilers in 1981. Known as infectious stunting syndrome (and also malabsorption syndrome and pale bird syndrome) the symptoms are of large scale stunting in the birds so that, by the time the birds reach their normal finishing weight of about 2 kg, up to 20% may weigh only about half this amount (see Fig. 7.4). Birds do not die from the disease but they are, needless to say, grossly uneconomic. The affected birds show very poor feathering and the characteristic post mortem signs are confined to abnormalities of the pancreas.

The disease appears to be due to a virus — it is a transmissible condition showing rapid contagion — and is believed, in the USA, to be an adenovirus where a vaccine is available. Attempts to identify it as an adenovirus in the UK have so far failed and the only measures one can advise at present are to treat the day-old chicks suspected of carrying the virus with soluble vitamins, electrolytes and broad spectrum antibiotics. It appears that infected breeder flocks produce chicks carrying this virus for a limited period only, similar to viral arthritis. The most recent indications in the UK are that the disease is caused by a calcivirus, and a vaccine is currently 'under test'.

Clostridial diseases

There is a significant number of clostridial bacteria capable of causing disease on the poultry farm. Clostridial bacteria are a large group which are capable of 'building up' as a problem if the site is kept unhygienically, is overstocked or badly constructed. Diseases caused by clostridia are malignant oedema (or gangrenous dermatitis), necrotic enteritis, and botulism. Clostridial organisms may also be found in association with many other diseases as 'secondaries', for example, in yolk sac infection. There is also strong evidence that the weakening of the birds' immunity by Gumboro disease may be the forerunner to certain of these, especially malignant oedema. Clostridia can also be serious hatchery pathogens.

Fig. 7.4 Turkeys in a pole-barn. Essentially healthy, a stunted bird can nevertheless be observed perching on the feeder, providing a high risk of cross-infection, especially if the stunting is due to a virus.

MALIGNANT OEDEMA (GANGRENOUS DERMATITIS)

Malignant oedema is an unpleasant and serious disease of broilers caused by *Clostridium septicum* which has become more common recently. It occurs towards the end of the growing cycle and may cause massive loss – even up to 50% of the birds. The effect is to cause gangrene of the muscle and of the skin so that the birds in a sense 'fall apart' whilst still alive.

It is often stated and believed that malignant oedema is associated with bad hygiene practices, the re-use of old litter for example, and also over-stocking and bad environmental conditions. There is probably a measure of truth in this but the disease can certainly occur without any of these being obvious and I have seen its devastating effects in flocks which are kept impeccably. What is known, however, is that it often happens after birds have had their immunity suppressed with diseases, such as Gumboro disease, or there have been other debilitating diseases, such as inclusion body hepatitis (see later in this chapter). Also it should be noted that whilst *C. septicum* may be the main infective agent with malignant oedema it is by no means the only one involved; *Staphylococcus aureus* is often the predominating bacteria. Thus, whilst penicillin-G is the antibiotic of choice to deal with this infection where clostridial organisms are involved, it may be less effective against staphylococcus. It is also important where outbreaks occur to consider carefully the programme for controlling Gumboro disease because outbreaks of this condition so often precede the attacks of malignant oedema. Perhaps the most effective preventive medication is with the synthetic penicillin 'Penbritin' (Beecham Laboratories), as this has a wide spectrum of activity, including both clostridial and staphylococcal species of bacteria.

NECROTIC ENTERITIS

This is also a disease which is more usually found in broilers than in other types of chicken though not exclusively so. The clostridium involved is *C. welchii* and the condition may lead to a mortality of up to 10%. Lesions are confined to the small intestine which is grossly inflamed and distended.

This clostridial disease, like others, has often been found in poultry houses with earth or chalk floors where the disease organisms can build up in certain areas which are probably inadequately cleaned or disinfected. Fortunately earth floors are becoming more of a rarity but where they are used it is worth emphasising that they can still be disinfected reasonably with the modern materials available (see Chapter 1). Preventive or curative treatment is effective using appropriate penicillin preparations.

BOTULISM
This is another disease of poultry caused by a clostridium (*C. botulinum*) which has occurred predominantly in broilers and can cause heavy mortality. I have seen cases of 20% losses in birds near the killing age of 45 days. The course of this disease is rather different from other clostridia insofar as the organisms multiply in the gut releasing a toxin which causes paralysis of the muscles, especially of the head and neck.

Fortunately it is relatively uncommon. The type of clostridium causing botulism in chickens is *not* the same as causes the disease in man. There is no treatment for poultry suffering from this condition but outbreaks are usually associated with dirty, badly managed sites.

Inclusion body hepatitis (IBH)
IBH is a relative newcomer to the poultry field, also associated mainly with broiler chickens. It occurs generally in the period 30–50 days of age. It has no special symptoms except that in a flock which is probably growing very well and apparently in the best of health, a sudden heavy mortality arises which may give a loss of up to about 10%. Post mortem signs are confined usually to the liver and kidneys, the former being much enlarged and containing many haemorrhages, whilst the kidneys are also enlarged with haemorrhages throughout. A laboratory examination should be made to confirm the presence of this disease which is caused by a virus.

Fatty liver kidney syndrome (FLKS)
This is an interesting and relatively common disease of chickens between about 7 and 35 days of age. The symptoms are indefinite; usually there is a rather higher mortality than there should be, and a few birds will be seen lying face downwards and apparently paralysed. Post mortem of affected birds shows a pale, swollen liver with haemorrhages — with the heart also pale and the kidneys swollen and usually inflamed. It should be noted that it is usually the best birds which are affected by this condition and it is associated with excessive levels of fat deposition.

CAUSE
It has now been established that FLKS is a disease induced by feeding high levels of wheat or other carbohydrate feed with lower

than normal levels of protein so that the ratio between carbohydrate and protein is too wide. It has also been confirmed that if diets containing these incorrect levels are fed, then supplementation of the diet with biotin at levels between 0.05 mg/kg and 0.10 mg/kg of feed will prevent FLKS. Now that this fact is known, the condition is less common but it does occur from time to time due to omission by the compounders of added biotin.

Respiratory diseases of chicks

With the increase in the intensity and size of poultry units an enormous surge has occurred in the incidence of respiratory diseases. As a group these are the most important causes of ill-health in poultry in almost all parts of the world. It is unusual nowadays to find respiratory disease in an uncomplicated form. The usual pattern is for one or more primary virus infections, acute or chronic, to be followed by secondary bacterial invaders in which strains of *E. coli* usually predominate. Preventive techniques are all-important since once respiratory disease has developed in a flock, and especially in the young birds, losses by mortality, or poor growth and food conversion can be so severe that it may be extremely difficult to stop a catastrophic economic loss.

The general approach to preventing losses cannot be easily generalised because the types of infection and their incidence vary a great deal geographically. If there is a high incidence, say of Newcastle disease and/or infectious bronchitis which are two of the main diseases, a central plank in the preventive policy will be to protect the birds by vaccination. The strains of vaccine to be used, and their frequency of use will depend on the local challenges that predominate and the parental immunity of the chicks. This parental immunity may have been derived from infection in the parent flock or from a suitable vaccination policy. As well as protection by vaccination, which will always be concerned with protecting birds from the primary viral agents, there may also be useful ways of protecting the birds against the secondary bacterial infections by medicating the stock with antibiotics or chemotherapeutic agents, either in the food or drinking water. Finally, all these measures should be supported by good husbandry, such as the application of warmth, improving the air flow, adding litter and changing lighting systems. We are faced once again with the salient fact that the seriousness of respiratory infections will depend predominantly on the influence of management and housing (see Fig. 7.5).

Fig. 7.5 A large deep pit poultry unit with ventilation extracting air from the droppings pit to prevent gases passing into the poultry housing above the pit.

INFECTIOUS BRONCHITIS

Universally this is the most widely experienced respiratory disease and is caused by a highly contagious virus. There are a number of strains and whilst most affect primarily the respiratory system there are some varieties, now apparently on the ascendant in many parts of the world, which also have a serious effect on the kidneys, causing what is known as the uraemic form of the disease.

Symptoms

The most noticeable sign in the young chick is a large amount of respiratory noise. Birds sneeze, gasp and shake their head; and in a large flock the best way of detecting early signs is to 'look and listen'. Enter the house very quietly, or if the birds are disturbed by your entry, wait until they are still. If you look you will see their heads shaking and probably an uneven spread of birds. The 'snicking' of the birds will be clearly heard and is almost symptomatic. Early diagnosis is vital because it enables medication to be started immediately. If the disease is allowed to advance unchecked the respiratory noise will usually get worse, with eye-watering, nasal discharge and increasing mortality, followed by secondary infections that take over so the original infection may be completely masked.

If the only infection is the infectious bronchitis virus, the disease could be over within a week to a fortnight, but it is rare for there to be such a happy outcome. Nevertheless, if the disease is uncomplicated the effect can be mild and recovery can be complete, rather like the common cold in man. What usually happens in practice is that as soon as the birds show signs of sickness they start huddling together and this provides the ideal media for the propagation of other infections; viral or bacterial, but often apparently dominated by *E. coli.*

In older birds infectious bronchitis can have two profound effects on the female. Infection in the immature female can prevent development of the oviduct, partially or completely, so that the bird will lay few, if any, eggs. In the other case, if the flock is adult and laying it will lead to a massive drop in egg production, which may partially recover, but in addition there will tend to be, after a time, the production of poor quality eggs and egg shells. Eggs are often of strange shapes, the egg shells are ridged and lack pigment and the white of the egg is watery.

When layers are affected egg production will usually fall dramatically and may recover to normal over a period of weeks. However, this seldom happens and usually only partial recovery takes place. The economic loss is hence very serious. It is even worse for the poultry breeder because a bronchitis infection during production can lower not only egg numbers and quality but also affect fertility and hatchability adversely. All this together emphasises the importance of giving susceptible birds protection by a complete vaccination programme if there is a fair risk of a challenge with the field virus.

Post mortem signs in chicks affected with the respiratory form will include the detection of catarrh in the trachea, congested lungs and cloudy air sacs. When the kidneys are affected, they appear considerably enlarged, and white with the deposition of urates. Sometimes urate deposits are seen throughout the body cavities. The effect on the oviduct is to reduce it in size, sometimes so much that it is almost absent, whilst with the mature bird the misshapen ova are diagnostic.

Diagnosis

The symptoms of infectious bronchitis after an incubation period of 1—4 days appear to be so reasonably straightforward that they would allow a clinical diagnosis to be effected without laboratory tests, but because the occurrence of the disease is rarely without other intruders, it is often necessary to have samples tested at the laboratory to be certain. For example, the milder forms of Newcastle disease or mycoplasmosis can produce rather similar symptoms. In any case, once the secondaries have come up to have their damaging effects, the diagnostic signs have all been very well masked. Thus plenty of use is made of the various tests which are either by virus isolation or by specific antibodies in the sera. The great advantage of having a positive diagnosis done is that whilst it is most likely that the result will not be in time to influence the treatment that will be used in the flock in question, it may be possible to plan or modify future control measures in the light of this information.

Control
Details of the approach to the control of the disease are given at the end of the section on Newcastle disease because it is best to consider the control of these two similar diseases together.

NEWCASTLE DISEASE (ND)
Just like infectious bronchitis, Newcastle disease tends to occur throughout the world wherever there are large poultry populations. Whilst the first outbreak that was reported and described occurred in Newcastle, England in 1927, this resulted from an importation of the most virulent form of the disease from the Far East. The first outbreaks that occurred in those days were nearly all extremely virulent and killed off virtually all affected and in-contact birds. Since that time, various other forms of the disease have occurred, many being much milder in extent and others somewhere between the two extremes. At the time of writing the most virulent cases appear to occur in the warmer countries, and the milder cases in the more temperate climates. The last serious outbreak in the United Kingdom of really virulent ND started in Essex in 1970 but the so-called Essex 70 strain which could cause almost 100% mortality seems currently to have been replaced by field infections which do not appear to be very much worse than vaccine strains.

Symptoms
The incubation period of ND is usually 2–7 days but it may be prolonged for up to three weeks. Normally the first signs in a flock are an unusual lassitude and indifference to food and water throughout the flock. This complete lack of the normal reactions of lively birds is quite symptomatic. There may be signs of respiratory distress, some birds apparently struggling for breath, with weird high pitched 'cries' issuing forth in isolated cases — a symptom which does not

seem to occur with any other disease. There is likely also to be a green, watery diarrhoea, and the appearance of nervous symptoms which does not occur with the other respiratory diseases. The nervous signs show up as a drooping of either one or both wings, incoordination, falling over and paddling of the legs and twitching and twisting of the neck muscles.

If these three main groups of symptoms are found in a flock then the presence of ND is fairly certain. But a diagnostic check should always be made and in any case it is unlikely that the pattern would be quite so logically presented as may seem implied. Only some of the symptoms might be seen. Confusion can occur with several other diseases; also, if some protection has been afforded by parenteral immunity or partial vaccination, the end picture would be a very different one. For example, in layers the only effect might be a drop in the egg production and egg quality without a subsequent return to normality. It will already be apparent that confusion with infectious bronchitis could be very easy, and there are many more diseases which could be confused with it.

Post mortem signs
Some or all of the following signs may be seen. The respiratory tract is usually inflamed, the air sacs are cloudy and there are small haemorrhages — known as 'petechiae' — on the heart and especially the proventriculus. There is often a great deal of caseous (dried pus-like) material in the trachea and bronchi and haemorrhages can be seen on the mucous membranes of the respiratory system.

Diagnosis
Clinical symptoms as described, together with the most prominent post mortem signs may be sufficient to be almost sure but it is nearly always necessary to have laboratory tests done. This may be done by virus isolation and/or serological testing, mostly using the Haemagglutination Inhibition test.

Control measures
If we start with the chick, in most cases where the disease is prevalent it will be necessary to vaccinate all parent flocks very thoroughly. It is then likely that the chicks will be born with a good immunity. There may not seem, therefore, very much point in an immediate vaccination and, whilst this is not entirely untrue, there are good practical reasons in large flocks to give some protection almost as soon after hatching as possible. One reason is that in large

houses of many thousands of birds there will almost certainly be some chicks which do not have an immunity. Thus, an early vaccination will protect them. Furthermore, if an early vaccination is given, it has been found that later vaccinations will cause less stress. The problem of stress cannot be exaggerated. The vaccines now used on chicks by water or spray administration are very effective but they are live and mildly virulent. Properly used they will cause no harmful effects but if incorrectly or carelessly used they are quite capable of causing a severe reaction which may be followed by secondary infections that can be almost as bad as the disease.

Protection of the birds

(a) *Newcastle disease*. For Newcastle disease there are three widely used vaccines, two being live vaccines (Hitchner B1 and La Sota) and one an inactivated oil-based vaccine. The first two are administered by spray, drinking water, or occasionally eye-drop, whilst the oil-based vaccine is given by injection. B1 is a safe 'gentle' vaccine which, when given by mass techniques, especially a spray, gives instant protection but protects for only a few weeks. La Sota is a little more stressful but is still mild and will protect for up to 12 weeks in the maturer bird. Now there are additional 'Clone' vaccines with extremely mild effect but better protection. The oil-based vaccine by injection is most frequently used in the older bird — commonly at point of lay — and will protect for a laying season but does not give immediate protection. Nevertheless it seems that within this 'armoury' of vaccines we can usually find the protection needed for any set of circumstances, though in countries where the most virulent forms of Newcastle disease are present, it is usual to have some of the more powerful vaccines available, such as the Komarov. These have the disadvantage that they cause very considerable stress on the birds, and hence most countries will not license their use. In the UK a 'slaughter policy' has just been instituted which removes the use of vaccines and replaces it by slaughtering any infected flocks. The Veterinary Service is also prepared to 'ring' vaccinate a serious outbreak in order to assist in its containment.

(b) *Infectious bronchitis*. There are three commonly used vaccines to protect birds against infectious bronchitis. These are two live vaccines, the relatively mild Massachusetts type H120, which is used early in life and gives immediate and limited protection, and the H52, which gives a much longer protection and can be used to cover

Fig. 7.6 The Turbair droplet sprayer can be used for vaccination, insecticides and disinfectant.

the laying period. Additionally and recently an oil-based inactivated vaccine has been produced which, if given to a bird 3—4 weeks before the laying period, will protect it through the whole of lay. It must be emphasised that full protection must be provided at all stages of development, not only to ensure that the birds throw off any challenge that might cause respiratory disease, but also because of the danger that if a potential layer or breeder contracts the disease during its development, the reproductive organs can be so damaged that egg production will be profoundly affected.

Table 7.1 sets out certain programmes of protection which can be used either as general routine protection where indicated, or for special emergencies or where there are severe challenges. It is well to stress that even in the presence of Newcastle disease it is possible to spray birds with a large droplet (about 50 microns size or above), and this may arrest the disease on the site since the vaccine particles have a 'blocking' effect by giving localised protection via the cells of the respiratory mucous membranes. In this connection I would also emphasise the virtues of the large particle size spray, such as the 'Turbair' (see Fig. 7.6), as compared with the small particle aerosol

Table 7.1 Newcastle disease and infectious bronchitis vaccination by the use of a large particle spray, or via drinking water or by injection. (N.B. No Newcastle disease vaccines may be used in the United Kingdom.)

Age	Method	Vaccine		Remarks
		Broilers	Breeders/Layers	
1–4 days General sensitising dose.	Spray.	B1 and H-120	B1 and H-120	Helps to reduce stress from subsequent vaccination.
Primary vaccination 12–14 days.	Spray.	B1 and H-120	B1	No necessity to use both if risk is small
Secondary vaccination 22–28 days.	Spray.	B1 or La Sota	B1 or La Sota	No necessity to use both if risk is small.
35–42 days.	Spray.	B1 or La Sota	B1 or La Sota	Final vaccination for broilers; unnecessary if low risk.
10 weeks.	Spray. La Sota H-52 in water.		La Sota or inactivated and H-52.	
Just before point of lay.	Spray or injection.		La Sota or inactivated for IB and ND.	Inactivated oil-based vaccines recommended for this application. La Sota live vaccine will give a much shorter immunity and necessitates revaccination during lay.

(i) Spray vaccination is generally more effective than drinking water application provided it is correctly applied. In those flocks in which coli-septicaemia is a major problem spray vaccination can increase this problem and on such premises drinking water application may be used as an alternative.

(ii) Spray vaccination works in two ways: it induces a rapid rise in antibody and also gives a useful measure of protection on respiratory surfaces themselves, known as 'Local Block'.

(iii) For boosting during lay, La Sota needs re-vaccinating after 5 months, but no re-vaccination is required with inactivated vaccines.

which is best *not* used. The latter penetrates deeply into the respiratory system and can cause a serious reaction. A method of using infectious bronchitis vaccine at day-old — if desired in the hatchery — has been developed by using the large particle spray with considerable success as it gives a minimum of reaction and a maximum of protection.

MYCOPLASMA INFECTION (CRD)

Mycoplasma are a group of organisms that cause a great deal of disease in the animal population. They are not dissimilar to, but are still quite distinct from bacteria, being smaller. They are also free-living, which distinguishes them from viruses.

In livestock they are associated mostly with respiratory diseases and the long-known poultry disease of 'chronic respiratory disease' is primarily caused by *Mycoplasma gallisepticum*. The usual signs of the disease in a flock are sneezing, snicking and coughing, inflamed and running eyes and swelling of the sinuses of the face. The lesions to be seen in the bird are likely to be confined to the respiratory tract and will consist of varying degrees of inflammation and exudates in the tract, lungs and the air sacs. The disease in itself can cause some mortality and loss of productivity but it is very often a precursor to the other respiratory diseases. It is more serious in its effects on the younger bird than the older one.

Control

Mycoplasmosis is a less contagious and less acutely virulent disease than the worst forms of Newcastle disease or infectious bronchitis. There is no vaccine to prevent it but nevertheless it may be controlled very effectively in several ways. The most satisfactory way is to build up an entire breeding enterprise that is free of disease by blood testing and elimination of infected birds. There are good serological tests and this procedure has been so successful that most breeding stock in the UK and USA and Western Europe are now free of *M. gallisepticum* infection. There are also several antibiotics that will successfully control the disease so these may be used in conjunction with a blood testing programme. Because the organisms can be transmitted from hen to chick via the egg, it is also recommended, in infected breeder flocks, to treat the hatching eggs by dipping them in suitable solutions containing anti-mycoplasmal drugs.

A related mycoplasma, *M. synoviae*, is also a widespread cause of disease. Whilst it is primarily a cause of lameness, due to the inflammation it causes in leg joints, it also retards growth and causes respiratory infections. Control measures are similar to those for *M. gallisepticum.*

INFECTIOUS LARYNGOTRACHEITIS (ILT)
Infectious laryngotracheitis is a highly virulent virus disease which is world-wide in incidence but is confined to certain areas. Symptoms are usually an extremely serious respiratory involvement with great distress exhibited by the birds as they struggle for breath, accompanied by coughing and rattling, and often with the bird depositing bloody mucus. There may also be less acute forms of the disease which are less severe but otherwise similar. Post mortem examination of birds with ILT shows severe inflammation of the larynx and trachea with bloody, cheesy 'clots' virtually filling the trachea. The virus that causes ILT does not affect any other organs and the birds die of asphyxiation.

Diagnosis can be made with a considerable degree of certainty from the symptoms, post mortem picture and history but it is advisable to have a laboratory check on specimens and if necessary seek virus isolation or serological tests.

Treatment and prevention
There is no drug available that will affect the virus of ILT and the only effect of treatment with antibiotics and vitamin supplement will be to assist the birds' resistance to secondary infection. There are, however, good vaccines available to prevent the disease, the modern ones being the modified live virus which may be given by the eye drop route.

It is important to emphasise that 'recovered' birds may remain as carriers of the infection for the rest of their lives. Thus in an eradication programme it is best to start by depopulating the entire site and then follow through with a most rigorous cleaning and disinfection programme. This is also one case at least where it would be advisable to leave the premises empty for a few weeks after the disinfection programme has been completed.

INFECTIOUS CORYZA (ROUP)
A bacterium *Haemophilus gallinarum* can cause a disease in poultry which is similar to the common cold in man. The symptoms are acute, leading to general inflammation, swelling and discharges around and from the eyes and nose. It does not appear to be a very serious problem nowadays in intensive units but vaccines are made which are effective in preventing it. It may be treated with antibiotics.

Internal parasites of chickens

COCCIDIOSIS

Coccidiosis is undoubtedly the most important parasitic disease of the domestic chicken and yet, because of the successful development of drugs to prevent and treat the condition, it is no longer a disease to be feared. Nevertheless, because it is always a potential threat which can cause serious loss, it is essential the poultryman knows when to suspect it and what to do in an emergency. He should also be aware of the range of drugs available and how they may be effectively used.

Coccidiosis of chickens is caused by protozoa (single-celled parasites) which live in the lining (epithelium) of the intestine. Those affecting chickens are of the species *Eimeria*. The life cycle of the various species in the chicken is as follows.

There is a massive multiplication of the coccidia (known as schizogony) and sexual multiplication (known as gametogony) within the chicken; then a stage of development takes place outside the host in which the eggs that are shed in sexual development reach a stage when they can infect other chickens, though they do not multiply. These are known as oocysts.

There are six main strains of Eimeria species which can cause diseases of the intestines in chickens. Each species causes rather different symptoms due to the Eimeria parasites of each strain having different favoured sites in the intestine. For example, the most common Eimeria are *E. tenella*, which affects only the caecal tubes and *E. necatrix*, which affects mainly the middle and lower intestine.

SYMPTOMS

The overall symptoms may be one or more of the following: bloody droppings, high mortality, general droopiness, emaciation, a marked drop in feed consumption, diarrhoea and egg production drop in layers. A proper diagnosis should be made by a veterinary laboratory.

Treatment and control of coccidiosis

Outbreaks of coccidiosis which occur may be treated with sulphonamides or combinations of sulphonamides and pyrimidines or amprolium, all given in the drinking water. Sulphamezathine or sulphaquinoxaline are usually given at 0.1% and 0.4% respectively in the drinking water for 5—7 days.

There is a wide range of coccidiostats used to prevent the disease during the growing period. At the present time in broiler feeds some of the most popular coccidiostats are based on monensin and arprinocid; also halofuginone, clopidol, robenidine and amprolium + ethopabate. Thus it can be seen, and this list is by no means exhaustive, that there are a number of drugs available for the prevention and treatment of coccidiosis. Changes in drugs are appropriate by careful planning to prevent resistance developing. Certain coccidiostats must also be withdrawn a specified number of days before birds are slaughtered to ensure there are no residues in the carcase. Because of this it may be necessary to use two anti-coccidial agents, even in the short life of a broiler, as it is risky to try and dispense with any prevention during the last 5–7 days of growth. Replacement birds should not be given an agent that completely destroys the parasites since no immunity develops.

Coccidial immunity
It is especially important with the disease of coccidiosis to know how immunity develops. If birds are to achieve immunity they must ingest a sufficient number of oocysts to produce some infection. These oocysts then go through several life cycles and multiply. Following exposure with a sufficient number of oocysts the bird will then become resistant to the disease. Immunity must be established for each individual species of coccidia because there is no cross immunity and thus birds can become immune to one species of coccidia yet still be vulnerable to others. Also, it is noteworthy that immunity is not permanent. It can be lost if the environment of the bird does not provide a sufficient level of re-exposure. In certain tests, loss of immunity was demonstrated within as short a period as ten weeks.

Two principles are used to achieve the gradual production of immunity as a means of controlling coccidiosis. The first is by the use of drugs at low level to reduce the severity of natural exposure and the second deliberate seeding of the litter with coccidia to provide a controlled exposure. It is much safer and reliable to use anti-coccidial drugs. With both of these methods it is possible to have an inadequate exposure with a resultant deficiency in immunity, or an excessive exposure leading to losses from the disease.

The most common technique to control coccidiosis is to give continuous preventive medication for a defined period with one of the anti-coccidial drugs in the food. Nearly all broiler chickens and most replacement breeding and egg production stock are given this treatment for a defined period but adult birds are not usually given preventive medication since they should have achieved immunity by then.

Withdrawal of coccidiostats

The difficulty must be stressed of dealing with the use and withdrawal of coccidiostats in rearing birds. The chicks will usually be put on a coccidiostat from hatching and this is likely to both control the disease and allow the chicks to build up an immunity so that by the time the drug is taken off – usually between 12–16 weeks of age – a satisfactory level of immunity has developed and the birds can safely withstand any subsequent challenge. Birds must be very diligently watched after the withdrawal period because they will suffer from an outbreak of the clinical disease if the challenge is too great, and will need treatment with one of the drugs or drug combinations mentioned above. The likelihood of a severe challenge may be related to the efficiency of management; for example, damp, wet litter following a period of satisfactory dry conditions might favour a sudden outburst of coccidial activity.

BLACKHEAD (HISTOMONIASIS)

Blackhead is another disease caused by a protozoan parasite, this one being called *Histomonas meleagridis*. Whilst it is primarily a disease of turkeys it may also affect young chickens in which the disease is mild. The symptoms include watery, yellowish diarrhoea, lethargy, weakness, and loss of appetite. Post mortem examination shows a marked inflammation, usually with cheesy cores, in the lumen of the caeca; on the liver a number of circular, yellowish-green depressions or ulcers about 12 mm in diameter may be observed.

There are a number of excellent drugs to prevent or cure blackhead, including, for example, Emtryl (May & Baker), Salfuride (Salsbury Laboratories) and Unizole (United Chemicals). The occurrence of blackhead in chickens indicates a need to improve hygiene and eliminate intestinal worm parasites since their eggs may carry the blackhead parasites.

THE TAPE WORM (*Davainea proglottina*)

Affected birds lose weight and are listless; breathing is rapid and feathers are ruffled and dry. In laying birds there is reduced egg production. At post mortem the intestinal mucosa may be thickened and haemorrhagic and the tape worms are seen. For development of the life cycle the intermediate hosts have to be present, such as snails and earthworms. Specific treatment should be used where the worms are found. Understandably, infection only takes place under extensive or semi-intensive conditions.

THE LARGE ROUND WORM (*Ascaridia galli*)

This is a large worm up to 80 mm in length which causes loss of condition, reduced egg production in layers and it can even cause death if infection is heavy. Retarded growth, listlessness and diarrhoea are the clearest symptoms. At post mortem the large round worms can be seen in the middle part of the small intestine. The disease is uncommon under hygienic conditions but certainly occurs if the litter is wet and overcrowded.

THE HAIR WORM (*Capillaria*)

The hair worm is a small parasite which affects the upper part of the alimentary tract causing diarrhoea, weakness, reduced egg production and anaemia. Affected birds are listless, weak and lose weight. Hygienic measures and treatment will be as with the other worms.

THE CAECAL WORM (*Heterakis gallinae*)

This is a worm of about 10 mm size which develops in the caeca and affects chickens and turkeys. Perhaps its most important 'function' is as a transmitter of the parasite causing blackhead (histomoniasis).

Treatments

There are adequate specific treatments to control the round and tape-worms. For example, piperazine products are safe and effective against roundworms, e.g. Biozine (Microbiologicals), Safersan (F.B.C.), and Piperazine (Beecham Animal Health). Also Nemicide (I.C.I. Pharmaceuticals), a product containing levamisole hydrochloride, is effective against roundworms. Whithelmin Premix (Beecham Animal Health), a premix for use in the food, contains haloxon and is useful as a treatment for worms in laying birds.

External parasites

Poultry can be infested with a variety of external parasites such as lice, fleas and various forms of mites, e.g. red mite, the depluming mite and scaly leg mite. These mites all burrow into various parts of the birds' skin and create considerable damage. The presence of all these conditions is rather uncommon under modern intensive management, and if general standards of hygiene are high it is doubtful if they will be seen at all. External parasites are more commonly associated with older birds and old-fashioned systems of continuous production. If they do occur, then it is advisable to deal with them energetically as they will have a highly debilitating effect on the birds and may also be associated with the spread of other diseases.

Treatment will depend on the administration (see Fig. 7.7) of one of the effective products which are listed later in Table 7.2. Of course it need hardly be emphasised that if birds are badly infested, especially with the mites, they should be culled as they are unlikely to respond very effectively to treatment, and they will remain as serious sources of infection.

Important viral diseases of principally young chickens

Viral arthritis (tenosynovitis)

A widespread form of viral arthritis is quite common in broiler chickens from about 4 weeks onwards. The signs are of serious lameness in the birds, coupled with poor growth rates and bad food conversion efficiencies. In the affected birds the flexor tendon sheaths running along the posterior of the tarsometatarsal bones are seen to be swollen, giving the shanks a very enlarged appearance. The sheaths of the gastrocnemius tendons just above the hocks are also swollen. In advanced cases the tendons themselves may frequently rupture. At post mortem the sheaths can be seen to be oedematous,

Fig. 7.7 Pyrethrins-in-oil being applied in a 3 tier cage unit through the Turbair Flydowner 12 battery-powered ULV sprayer for insect control. Birds are not disturbed, due to the low noise level of the sprayer and unobtrusive nature of the fine spray.

looking almost like gelatine in appearance. There is usually no pus in the inflamed tissues and the remainder of the bird appears almost normal.

A tentative diagnosis on the basis of the clinical signs can usually be made but confirmation depends upon viral isolation and identification.

There seems little doubt that the virus causing this condition is widely spread among the world's poultry industries but only certain broiler flocks are without maternal immunity and are challenged. Thus, the practical incidence of the disease is quite limited. There is no cure for the condition but when flocks are affected the administration of an antibiotic with a wide spectrum of activity plus soluble vitamin preparations is a justified veterinary procedure in order to limit the effect of the disease, guard against secondaries, such as staphylococci and clostridia, and help to overcome the effects of inappetance and poor growth.

Epidemic tremor (infectious avian encephalomyelitis (IAE))

Epidemic tremor is caused by a virus of chickens leading to nervous signs and symptoms in young birds. Whilst birds of all ages can be infected it is only in birds up to about 8 weeks of age that the characteristic nervous signs are normally seen. In laying birds an attack causes a drop in egg production of about 10%, which is soon over, but a drop in hatchability also occurs.

Affected chicks show incoordinate movements, falling, collapsing, then becoming prostrate and finally dying. If the chick is picked up and rested in the palm of the hand the tremors of the muscle, which are quite characteristic of the disease, may be felt. Usually about 10–15% of the flock are affected and most of them die, though a few make a complete recovery.

A definite diagnosis is made on microscopic examination of the brain and central nervous system where specific changes take place.

ROUTE OF INFECTION

The virus infects chicks in two ways. The first route is from the dam to the chick via the ovaries. The second is that after hatching the virus can enter by the mouth or respiratory system. If chicks are infected via the ovary, they contract the disease within about 7 days of hatching. If the chicks are infected by the oral route, they will become diseased from about 3 weeks onwards.

Fig. 7.8 Typical case of Marek's disease, showing paralysis of one wing.

CONTROL

Fortunately excellent live vaccines are now available to control epidemic tremor. The procedure undertaken is to vaccinate breeders to protect them against falls in egg production and hatchability and also to prevent the transfer of infection to their chicks. Vaccination is given between 10–16 weeks of age. Provided it is done within this period, protection should be satisfactory for the rest of the life.

Marek's disease and lymphoid leucosis

Both Marek's disease (see Fig. 7.8) and lymphoid leucosis are very important conditions leading to neoplasia (tumours) in chickens and caused by two groups of viruses. Marek's disease is caused by a strongly cell-associated herpesvirus, whilst leucosis is caused by some of the so-called RNA tumour virus group of oncornaviruses. The major manifestations of both diseases are lymphoid neoplasia but in other respects the two conditions differ widely.

Marek's disease was one of the most serious causes of loss in poultry before the relatively recent introduction of vaccines which has enabled its very successful control. It is a disease which causes proliferation of the lymphoid tissue, affecting most organs and tissues but especially the peripheral nerves. It affects chickens most commonly between 12 and 24 weeks of age, although it does occur occasionally in chickens from 6 weeks of age and sometimes, but rarely, in birds older than 24 weeks. The incubation period may vary from as little as 3 weeks to several months. There is one form of Marek's disease which is known as *acute Marek's*. This produces a very high mortality: up to 30% is quite common, and on occasions even as much as 80%. The disease may proceed in two ways: there may be a quick peak of mortality, rapidly falling away to almost nothing, over a period of a few weeks or, alternatively, it may reach a peak quite quickly and then continue without much change for months. Only a proportion of birds may show nervous signs of paralysis.

The alternative, and until recently the more common forms is that known as the *classical Marek's* disease. Mortality is usually less, rarely exceeding 10–15%. In some cases mortality proceeds only for a few weeks and in others it may go on for many months. The symptoms differ widely depending on which nerves are affected. Most often there is a progressive paralysis of the wings and legs. Badly affected birds cannot stand and, characteristically, birds are found lying on their sides with one leg stretched forward and the other held behind. In other cases the neck may be twisted, or the respiratory system may be involved, or even the intestines.

Post mortem signs are of diffuse lymphomatous enlargements of one or more organs or tissues — most often liver, gonads, spleen, kidneys, lungs, proventriculus and heart. Sometimes the lymphomas also arise in the skin associated with feather follicles and also in the skeletal muscles. In younger birds the liver enlargement is usually moderate in extent but in adults the greatly enlarged liver may appear identical to that in lymphoid leucosis.

CONTROL

There is no treatment for Marek's disease. Control depends on the rearing of young stock in isolation from older birds, the use of genetically resistant stock wherever possible, and above all else, by vaccination. There are two main types of vaccine — either a modified field strain of Marek's disease virus, or a turkey herpes virus — which is a virus antigenically closely related to Marek's disease virus and which is present in most turkey flocks. It is not pathogenic for turkeys or chickens and can be used very successfully for vaccination.

There are two forms of the vaccines produced. In one form the vaccine is used in association with the cells, and in the other the vaccines are freeze-dried. There is no evidence as to which is definitely the best and both can be recommended. The freeze-dried vaccine, which can be kept in an ordinary refrigerator, is much easier to store and handle than the cell-associated form which must be kept in liquid nitrogen containers at $-100°C$. However, some poultry men consider the immunity derived from the cell-associated form is better, perhaps because rather greater care must be taken in its handling.

All vaccines are normally used once only at one day old, and this is most conveniently given at the hatchery. Within a week a reasonable level of protection is obtained and this lasts a lifetime. In the last year or two there have been some unfortunate 'breakdowns' in properly vaccinated flocks. There is no evidence that this is due to any fault in the existing advice or techniques but it is a warning that correct methods of administration must be used. Such has been the concern in the poultry industry about the 'breakdowns' that some organisations are now advising a second vaccination at about two weeks of age.

LEUCOSIS
There are several different forms of avian leucosis. The commonest is lymphoid leucosis, in which there is usually an enlargement of the liver which is so grossly overgrown that it extends the full length of the abdominal cavity, whilst tumours may also affect any other organs of the body, the most common sites being the spleen, kidney and bursa of Fabricius. Another type is erythroid leucosis, which causes a serious anaemia due to the proliferation of excessive numbers of immature red blood cells. The liver, spleen and bone marrow become cherry red in this form. In contrast, in myeloid leucosis there is tumour formation in the liver and spleen, the liver often assuming the appearance of Morocco leather with a granular texture, due to the presence of a large number of discrete and nodular tumours of a chalky or cheesy consistency.

These lesions are all caused by a group of closely related RNA tumour viruses. Virus strains produce predominantly one form of leucosis but many will, in addition, produce lymphoid leucosis. The viruses can be identified by the presence of a group of specific antigen using the so-called Cofal test.

The course of the disease

Most commercial poultry have some measure of infection with certain groups of the leucosis viruses. The viruses are excreted in the droppings and the saliva and can readily infect in-contact birds. Also, a proportion of eggs are also infected passaging the virus through to the chick. Chicks receiving their infection through the eggs become tolerant to the virus and do not produce antibodies, whereas those infected after hatching respond with the production of viral anti-bodies. Chicks tolerant to the virus are more likely to succumb to disease and if they do not they shed virus in the eggs more consist-ently than chickens with circulating antibody. Lymphoid leucosis is the main form of disease developing after infection with leucosis virus. It is evident, however, that only about 2% of chickens die from lymphoid leucosis.

Control

There is no treatment and, because the infection is transmitted through the egg, management and hygiene methods are unable to control the disease. However, the viruses are not highly contagious and it is relatively easy to prevent infection of a flock from outside. If it is possible to free flocks from infection it is possible to maintain them and their progeny free of infection.

Genetic selection of stock resistant to infection with leucosis viruses creates a population resistant to infection with leucosis viruses and also reduces the number of birds capable of supporting infection.

Fowl pox

Fowl pox is a virus infection of the pox group which causes lesions in the head and mouth of the bird. It is also possible to find lesions on the legs and mucous membranes such as the cloaca. The lesions on the head and comb are usually wart-like in nature whilst those which occur in the mouth are 'diphtheritic' and have the appearance of a cheesy membrane. The general symptoms depend on the area of the body affected. The birds appear dull and when the mouth is affected may have difficulty in breathing and eating.

When the virus attacks the mucous membranes of the nasal and buccal cavities mortality can be as high as 40–50%. The virus causes a marked increase in the output of mucus and this is sometimes referred to as 'wet pox'. The less serious skin form of the disease does not lead to high mortality but can cause a reduced egg production in laying birds.

DIAGNOSIS AND TREATMENT
The symptoms are usually clear enough to make a diagnosis of the disease, though if there are doubts a veterinary laboratory can confirm.

It is not easy to treat affected birds but it is possible to remove the diphtheritic membranes from the mouth and the area around and then treat with antiseptics and emollients. Prevention can be achieved by using a live pox vaccine which can be administered by wing web or feather follicle application. Fowl pox is a relatively uncommon condition in temperate areas under intensive conditions but remains as a common complaint in warm climates where the systems are usually lacking good hygiene.

Egg drop syndrome 1976 (EDS '76)

For several years it has been known that a variety of viruses, so-called adenoviruses, can infect chickens. Whilst they may have an effect at any time of life the most serious strains cause sudden and prolonged falls in egg production and a profound effect on egg and shell quality. One particular strain first caused problems in 1976 in broiler breeder parents and has since been designated EDS '76. The condition has also spread to other adult birds but it is in breeders that the effect has been most serious. The syndrome has shown itself in a number of forms. There may be a failure of peak production or there may be gradual or sudden drops in egg production. The egg production of an affected flock may or may not return to normal. There is also a tendency for lowered hatchability, poor egg shell quality and loss of colour. Diagnosis of this condition requires expert examination since the symptoms can readily be confused with those of infectious bronchitis and Newcastle disease and perhaps other adenoviruses and infectious avian encephalomyelitis. A vaccine has now been produced which has been found to be capable of giving satisfactory protection, e.g. Nobi-Vac EDS '76 Vaccine (Intervet Laboratories).

Pullet disease ('blue comb'; 'monocytosis')

Pullet disease was once a very common condition of birds affecting them soon after they had come into production. It has all the signs of a viral infection but no virus has been identified. The symptoms are usually a marked fall in egg production together with inappetance and lethargy. Some birds may be found dead, dying too quickly to show symptoms, but in most, and especially later cases in the course of the disease, death is preceded by a short period of illness during which purple coloured combs and wattles are the most noticeable feature, together with diarrhoea and an extremely dejected appearance.

Post mortem signs are especially associated with abnormalities in the kidneys which are usually grossly enlarged with crystalline urate deposits. There are also degenerative changes of the birds' ovaries and a general congestion of the carcase, including a patchy discolouration of the pectoral muscles.

The only useful treatment is to administer tetracyclines in the drinking water, ensuring that this is freely available to all the birds. Restriction of food intake may be beneficial for a time and a 'traditional' remedy is to mix in with the diet 10–20% of molasses and feed the whole diet wet.

Two classical bacterial diseases of chickens

Avian tuberculosis

Avian tuberculosis is a disease caused by a bacterium *Mycobacterium tuberculosis avium*. It is a contagious disease passed on by contact via the droppings of infected birds.

The disease normally affects older birds when there is a progressive loss of weight ('going light' as it used to be termed). The birds become unthrifty. The muscles of the breast are reduced in size exposing the sternum or breast bone. Appetite usually remains normal until the terminal stage of the disease. There may be some lameness and swelling of the joints. The comb and wattles appear pale in colour.

Post mortem examination reveals lesions which appear as yellowish-white caseous nodules in the liver, spleen and intestines. Laboratory examination can confirm the presence of the disease.

No treatment is effective and the disease is best dealt with by good culling of the affected birds combined with a complete depopulation of the house and subsequent disinfection.

Fowl cholera (avian pasteurellosis)

Fowl cholera is caused by a bacterium *Pasteurella multicoida* and can be a very serious cause of disease in many parts of the world. Infection occurs by the respiratory or alimentary route which contaminates water, soil and feed. There is an incubation period of 4–10 days and the severity of the condition depends very much on the 'stress' imposed on the birds by poor ventilation, overcrowding, and so on. Symptoms in the most acute cases include sudden death in large numbers with signs of cyanosis (purple or mauve colouring) and swelling of the comb and wattles. In the less acute stages there is swelling of the joints and legs causing lameness. Affected birds do not eat or drink and have difficulty in breathing. A thick nasal discharge will be seen together with a greenish-yellow diarrhoea.

Mortality may be very high, even up to 90%. Diagnosis is made on the basis of the symptoms and on isolation of the organism.

Treatment may be instituted by using antibiotics and drugs and prevention can be effected by vaccination. The incidence of tuberculosis and fowl cholera has decreased markedly under hygienic intensive conditions and with the better understanding of these diseases and the use of good drugs and vaccines both diseases may be expected to diminish in seriousness world-wide.

Mycotoxicosis

Chicks of all ages may be affected with forms of this fungus-induced disease known as mycotoxicosis. This is really a group of diseases which arise from toxins released by moulds found in certain feedstuffs or in the litter of the poultry house. Symptoms are usually indefinite but there may be a number of birds off-colour, obviously sick, droopy, eating and drinking little or nothing, and several dying. Post mortem signs are mostly confined to the liver which may be congested in acute cases or, in chronic cases, pale or yellowish-brown in colour and hard. Confirmation of the involvement of a mycotoxin requires detailed microscopic examination of the liver and of the feed the birds have been receiving.

There is no specific treatment but the administration of vitamins, especially B vitamins in the water, is warranted in an attempt to reduce some of the effects of the toxins. A number of chemicals is currently available for the treatment of either the food or the litter and housing, e.g. Kemin.

Table 7.2 The health of poultry: a summary of diseases, prevention and treatment

Disease	Prevention	Treatment
Adenoviruses	Vaccine may protect against one type EDS 76 (Egg Drop Syndrome 1976).	Non-specific measures such as vitamin, mineral and electrolyte mixtures and often broad spectrum antibiotics may assist in the bird's recovery.

Disease	Prevention	Treatment
Aspergillosis	Avoid all damp litter and nest material.	Treat whole environment with a disinfectant active against fungi.
Avian clostridial diseases	Hygienic measures within and around buildings require to be improved and there is a need for an improved disinfection and fumigation programme.	Soluble penicillin or ampicillin in drinking water.
Avian mycoplasmosis (CRD)	Normally eliminated by blood testing and removal of reactors. Also by medication with antibiotics such as Linco-spectin, Tylosin or Rovamycin.	Similar to preventatives.
Avian pasteurellosis	Vaccination by injection of Pasteurella vaccine.	Ampicillin; chlortetracycline; oxytetracycline.
Coccidiosis	Medication of ration with a variety of coccidiostats, e.g. Elancoban, Salcostat, Pancoxin, Cycostat and Stenorol.	Various sulphonamides and potentiated sulpha drugs.
E. coli infections	E. coli is usually a secondary infection; thus prevent primary disease with vaccination, therapy or good husbandry. A useful drug is Furazolidone in feed. Also arsenicals are widely used as preventatives and treatments with vitamins added.	Chlortetracycline hydrochloride, Furazolidone or Linco-spectin.
Fatty liver and kidney syndrome (FLKS)	Ensure protein and carbohydrate ratio correct and ration sufficient in biotin and other vitamin B elements.	Administer water soluble vitamin preparation fortified with biotin.
Fowl pox	Vaccination effectively prevents.	Administer non-specific broad spectrum antibiotics for secondary infections.
Gangrenous dermatitis	Usually associated with broilers after early Gumboro disease challenge so vaccination against latter assists. Do not use 'old' litter or over-stock, and ensure perfect disinfection between crops.	Soluble penicillin or ampicillin in water.
Gumboro disease (infectious bursal diseases)	Gumboro disease vaccine.	Treat for secondary infections with vitamin/antibiotic, vitamin preparations.
Histomoniasis (blackhead)	Dimetridazole and other nitrothiazoles.	As Prevention.
Inclusion body hepatitis (IBH)	Gumboro vaccination may assist in prevention as Gumboro disease appears to predispose to infection of IBH.	Non-specific measures including broad spectrum antibiotics and vitamins, especially fat-soluble vitamins.

Disease	Prevention	Treatment
Infectious avian encephalomyelitis (epidemic tremor)	A variety of live vaccines administered in drinking water at an age of about 15 weeks.	No specific treatment.
Infectious bronchitis	Vaccination. Primary with H-120 spray or drinking water, continue for rearers with H-52 in coarse spray or drinking water.	To curb secondary infections, chlortetracycline hydrochloride or furazolidone in water or feed.
Infectious laryngo-tracheitis	Vaccination by individual ocular or nasal drop or in spray.	Non-specific broad spectrum antibiotics and vitamins.
Insect infestation	A wide range of materials exist for dealing with flies, lice, beetles and crawling insects which are especially liable to infest poultry houses due to their warmth and their cavity construction. Many are organo-phosphorus compounds or gamma benzene hexachloride.	
Marek's disease	Vaccinate chicks at day-old by intra-muscular route.	No specific treatment but vitamin and mineral preparations added to drinking water may assist birds. Also treatment for any intercurrent infection, such as coccidiosis or secondary bacterial infections.
Necrotic enteritis	Improved hygiene including phenolic disinfectants and penicillin in feed at a level of 40 g per tonne.	Soluble penicillin in water or broad spectrum antibiotic, e.g. oxytetracycline hydrochloride soluble.
Newcastle disease (notifiable in UK)	Variety of vaccines protect, e.g. Hitchner B1, and La Sota, by droplet or water medication largely for young or growing stock, and in-activated oil-adjuvant vaccines by injection, primarily for layers or breeders. (In some countries, e.g. UK, vaccines are illegal and a slaughter policy is followed.)	No effective treatment against virus of Newcastle disease but treatment for secondaries as under *E. coli* infections.
Perosis	Balanced ration sufficient, especially in manganese, other minerals and available phosphorus.	As *Prevention*, administering extra vitamins and minerals in soluble form.
Roundworms	Normal hygienic measures during and between batches of chicken on litter.	Piperazine dihydrochloride and organo-phosphorus compound.
Salmonellosis	Prevention relies on good hygiene, correct feeding practice and testing by veterinary diagnostic laboratories for the organisms.	Soluble furazolidone, ampi-cillin, neomycin or sulpha drugs.

Disease	Prevention	Treatment
Stress	Mixtures of vitamins, minerals and electrolytes, which may, on veterinary advice, incorporate an antibiotic.	
Viral arthritis (tenosynovitis)	Non-specific antibiotics, e.g. chlortetracycline and oxytetracycline.	As with *Prevention* but higher dose.
Yolk sac infection	Hygienic measures in hatchery, breeding farms and chick accommodation.	Non-specific broad spectrum antibiotics.

Index

INDEX